The Thresher

—

CONTENTS

Not I, not I, but the wind that blows through me.

A fine wind is blowing the new direction of Time.

- D. H. Lawrence

PROLOGUE

Was the baby a changeling?

In those days it would have been easy enough for a nurse to have mixed up the tags on the cribs in the arrivals room. But whosever child it was, and despite the quiet corner of the world it had chosen to be born in, its arrival was accompanied by unseen tumult. Strident winds blew up the iron-grey Derwent in gusts, and two days later were still blowing.

Downriver, the baby's father was retrieving a marvellous item from his car, a miracle in silicon and tin. He was struggling out with it when his middle-aged neighbour, back from his afternoon stroll, offered to help with the suitcase-sized object.

'It's heavy, Mr. Glendower. What on earth is in it?'

'A surprise for the wife when she gets back from hospital, Mr. Murchison. It's a portable computer.'

'Good lord. I never knew such things existed.'

'It's an IBM 5100 model, an all-in-one system, with 16 kilobytes of RAM.'

'You don't expect me to know what any of that means, of course, Mr. Glendower.' They were puffing slightly as they got the package onto the lounge room table.

'These biting winds…you wouldn't know it was the first day of summer, would you?'

The new father shook his head, opening his other baby's case, hauling it out with some difficulty, and scratching the

9

wooden table in the process.

'Is that some kind of cassette player at the top?'

'It's for data tapes. I've a box of them here. They hold 200 kilobytes each…you could fit an entire novel on one of them, Mr. Murchison!'

'They're almost the size of a novel.'

'And, in maintenance mode, you can write directly into the computer's RAM, using a hexadecimal code.'

'Whatever the devil that is.'

'There's even a port for a printer. And this particular model has two languages. Using this toggle on the front panel you can switch between BASIC and APL.'

'I know a little French, Mr. Glendower…that's enough for me.'

Murchison was impressed, nevertheless. He marvelled at the thing, and not solely from politeness.

He walked next door to fetch a bottle of Angove's Claret to toast tomorrow's scheduled arrival of a three-day-old baby in the house. By the time he returned Glendower had switched on his black and white television, albeit with the sound turned down.

'And what will you use this wonderful new Computing Device for, Mr. Glendower?'

'Oh, taxes. And statistical analysis.' He worked at an insurance company. 'But chiefly as a sound investment. Portable computers can only increase in value, Mr. Murchison. They're the way of the future.'

'And how much did it set you back, if you don't mind me asking.'

'I bought it with the money I inherited from my late father…it was a bargain at just over $12,000.' Murchison spluttered a little over his wine, and had to look away, catching sight as he did of *Power Without Glory*, the new mini-series being promoted heavily by the government broadcaster. By way of politeness and in order to change the topic from money, he made a disparaging remark about the show and the book it was based on.

'Frank Hardy's a commie, a pinko lunatic, Mr.

Glendower. Exactly the sort of garbage the ABC would promote. On our tax dollars, needless to say. Still, they say the ABC is chock full of poofters.' Staunch monarchist that he was, Mr. Murchison's lounge room wall held a framed photo of Queen Elizabeth II and a smaller one of Sir John Kerr, whom he referred to as a 'true working class hero, unlike that bitter little yob from the Beatles.'

That had been the first time Mr. Glendower had heard him betray any knowledge of pop culture, and it seemed somewhat incongruous, for Mr. Murchison, with whom he was still not on first name terms despite knowing him for several years, always seemed to him as a character beyond any particular time and era, although his World War II medals, worn with pride each Anzac Day, dated his young manhood to around the time when Glendower had been born. There were books on his shelf which had a faint air of disreputability about them, and which secretly fascinated Glendower, although he had been too polite to pick them up. One was called *The Dispossessed Majority*; another boasted as its provocative title *None Dare Call It Conspiracy*. But Glendower, a lifelong Labor voter, was by no means a *Don's Party* type, and in matters of manners and sexual mores was somewhat uptight. He had turned mildly red on hearing the word 'poofter' uttered in his own home, and attempted to change the subject.

'No doubt this dollar devaluation will be good for the apple growers, Mr. Murchison.'

But the latter snorted.

'Fraser is an imbecile. So far he has proven to represent nearly everything I despise about the Liberal Party. Labor at least stab you in the guts. Fraser will stab us all in the back, I'm afraid.'

'How do you mean?'

'Well, take the Rhodesian situation.'

'The Bush War?'

'Yes. Southern Africa is one of the few things holding up the global Communist advance. South Africa itself is too big a target, for now; so there's an international effort to undermine Rhodesia, using Mozambique as a proxy. Did you see Kissinger's Zambia conference on the news? In my opinion he is almost certainly a Soviet agent.'

'Kissinger, a Soviet agent?' spluttered Glendower. 'Come now, Mr. Murchison!'

'He's a Satanic figure, Mr. Glendower. Also complicit, needless to say, is that disgusting traitor Harold Wilson, who has actually given material support to the black Marxists of Mozambique to wage war on a nation of British stock! But to cap things off, our own so-called conservative government and its oily little foreign minister Andrew Peacock, have followed in the footsteps of Whitlam and condemned the brave people of Rhodesia to perdition...Australia's foreign policy is virtually dictated by the UN! Rhodesia will be toppled first, then South Africa. That's the plan.'

'Surely the blackfellows have a right to govern their own country?'

'British-settled countries are governed by the rule of Law, Mr. Glendower. 'Majority rule' is merely a code-word for bolshevism.' He chugged back his second glass, then poured another for Glendower. He had poured such large glasses that the bottle was almost empty, and he announced that he would soon be back with another, to Glendower's silent consternation.

'The fact is,' he boomed on returning with a second bottle of Angove's, 'that these so-called black 'nationalists' like Mugabe treat their fellows far worse than the whites have ever done. And, as you get your news from the bolshies at the ABC, you probably aren't aware the so-called 'white' Rhodesian army consists of 50% black *volunteers*.'

'No, I wasn't aware of that...' tailed off Glendower, trying to think of a way to get rid of his guest before he became too drunk.

'Then there's this East Timor business. The left are up in arms about it...but they were completely silent when Indonesia invaded West Papua! That's because Indonesia was Soviet-backed at the time, and now it isn't. You would have to scratch under a lot of rocks to find a leftist with any principle, Mr. Glendower.' Even while tipsy, he wouldn't drop the formal mode of address, Glendower thought irritably.

By way of conversation, he warily said: 'And what do you think of the new president-elect over in America?'

'Jimmy the Tooth? Well now, what would you say about a Southerner who sang the Battle Hymn of the Republic on the eve of his election? For all his anti-Washington rhetoric, his cabinet is full of the same faces as LBJ's. He's a creature of the Rockefellers and the Trilateral Commission, Mr. Glendower.' Swilling back another glass of the sweet South Australian wine, he spotted a copy of Donald Horne's *The Lucky Country* on the shelf. 'I hope you don't take that rubbish seriously. But you aren't to know, of course. God, what we really need in this country is a purge of the Right,' he sighed. 'We need men of principle who nevertheless have the panache to somehow impress an almost-mindless populace. That Dunstan poofter may be an evil, rat-like creature, but at least he has media savvy, like when he stood on the beach at Glenelg to defy the end of the world, or whatever it was.

'And that David Bowie chap knows a thing or two about presentation, too. We need someone with that kind of flamboyance, but also with backbone, who is willing to stand up for God, Queen and Country.'

Again, Glendower was rather shocked to hear the name of a contemporary pop star pass the lips of this fifty-something arch-conservative with skin as dry as paper, especially one as debauched as Bowie.

'Perhaps, then, you yourself…'

'We shall see, Mr. Glendower. If no one else is willing to take a stand, then I may well have to, ha ha ha.' Relieving to hear laughter, as if his uninvited guest had gotten overheated and was now cooling down somewhat. Perhaps he would soon be leaving; but not, it appeared, before he embarked on an extended rant about Prince Bernhard of the Netherlands, from which he turned to one Mitsuyasu Maeno, a Japanese pornographic actor who had recently crashed a light aircraft into the home of a high-ranking yakuza he believed had betrayed the nation due to his involvement in the Lockheed Scandal.

'Just like that writer chap a few years back...I will never understand the Jap, Mr. Glendower. I fought him in the war, of course, but I have yet to comprehend him. Such fanaticism...' He sighed and shook his head, beginning to lose steam. Glendower made hints that he wished to tinker with his computer, and Murchison seemed pleased to take them.

'I'll bid you good evening, then. And please, by all means, keep the rest of the wine.' There were only a few drops left, Glendower noted drily.

Murchison made his way next door, full of melancholy at the perilous state of the world. 'All is entropy,' he whispered, and shook his head. The average man cared about little but beer, sex and cricket. Or, as with his neighbour, computers, of all things! There was always a sedative, some attention-turner to keep people from seeking the truth...

With these heavy thoughts, he retreated inside his home, his castle.

As Glendower bid Murchison farewell on the porch, he noticed with some annoyance the hi-fi of his *other* neighbour blaring the competent, earnest, and persistent rock and roll plod of REO Speedwagon across the gusty wind. That house was a rental property, and Glendower had never liked living next door to a residency which changed hands every six months (or less if the tenant was evicted, as had happened twice in the three years he had lived here); but, as his own home was a good one, he put up with REO Speedwagon.

That very day, on the other side of the world, unbeknownst to either neighbour, another band called the Sex Pistols with little euphonic talent but a certain snarling belligerence, enough to make the hairs stand on end, were shocking the respectable working classes by swearing live on television. Filth and fury headlines would ensure they would be a household word in England next day, even beyond the dreams of their cunning manager. They were poised to recruit any number of followers among a generation educated in the English comprehensive system, sweeping away any last vestiges of respect the REO Speedwagons of this world might still cling to, egged on to some degree by the British tabloids who loved that sort of thing…or perhaps they had merely come to save the white working classes from the ravages of disco.

But while their teenage followers would spit and pogo meaninglessly to no end, their tangible influence on the general populace was virtually nil, and what it all ultimately meant, no one could as yet say.

The southerly, Antarctic winds blowing up the Derwent that evening, however, presaged events more earth-shattering in the scheme of things.

*   *   *

Glendower tinkered with his computer until his wife's arrival by taxi around 10pm. It was the second time he had made the baby's acquaintance, and he looked down at it curiously as he carried its capsule from the back seat. Its eyes, opening slightly, were still largely in the otherworld.

'Get the formula ready, please. I'm bloody exhausted. The instructions are on the tin.' She handed him a paper bag with an empty bottle and a tin of powder.

'I thought you had breasts for that kind of thing?'

'He wouldn't take to breast milk properly the first day, so the doctors told me to use formula instead. It's just as good. Anyway, breast feeding is *messy*.'

Glendower looked doubtful, but said nothing, anxious to avoid an argument with his sharp-tongued wife. But an argument was coming, nonetheless…for she had spotted the computer.

'You mean to say you haven't even put the *cradle* together, you useless man? You've been tinkering with this new toy instead, I suppose…' When she found he had spent nearly his entire inheritance on the machine she was livid.

'I thought it would be a nice surprise,' he said sullenly, genuinely dismayed by her lack of enthusiasm. 'How many people in Tasmania have one of *these* in their homes? Probably only a dozen, according to the salesman.'

'Yes, but what good is it?'

'What good is it? It's bloody obvious, woman! The taxes for a start…'

'$12,000 to do your tax return quicker? You could have at least bought a colour TV, so I can watch *The Young Doctors* in colour. Now we've got some weird machine I won't even be able to use!'

'There are plenty of other things it's good for. You'll see…' He shoved the bottle in the baby's mouth, half-distracted and fully annoyed.

*   *   *

A week later his wife went alone to see a film, because she felt she needed a break from the baby. Driving alone to the Hoyts cinema below street level in Hobart's CBD, she picked a film called *The Sailor Who Fell From Grace With the Sea*, because she liked Kris Kristofferson…but she found it completely disgusting. She wanted to walk out but was embarrassed to, and so stayed on. Three quarters of the way through she fell asleep, snoring loudly, so that most of the other filmgoers had little fits of sniggers.

Waking up as the end credits were playing, she wondered why so many of those filing out were staring at her.

She drove home, where her husband was putting tinsel on the plastic Christmas tree, minded to reconciliation. Too tired to put up a fight, she stopped short of apologising…something he had in any case realised by now was congenitally impossible for her…and instead their talk turned to mundane things. It was the first Christmas of their three-year marriage which they wouldn't be spending with her father in the country.

Instead, the Glendowers had a quietly sterile Christmas at home, and on New Years' Eve went to bed at eleven o'clock in the fervent but mistaken belief that the Australian Labor Party would surely be returned to power in the coming year.

The month-old baby was now making cooing sounds during the few moments when he wasn't sleeping or drinking formula.

*   *   *

By April he was clapping his hands and holding a rattle, laughing enthusiastically as he rolled from front to back on a mat on the floor.

His mother was placated by his laughter. His first smile, three months earlier, had almost turned her against him…for, two days after his baptism as 'Michael Allan Glendower' at the old wooden Anglican church in Kingston, he had grinned broadly while turning his head in the direction of the TV set, where news of a disastrous train wreck in Sydney with over 80 dead was flickering from the screen.

She had felt a small burst of nausea at this incongruity, and what mothering instinct she had was needed to assure her that the baby understood nothing of what he saw.

But now, watching him play on the mat, all seemed well again. He would be normal, she decided, pleased with herself for birthing a future respectable citizen.

*   *   *

A new set of neighbours arrived.

The previous tenant had been strangely quiet since acquiring a copy of Fleetwood Mac's *Rumours*. Such was his reverence for this album that he used headphones for once, often crooning along with it. It was something akin to a

17

religious experience for him.

Now, however, he had moved to greener pastures, replaced by a young couple who seemed rather uptight and frustrated, always squabbling just on the threshold of hearing. They never gave more than a curt nod of the head to the Glendowers, but at least they didn't hold riotous parties.

Glendower had finally given in to his wife's nagging and bought a colour TV with the remainder of his savings. He had wanted a program known as a 'word processor', which would make his computer effectively function as an electric typewriter. But the program, known as Electric Pencil, wasn't compatible with an IBM 5100, so there went his plan of keeping an electronic diary of suburban life.

As consolation, he got to see Felicity Kendall of *The Good Life* in glorious full colour, along with other brand new British comedies such as *George and Mildred* and an especially funny one called *Fawlty Towers*. He also watched *Charlie's Angels* on the commercial channel, TVT6 (somewhat surreptitiously, as his wife didn't approve of it).

The news, rendered in colour, was more vivid, but also sickly and surreal, like an extreme Mannerist painting by El Greco. It seemed full of shootings and kidnappings by violent leftists in Germany. Cambodia and Vietnam were at war, and many Vietnamese were streaming into the western suburbs of Melbourne.

But all this seemed far away and make-believe to the Glendowers.

*   *   *

That winter, little Michael grew his first tooth, followed quickly by a second. Mouth agrin as if showing off, he sat on a bunny rug on the floor staring fascinated at the bright moving colours of *The Muppet Show,* while his parents prepared for a small dinner party they had organised.

Originally intended as a catch-up with Mrs. Glendower's

sister Sylvie, the guest list had expanded the previous day when her husband had run into Murchison and asked him along. His wife, who disliked Murchison, was annoyed, suspecting (correctly, in fact) that her husband, despite a plea of social tone-deafness, had actually invited him from a wicked sense of fun...for, as she well knew, her husband was not overly fond of his sister-in-law.

'And just how do you think *those* two are going to get along?'

'Perhaps Sylvie has changed since her release from the nut ward?'

'The psychiatric unit of the Royal Hobart Hospital is not...'

'A nut ward? Yes, it is.'

'Well, you don't have to put it like that. Anyway, she's better now. She's been treating her schizophrenia with medication. And I haven't seen her since before her...incident...so be polite to her. I *mean* it.'

'Should I be polite to her other personality as well?'

'Schizophrenia isn't a split personality disorder, they're different. And that's just the sort of comment I'm talking about, so hold your tongue if you can't say anything sensible.'

'Are you sure you aren't developing a split personality yourself? Madness runs in your family doesn't it?' He looked pointedly at the baby as he said this. She snarled, about to fly off the handle, when the doorbell rang.

It was Sylvie. Glendower wondered guiltily if she might have heard his last remark, but his sister-in-law was all hesitant smiles as she looked around, giving him a respectful nod before alighting her gaze on her nephew for the first time.

'Oh, isn't he gorgeous!'

Could this be the woman who heard voices telling her that ASIO and the CIA were plotting to destroy the world, and who had created some kind of public order disturbance (exactly what, his wife had refused to tell him) in the electrical section of FitzGerald's department store, Glendower wondered idly...thinking, also, for the first time, that she was more attractive than his wife.

The bell rang again, and Murchison was admitted, bearing a bottle of Angove's Claret. His liver was playing up, and as a consequence he was in a somewhat churlish mood, not helped by Mrs. Glendower's obvious frostiness towards him.

'Did anyone see Elvis' funeral procession on the news?' murmured Sylvie from where she was crouching and playing with the baby. 'So many flowers!'

'I can't believe he's dead,' sighed Mrs. Glendower.

'Good riddance,' snapped Murchison, and even the baby went quiet. Sensing, perhaps, that he had been unnecessarily curt, he attempted to make amends. 'And, ah, how are you getting on trying to understand your computer's various modes of expression, Mr. Glendower? Have you had to purchase a trilingual dictionary yet, or will you merely hire an interpreter, ha ha?'

'I've been sticking to BASIC, Mr. Murchison. I find it more stimulating.' That he had given up on APL because he lacked the necessary mathematical background to understand it he was hardly going to give Murchison the satisfaction of knowing. A further silence followed.

'Well, Sir John Kerr is gone,' said Mrs. Glendower at last. 'I expect you'll be sorry, Mr. Murchison…although I can't say I'm very sorry myself.'

'The new Governor-General, Zelman Cowen, is a Zionist Jew,' scoffed Murchison. 'He'd be better off in America, where the 700 Club of so-called Christians would worship the ground he walks on.'

'Oh, I hate those evangelical types,' said Sylvie. 'There's a lot of them up in Queensland, so they say.'

'I dare say many of them are decent people,' said Murchison. 'But their brand of politics is rather naive, in my contrarian opinion.'

'No wonder that Bjelke-Petersen idiot is in power up there, with the gospel hall types all voting for him,' said Mrs. Glendower, with a forced cackle that tried to sound bitter but came out slightly nervous. She became more timorous still as

Murchison glared at her.

Glendower, who subscribed to *The Economist*, asked Murchison what he thought of President Ford's pardoning of Tokyo Rose as one of his last acts in office. To Glendower's surprise (remembering many casual anti-Japanese remarks), he appeared not to care. Certain muttered comments even seemed to suggest that he had found her broadcasts entertaining, long ago during the war.

'In any case,' he cleared his throat, 'I don't have time to worry about Japs when there are far more pressing matters. Other nationalities are invading our larger cities without so much as a Pearl Harbour to announce them. Soon they'll be *here* as well. And now the ALP is trying to take over our Legislative Council. The Marxists and Fabians have given up on Queensland for the time being, and are setting their sights on Tasmania. Well, I'm not going to stand for it.' He thumped a fist on his open palm, making Sylvie blink.

'If Fraser's constitutional changes go through, we won't even be able to appoint our own state senators. This, along with the Gleneagles Agreement, is the last straw as far as I'm concerned. I am forming a direct action group, and intend to fight for my values, to the last breath if necessary!'

'Good for you!' said Sylvie, smiling warmly. 'And what are your values?'

'My group, currently with a membership of one, stands for the promotion of the Senate and State Rights, and we are also pro-Rhodesian. In point of fact, if the group doesn't succeed, I will probably volunteer for the Rhodesian army myself, in spite of my age. I would rather die with dignity in a noble cause than sit back and watch the debauched herits of a once-great British Empire hand everything their ancestors ever fought for to a pack of murdering Communist niggers!'

During this speech, Sylvie's warm smile had slowly changed to a look of horror. 'You don't mean you support the white supremacist governments of southern Africa?' she gasped incredulously. 'But they're undemocratic! Isn't democracy a British tradition?'

'Fraser, Peacock and Co. don't say anything about

'majority rule' or free elections for Communist nations like Cambodia, do they? Only for Rhodesia and South Africa. That should tell you something, my dear.'

'But *they* don't segregate people by race!'

'Let me tell you how the black Marxists of Rhodesia treat their own people. Take a look at Mr. Chikombe Madividza here.' He pulled a photo from his wallet and handed it to her. She saw a negro with bandages across his face. 'His wife was forced to *cook* the bits of flesh they cut from his face, and then was forced to *eat* them.'

'Oh, how disgusting.' She looked as if she was going to throw up.

'Mr. Murchison, I'll thank you not to upset my sister!'

'How do you know it's blacks who did this? It could be the CIA…'

'Now, dear, calm down. You should…'

'I mean, wasn't Rhodes an agent of the Rothschilds?' She was beginning to hyperventilate slightly, and Murchison, concerned, rushed to fetch a glass of water.

'It's all right,' she managed, slurping at it weakly. 'I'm not having another attack. The medication…'

'What medication is she on?' Murchison demanded of Mrs. Glendower.

'It's clozapine,' said Sylvie. 'A new drug. It seems to work, I think. I've quit smoking pot, too, it was making me worse.'

''Whoopie weed' is no good for anyone,' said Murchison. 'But isn't clozapine an anti-psychotic?'

'Yes, yes. I have paranoid schizophrenia, but please don't think I'm some kind of nut.' Glendower shifted uneasily.

'I don't think you're a nut,' said Murchison, 'but it might explain why you think handing a British country over to black Marxists is a good idea.'

'Mr. Murchison!' growled Mrs. Glendower. 'That's enough!'

'I never heard that Rhodes was an agent of the Rothschilds…and in any case, the ordinary settlers…'

'Have you ever heard of MKUltra, Mr. Murchison?'

'I remember something about a cover up, after

Watergate…'

'I used to think I was…well…'

'You should throw those damned pills away!'

'You're not supposed to quit suddenly. I have regular blood tests…'

'Now, dinner's nearly ready. Can everyone…'

In the midst of the hubbub, a normally quiet voice rang out, defiantly, challenging the others to silence.

'Well *I've* decided I'll be voting for Don Chipp's new party. I like their idea of espousing a middle ground,' said Mr. Glendower matter-of-factly. The look on his face could almost be described as a nervous smugness. 'One of their objectives is to oppose extremist elements, left or right, which seek to endanger the democratic process. I like the sound of that!'

He had wondered what Murchison would think about this, being an extremist element himself, and it irritated him that he had wondered. Sure enough, Murchison scoffed…but the chief opposition came from his wife, who announced haughtily that *she* would be voting for Whitlam again, and that anyone who didn't was an idiot. She began to pour scorn on the Australian Democrats, a party which would never amount to anything, a band of ditherers. Glendower took this personally, and an argument ensued, while Murchison and Sylvie shouted at cross-purposes over the top of them about negroes.

Then: '*Look! No!*' shrieked Sylvie, rushing forward just in time to rescue the baby from coming into contact with the oil heater.

'So, he can crawl!' cried the mother. 'Well, what a time to suddenly learn!'

They oohed and aahed over the baby, who had been trying to press his face up against the glass front of the heater, attracted, it appeared, to the blue and yellow viscosity of the flames.

* * *

Weeks later the baby was attempting to stand, and 'walking' around the room with his hand held. Glendower paid little attention, however, being preoccupied with his own concerns.

By now he had realised that computers were going down rapidly in price, and was kicking himself for not having predicted it...he had even heard of a cheap Tandy model with 4k of RAM selling for around $1000!

He remembered sheepishly the comments he had made to Murchison about his 'investment'. Hopefully the old boy would have forgotten about it, but he couldn't shake off his worry that Murchison would secretly think him rather dim. He resolved to read up on some brainy subject with which to impress him in future.

But things weren't all bad. 'His' team of North Melbourne had prevailed in the Grand Final rematch against Collingwood, and Chipp's new party had done better than expected in the recent South Australian election, obtaining 14% of the vote. If they did that well at the federal level they could end up holding the balance of power.

Chipp had recently voiced his support for an American-style Cabinet, whose ministers weren't necessarily drawn from MPs of the governing party, but that surely had nothing to do with the fact he had been excluded from the Fraser Cabinet himself. No, after the turmoil of the last decade, cooler heads were now prevailing over the nation's politics, Glendower told himself, feeling a little sunlit burst of joy as he did so.

He was feeling so magnanimous, in fact, that he decided to treat himself to see the hyped new film *Star Wars*. The young star of the film, Mark something-or-other, was recently on the *Don Lane Show*, and had made the movie sound rather beguiling.

The Tasman Bridge had just re-opened after being smashed apart by a container ship two years earlier, and he drove across it to the Eastside Drive-in at Warrane. The bigger Elwick Drive-in was unreliable, being often affected by the Bridgewater Jerry, the thick fog that came rolling down the Derwent, or that was what he told himself. In reality, he had a deep-seated aversion to Hobart's northern suburbs.

His wife grumbled at the price of tickets, which had recently gone up to $3.50. Still, she seemed to enjoy the movie, while the baby slept quietly through it in his capsule.

Glendower himself was disappointed.

It was a kids film, he thought, irritatedly; the silly metal robots proved it.

One scene impressed him, however – the opening shot of a vast interstellar spaceship trailing across the screen. This saurian vessel awakened something in his blood, a veiled sense of dread and awe. It spoke of a future remote and haughty, one he had no part in. It also made him think about religion, a subject he disliked…and so he gradually expunged the film from his mind.

*   *   *

In other regions of the world, as the German Autumn drew to a close and Andreas Baader and his comrades were buried in a mass grave in Stuttgart by gracious permission of the son of Rommel, a new mode of music was being spawned in New York, one whose goofy beats would permeate or pollute the world for several decades to come.

Blacks, it seemed, had taken advantage of a power blackout to engage in widespread looting. The stolen items including expensive DJing equipment, the use of which mushroomed hip-hop from a Bronx-backstreet obscurity to the bright glare of the hit parade in just a year or two, somewhat negating the old adage that crime doesn't pay.

In Tasmania, however, Christmas was drawing near, a time for forgiveness and togetherness.

Glendower and his wife exchanged token presents in the morning, before taking the train to Ross where her father lived. The drab, grey house, built in the 1890s from oversized bricks stood just outside the township, perched alone like a jackdaw on some old dead tree in the Scottish highlands.

The lord of the manor, Mr. Tibbit, had subsisted on an invalid pension since putting his back out, and his eldest daughter Noela, married to a prosperous farmer half an hour's drive away, came three times a week to do the tasks he couldn't manage. He could cook for himself, however, thanks to an oven raised on bolsters, and today had cooked a full Christmas roast.

His wife, who died five years ago in a car crash during a shopping trip to Launceston, never got to see her second daughter married to Glendower, who had met her just once, weeks before her death. In light of what had happened he felt ashamed his only memory of her was a negative one – a feeling that she had slighted his manhood by calling in Noela's husband to fix a dripping tap when he, Glendower, had been standing right next to her. He brooded sourly on this, still suspecting that Mr. Tibbit had a similarly low opinion of his manhood.

On arriving, they saw a car already there. Glendower thought it looked familiar, but couldn't place it. Sylvie must be here, he thought, as Noela would be spending this Christmas with her in-laws near Railton, only stopping by on the 27th to see her new nephew.

*   *   *

They opened the heavy, creaking front door and walked straight in to receive a shock.

Murchison was there.

Not just there…but making himself thoroughly at home, sitting in the best armchair with a glass of sherry, regaling Mr. Tibbit with an anecdote from the war years. (Tibbit had not served in that war, as farming had been a reserved occupation).

Sylvie turned around and smiled, sheepishly but mischievously, raising a glass of wine as if in toast.

'Hello,' said Mrs. Glendower, with tightly compressed lips. 'I thought you couldn't drink, Sylvie…on your medication.'

'Oh, Reginald helped me get off that rubbish,' she said with a dismissive wave, before going across to Murchison and touching his arm.

So, he has a first name, Glendower thought, smirking inwardly, although he couldn't believe what he was seeing. He noticed she was wearing what looked like an engagement ring.

'Old enough to be her father,' his own wife would hiss to him later when he was alone with her bile (in point of fact, Murchison *was* the same age as their father, but had a younger countenance and bearing).

'She actually told me that he doesn't believe in sex before marriage and she finds that refreshing…as if I would even *want* to know things like that! She also told me about some absurd dream she had the night after she first met him, where everything seemed serene and full of light. Can you imagine?'

But now she managed grudgingly: 'How pleasant to see you here, Mr. Murchison.'

'Call me Reg. We're family now, almost.'

'I had no idea you, uh…'

'We kept it a surprise,' said her sister, with a warm, fluttering smile.

'On our very doorstep,' said Glendower, trying to appear amused.

'Oh, Reg'll usually pick me in his car and we'll go on a walk, or to the art gallery or something. I haven't been to *his* house that many times, and I took care never to let you see me when I did. I knew what you'd say, you know.' Mrs. Glendower turned bright red. 'But I expect I'll be moving in there at *some* point. We're going to be neighbours!'

'So I see.'

*   *   *

At the Christmas dinner table, talk turned to politics as was usual with the daughters of that family, but no one brought up the recent federal election, a Liberal landslide that had finally deflated Whitlam's maintained rage. The Democrats had done all right, though not as well as Glendower had expected, giving him little to gloat about...but Murchison made them all sit up with an announcement. His group (whose membership had expanded to two with the enrolment of his fiancé) would be seeking to make Tasmania an *independent country*.

He was quite serious about this. Two things had convinced him he could no longer countenance subjugation to the federal government. First, the Williamsburg 7 conference, held in Canberra the previous month, a kind of Bilderberg event for Australia and South-East Asia; but more importantly, the Shiel affair, just days earlier. A newly appointed minister had been *removed from government* by Fraser and Cowan for some relatively mild comments indicating he believed that South Africa's way of government was a matter for South Africans to decide.

'Both parties are the same!' said Sylvie. 'Pig Iron Bob admitted it when he said people would accept socialist measures from him more readily than they would from declared socialists!'

'You're parroting *his* nonsense?' Mrs. Glendower said to her sister. 'You always said you hated apartheid.'

'Reg has shown me, with proper evidence, how evil the Marxists really are. And they're *supported* by the biggest arch-capitalists!'

'Don't be silly. Why would...'

'Take this Steve Biko. No one had even heard of him when he was alive...now he's a martyred saint, manufactured instantly by the corporate media.'

'He was beaten to death...that's horrible.'

'Don't you believe in free trade, my girl?' wheezed her father.

'Not the big international corporations, Dad...they're monopolising anyway, so it's *not* free trade.'

'Oh,' he said, returning to his roast onions.

'We both believe in genuine free trade,' said Murchison. 'But certain rich families engage in treason because they profit monetarily from it...or for other reasons.' But his prospective father-in-law had lost interest. Indeed, it was unclear what he thought of the coming marriage; nowadays he gave off an air of being somewhat apart from the concerns of the world.

'So, you want Tasmania to be a republic?'

'No, no...I don't want to secede from the Empire...the Commonwealth, I mean.'

'You betray yourself, Mr. Murchison.'

'Call me Reg, please.'

'The Commonwealth is coming apart, anyway,' said Sylvie. 'Quebec just made French its official language.'

'Tasmania should be more British than the British!'

'And what do you think of Mr. Murchison's...*Reg's*...beloved Joh Bjelke-Petersen?' asked Mrs. Glendower, determined to needle her wayward sister. 'Hundreds arrested just for protesting the right to protest...surely you don't approve of that?'

'That's Queensland's business.'

'And what happens in Rhodesia is *your* business! Ha!'

'How do you feel about *your* beloved Al Grassby being in the pockets of the Calabrian Mafia?'

'What nonsense! Anyway, I don't like Grassby. His dress sense is terrible.' As if at the mention of Grassby, a smell announced that the baby in his high chair needed changing, and Mrs. Glendower went to do so while the others moved into the lounge to drink sherry and listen to music.

Mr. Tibbit wanted to put on one of his Slim Dusty records, but Sylvie insisted he should hear a new band she had been listening to called Radio Birdman.

It was extremely noisy. Why, they blatantly steal the theme from *Hawaii Five-O*, thought Glendower in disgust, only played in a garbled and distorted way. This must be the new 'punk' music he had read of in the papers. Murchison, with an expression of good-humoured tolerance, merely put his hands over his ears.

When it became clear that everyone hated it, she turned it off with a sigh. 'I was going to have a dance. Oh well, there's this.' She put on a seven inch with a song called 'The Passenger', by someone calling himself 'Iggy Pop'. Murchison liked it a lot better, although he said it still sounded like nigger music, and the singer looked like a Chinese lesbian.

Glendower thought he could hear a dramatic chord progression beneath the madness, however. It could easily be the song of the season. Sad, resigned, yet with hidden bliss under the surface. A bit like Sylvie herself, he thought.

His yearning for her, permanently lost to him though he had never thought otherwise, was dangerous, and so he shut it up within himself. That kind of bliss was not for him, he thought, with a bitterness tinged with deep self-pity.

From the diary of Reginald Murchison

Saturday 1st April, 1978

Resuming diary after several years' absence.

Wireless said some cove with the forgettable name Dick Smith towed an 'iceberg' of shaving foam into Sydney Harbour for an April Fool's Day joke. I should like to play a similar jape on the World Council of Churches, burying them beneath a tide of black mud, so they can finally understand what they are unleashing on the world. I merely wish to make them see with *other* eyes.

If they could but see the clear sun over Salisbury, the cricket teams playing happily in the long sunsets...

And now? Ian Smith has capitulated, his government to be replaced by a black one in nine moons...a gambit to buy more time?

If we could but wake up the peoples of Britain, Australia, the United States, the gambit would pay off! Because it is the corrupt rulers of these countries making it happen, insisting as one that Nkomo and Mugabe must be included in next year's transitional government, knowing full well they will edge out the black moderates.

Meanwhile, Jimmy the Tooth praises the Obasanjo junta in Nigeria as a 'great democracy'!

My beloved second wife, whose entry into my life I could never have foreseen, is slowly coming around on the race issue. It isn't just the abstract system of 'Marxism' causing the troubles, she understands that now, although she is having a tough time squaring it with her preconceptions. But I fear

31

that, very soon, she will be more fanatical than I. Already she insists I am being too soft on the World Council of Churches, whom she would like to see executed for treason. Treason against what? I asked. Against the Crown and the British Empire, she insisted. Empire!

That's my lass...

Her family are unhappy with our surreptitious courtship and private wedding, which Sylvie nevertheless insisted on. The honeymoon in New Zealand I will remember as perhaps the most wonderful time of my life.

Now, if only she can give me the son that my first wife denied me.

Wednesday 12th April, 1978

It turns out our local representative to the Australian Council of Churches, Bishop O'Neill, happens to be not only an envoy to the *World* Council of Churches, but actually a member of its central committee! The good bishop directly helped solicit Australia's donation of $72,000 to the so-called 'Patriotic Front' of Marxist terrorists. How many were tortured, raped, and burnt alive with the connivance of this eminent churchman?

Sylvie is right that I am too soft on them.

Tuesday 25th April, 1978

This Anzac day I did something different to commemorate. We once fought for Queen and Country, and Rhodesia rightly belongs to the Crown...so after dawn service at the cenotaph, I strolled through the centre of Hobart, that 'metropolis of murderers and university of burglary and all subter-human abomination,' as the Irish Fenian prisoner John Mitchel once put it, where, waiting for me, hired for the occasion, was a good-sized tipping truck.

The front door of Bishop O'Neill's large convict-built

house, one of three properties he owns, directly adjoins the footpath, as is often the case in the older parts of town, there being merely a thin strip of concrete fringed by a short, wrought-iron fence, between it and the street. That (alongside Mr. Dick Smith's Sydney Harbour jape) is what gave me the idea. The mud I obtained from Lake Dulverton with the help of an Oatlands jack-of-all-trades. I kept the engine running and knocked at the door. When the bishop answered, looking quizzical as to why the truck was there blocking traffic, I told him to wait as I had something for him to sign. I entered the cab and swiftly tilted the tray (having made sure this model had excellent hydraulic rams, and was quick to dump its load).

Sadly, much of the mud stuck in the tray due to its consistency, so the good bishop wallowed only to his knees.

I told him it was a gift from the people of Rhodesia…and to my surprise the bogged figure began shaking his fist at me in anger!

I am afraid the sight of him unrepentant caused me to grab his walking stick off him and begin to thrash him with it…and this was my undoing, as a police car just happened to drive past, and now I am to be summonsed for Assault Occasioning Actual Bodily Harm.

Sylvie is proud of me though. The look of admiration on her face when I told her of my arrest made it worth it, a hundred times over. And, after all, what was the point of doing it if we couldn't claim it for our organisation? (Which, this reminds me, I have yet to come up with a name for…)

Friday 19th May, 1978

Robert Menzies died four days ago…100,000 lined the streets of Melbourne today for his funeral. I have mixed feelings, but shan't speak ill of the dead. Certainly he was a greater man than the current gang of rabble in Canberra.

Meanwhile, in Hobart, the police have been aggressively forcing businesses to change their signs to metric, despite their customers preferring to buy fabric by the yard, or apples by the pound. I have decided that our group will staunchly oppose this, and have added anti-metrification to our platform. Might as well put as much on the agenda as possible now that I'm publicly revealed.

At least the newspapers didn't print our home address. Our neighbours, the Glendowers, professed their gratitude for that, although they make no secret of the fact that they consider me a dangerous lunatic.

Wednesday 14th June, 1978

Finally came up with a name for our organisation, which I can use in court, where I am representing myself: the Tasmanian Union of Loyalists, or TUL. It reminds me of Thule, the Latin name for Hyperborea, which I recall from my Herodotus as a happy land somewhere beyond the north wind.

And in that land, perhaps, I shall never again hear the ridiculous song 'Mull of Kintyre' coming from next door, where Sylvie's sister has been playing it loudly and incessantly while her husband is at work. Who knows what it is doing to the brain of their little toddling son?

Meanwhile, Sylvie has been obsessively playing a record called 'Wuthering Heights', which despite the banshee screech of the singer, is not so bad as 'Mull of Kintyre'. The plaintive note in the singer's voice when she says 'master'! But I doubt she'll find a man strong enough to master her, not if she moves in degenerate pop music circles. A wild Irish girl, seemingly wilder than Sylvie herself (the Tibbits are largely Irish despite their Anglo-French surname…Alpine types, needless to say, although I fancy their son has a touch of the Nordic about him).

The press have been harping on about the Cassinga raid, telling blatant lies about what was actually a superb military operation. How long for South Africa, if Rhodesia falls?

Monday 26th June, 1978

Today Sylvie called the death of one's race 'the Second
Death', thus bringing my esoteric teachings into the open. In
that brief phrase she encapsulated it better than I ever
could...it is a *far* worse fate than individual death.

Court case next month; almost certainly will go to prison.
Resumed diary all too brief.

*   *   *

From the diary of Sylvie Murchison

Friday July 28th

They've stopped the passenger trains in Tasmania due to
'lack of demand'. We are like those trains, Reg and
I...romantic, doomed to failure. There's no way we could
have expected the magistrate to go easy on him in light of his
age and high ideals. I believe they dropped the 'bodily harm'
charge deliberately, in order to make it a summary offence, as
they were frightened of having him before a jury. He will be
out in two years if he 'behaves'. Until then I shall keep the
Murchison flame burning...

Thursday August 3rd

According to a recent Gallup Poll 80% of Australians are
against taking more migrants from Asia and Africa.

So why do I feel so alone?

Thursday August 24th

Someone from the mainland calling himself a 'bush nationalist' phoned. Still not sure how he got our number. Said he was sympathetic to the TUL, but disagreed about the monarchy.

I answered him as I thought Reg might have: the armed forces take an oath of loyalty to the Crown, not to the Prime Minister. So who is going to help in a revolution? Whitlam (to think I used to like him!) acknowledged this - it's the main reason he didn't stage a coup. So the bush nationalist and I agreed to disagree.

Then he began telling me of the 'biologising' (whatever that means) of Russia's domestic policy, and of a 'National Alliance' in America, and something called the 'Gress' (I think?) in France. So perhaps we are not as alone as we thought we were.

But he also warned me about a weird cult group called the 'Sunshine Club' who recently tried to murder a nationalist and his family in Sydney. They said that he not only deserved to die for his 'white racist' beliefs, but that his wife and children also deserved to die because they were 'infected' with his views! Our newfound friend told me to be on my guard for members of this sect in Tasmania.

I think I will get a dog.

Friday September 1st

The first day of spring I came home with a bouncing Rottweiler pup. He's so adorable. I called him 'Menzies' after the late prime minister. That's sure to annoy dear Sally next door, but she'll just have to try and grow up a bit.

I warned Reg about the Sunshine Club during my weekly visit yesterday. You never know, they may even have infiltrated the staff at Risdon. I told him that Grassby had mentioned him by name in a speech at the sinisterly-named 'Commission for Community Affairs', but Reg just scoffed.

Thursday September 28th

The new pope has died after only 33 days on the papal throne. That seems weird, what with the masonic symbolism of the number 33. Was he killed for a reason?

I must say I prefer the Catholic Church to Reg's C of E (which I was also raised in), though neither of us attend anyway. All the churches are riddled with commies! When I tell my sister things like that she thinks it is my schizophrenia coming back, but it isn't...just a calm, rational analysis.

Why does she always think so badly of me?

Friday October 13th

Sid Vicious of the Sex Pistols has been in the news, charged with the murder of his girlfriend. What a sordid affair! I hate the way these punks dance, flopping up and down on the spot like rag dolls. I'm really starting to be bored by rock music, truth be told. I like Handel (Reg prefers Haydn and Elgar, or at least pretends to), but I feel the need for something completely different to match my feelings these days.

Something like a thousand steam engines all hissing at once!!!

Saturday October 28th

The terrorist Begin was joint winner of the Nobel Peace Prize...what a topsy turvy world we live in. No wonder I once had a breakdown. I thought it was I who was upside down, but no, it's actually the world!

I've been painting again, pictures of what I see as a better world, but now I'm determined to do a really demonic one of

Begin. I have to get it out of my system.

I wanted to enrol part time in art school, as a mature age student, but Reg talked me out of it when we were courting. He lent me his copy of *The Painted Word* by Tom Wolfe, which helped me realise that the art world is a rigged game. (Funny how their names all end in Berg…I wonder what *that* means?)

Art like mine can't be shown in public, even if I wanted it to, because it comes from the heart.

Reg is right about so much!

Monday November 20th

Hundreds of commies from San Francisco just committed mass suicide in South America! I would say 'good riddance' if it weren't for the fact that 270 of them were children.

Reading a book from Reg's shelf called *The Camp of the Saints*. It's scary, but makes me even more committed.

Monday December 25th

Christmas dinner at Dad's. His cooking was really delicious this year, but he seems even more distant than last time. He liked Menzies and played 'fetch the stick' with him a lot. Little Michael (is he really two already?!) on the other hand was *terrified* of Menzies.

I care less and less about music. Unlike last year, when I was DJ, this time Sally picked the tunes. She played 'Mull of Kintyre' by Wings (as if we hadn't heard it enough already) and 'Mary's Boy Child' by Boney M. It was weird listening to blacks singing a Christmas song, because I always associate manger songs with snow. If our race is to plow its own path once more, shouldn't it perhaps have a new religion, not one that we share with other races? I don't know, it's something to ponder…

Sally lent me a book called *Tirra Lirra By the River*, and I promised I would read it, but it looks so boring. Sally is always so attuned to the latest media trends, how does she do it? As for my brother-in-law Paul, he keeps talking about my paintings, which he only saw once. Is he attracted to me? I hope not, for even if we weren't both married I could never reciprocate! He's far too normal for me.

The World Council of Churches are now openly campaigning to keep white Rhodesians out of Australia! What the fuck is their problem??? Are they insane? Or just sadists? They just gave another $110,000 to SWAPO (who murder and maim black people, including children), but that doesn't seem to keep them awake at night.

These murderous priests should be hung with piano wire, every last one of them! And I say that in full cognisance of the Christmas spirit of forgiveness!

Saturday February 3rd

Sid Vicious is dead. In the Northern Territory they are going to pull uranium from the earth. Every part of me cries out against this. It will contaminate the water, the blood of the earth. People can never be whole unless they have a unifying vision. Only love for the earth will unify everyone, left or right. I feel that in my bones.

Wednesday March 7th

Sally was asking me about Reg's money. She seemed jealous that he inherited enough to live off the interest, which on top of his war pension is more than adequate to support his wife and future child. Is she trying to con me out of it somehow, while he's in prison? I begin to feel suspicious of her in so many ways.

Saturday May 5th

Murch has been jailed for an extra eighteen months, due to an altercation with another inmate! Even though the other inmate started it, the injuries Reg inflicted on him were considered excessive. It's unfair and disgraceful.

Britain has elected a female prime minister known as the 'Iron Lady'. Can she save Rhodesia? If not then what possible use is she?

Sunday June 10th

The Abos have opened a uranium mine on one of their tribal lands in the NT, raping the land. Then again, Reg believes that if South Africa has nukes, as is now rumoured, maybe they won't fold so easily as Rhodesia is currently doing!

The new Kingborough Sports Centre has finally opened, and my brother-in-law Paul has taken up badminton there. Perhaps I should take up a sport also, to take my mind off things. I am estranged from all my old friends, and my relationship with Sally next door is highly fraught. Even little nephew Michael looks at me with a frown on his brow. Reg is my only true friend and comrade.

Thursday July 12th

It seems that space stations are falling from the sky, and crashing into the Western Australian desert.

I think I will go mad again…

Thursday November 29th

For Michael's third birthday I got him some beeswax crayons, much nicer than the made-in-China brand that were recently pulled from sale after several children were hospitalised from their poison.

Sally bought him a polyester tracksuit, poor kid!

The Tasmanian government has banned smoking on buses, as they are worried about bus seats catching on fire. Perhaps they are right, as the last thing we need is more air pollution from burning nylon.

I am reading a new book called *Gaia*, by James Lovelock. It's truly fascinating. I, for one, am glad the federal government have made national parks of the Barrier Reef and Kakadu...for once I agree with them, a strange old feeling!

Reg has been studying philosophy and theology in the cell he shares with a confidence trickster called Wally Bailey. Reg wants to find a way to unite the intellect and the soul, and so make an unbreakable union by means of which the white race can carry out its destiny. But what that destiny is, he doesn't know, and neither do I.

* * *

From the diary of Paul Glendower

27/12/79

Writing this diary on our good old typewriter, for which Sally thoughtfully bought me a new ribbon for Christmas. It has proved impossible to get any kind of word processing program for the IBM 5100. I wonder what someone from the future would think of this machine, which once seemed like a dream, 'so various, so beautiful, so new,' but now 'hath neither joy, nor love, nor light'?

1/1/80

So, the new decade has dawned at last. Could it be unkinder to me than the seventies have been?

8/1/80

I am worried about Sylvie. She has been to see a movie called 'Alien' SEVEN times. She claims it ties in with her environmental views, but isn't it rather a sign of the kind of obsessive behaviour that caused her to have a breakdown several years ago?

26/1/80

Australia Day BBQ after badminton. Henry mentioned a computer selling for less than 300 DOLLARS (this old typewriter only has a pound sign). You have to solder it yourself and it only has a kilobyte of RAM, but still, damn it all. Another reason to kick myself for jumping into the market too early.

5/3/80

Spoke to Sylvie over the back fence when she was putting washing out (she rarely visits, and I almost get the feeling she and Sally are not on very good terms). She ranted to me about terrorists in Rhodesia, or Zimbabwe or whatever it's supposed to be called, intimidating blacks to vote for the terrorist Robert Mugabe over moderate blacks, or something like that. Apparently our own PM Malcolm Fraser is complicit in this, and calls Mugabe's fraudulent election a 'remarkable achievement'.

Why on earth does Sylvie care so much about the collapse of Rhodesia? She has never been there, and before her unfortunate meeting with Murchison (which I stupidly instigated) she was actually in favour of black government there. Murchison's influence has unhinged her in a way that is worse than her previous schizophrenic attacks. Even imprisoned I can still feel his baleful presence, watching me in presumed disapproval! (There is no exclamation mark on this typewriter, so I have to make one, using fullstop-backspace-apostrophe. Like thus:!!!) That man really is the limit...

21/6/80

Haven't written for some time. Don't think I will keep this diary up.

In the last month, there has been a terrible smear campaign in the media against Murchison. Some mainland papers have even claimed his war record to be falsified or exaggerated, while the churchman he attacked is presented as a kind of Christian Martyr.

Whether the smears against Murchison are true or not, people believe them, because they come from a legitimate source - the media. At work, where I stupidly revealed already that I am his brother-in-law, I am being made to suffer for it, frozen out of social activities in a snide and subtle way I would not have thought possible.

I hate Murchison for this. I hate myself, and I even hate Sylvie. What a hypocrite Murchison is, to go on about the 'Rule of Law' in an almost religious manner, then flout it himself.

Even though I don't believe in God, the Murchisons are surely cursed by Him.

And so am I. Ha!

*   *   *

From the diary of Sally Glendower

October 10th, 1980

Michael recited a 'poem' he made up today. It said
'Moo Moo Moo
goes the little dairy Coo.
Over the hills and stiles.
Moo Moo Moo.'
Since I taught him the the alphabet he has more or less

43 ⎯

taught himself to read. Not bad. Perhaps he will be a writer? Not if he takes after his father, though, who is withdrawing into himself more each day.

Have enrolled Michael to start Sunday School next year at the new Uniting Church up on the hill. He will find it more modern and interesting than the Anglican church he was baptised in.

December 8th, 1980

John Lennon has been murdered, by someone the police described as a 'local screwball'. Shocking. It seems like only yesterday that I bought 'Hey Jude'.

Actually, it was well over a decade ago. Time moves so quickly.

May 3rd, 1981

Michael's drawing skills coming along nicely, drawing birds as M's. But there was an incident at kindergarten, at the teddy bears' picnic. I get the feeling he doesn't like his teacher very much. He has become rather withdrawn, and tries not to go at every chance. Yet she is a perfectly sensible woman, so it's more likely to be a problem with Michael himself. I overheard him in the playground yesterday, arguing with another child about 'infinity'.

July 29th, 1981

Australia should be a republic, I have no doubt of that, but I still had a good old cry at the royal wedding, as did Sylvie, who came over to watch it on our colour screen (clearing the bad feeling between us a bit). Diana was so beautiful! I thought my heart would burst when they kissed.

Paul has a week off work, but all he does is mope around

the house or sit reading some book called 'The Soul of a New Machine'. He's doing something called a 'text adventure' on his ugly computer (its proper title is 'Colossal Cave Adventure'). Sometimes I wonder whether he's a man or a baby.

September 14th, 1981

To my shock, Sylvie actually defended some of the positions of that horrible Joh Bjelke-Petersen.

The *Saturday Evening Mercury* has claimed that Murchison is Joh's paid agent in Tasmania. Maybe he *is*, and that's where the lump sum came from, and not some inheritance from a wealthy grandfather!

Although even Sylvie didn't like Joh's military-style raids against that hippie commune in Far North Queensland a few years back...but only because the hippies 'weren't actual Communists' (her words). I no longer recognise her as my flaky but gentle sister...it's like Murchison has infected her with a brain disease (though apparently even *he* isn't a fan of Joh allowing the Japanese to build a tourist complex on the Queensland coast). Sylvie insists there is 'complete freedom of expression' in Queensland, which is rubbish, as we all know what happens to anyone who tries to protest there!

On the other hand, she doesn't like Reagan or Thatcher very much, says their anti-inflation measures are causing high unemployment, and that the answer is something called 'social credit', whatever that is (something else flaky, no doubt).

December 2nd, 1981

Got Michael a 'Junior Encyclopedia' for his fifth birthday. He has been reading it so obsessively that I was obliged to take it off him for a few days. I even caught him reading it by torchlight when he was meant to be asleep.

December 12th, 1981

The Franklin Dam referendum.
I voted for the original proposal, Paul voted for the compromise solution, and Sylvie voted informally, as 'no dams' was not on the ballot. Typical.

December 14th, 1981

Dreamt that Michael leading a revolt against all decency. But the people he led turned on him, and he had to hide in a crater of boiling mud, which quickly burned him up.

December 15th, 1981

Murchison will be released in a few days.
God help us all.

PART ONE

THE CHANGELING

1

BLACK DOG

Uncle Reg said machines were getting more advanced, but everything else was getting worse, because the State was being run like a business, and not by the mystical head of the monarchy.

But what did Uncle Reg mean by that?

Was it the same State Miss Quinn had said would punish him if he played with guns?

And what things were getting 'worse'?

For him they were getting better!

Only yesterday, the teacher had asked him to read the storytime tale to his class…because he was the only student who could read properly! Also, he was the only one who knew the answer to twelve times twelve! He had his own encyclopedia, his ladybird books, and the toy soldiers Uncle Reg had bought for him.

Life was good…

So much better than last year, when Miss Quinn, his horrid kindergarten teacher, had been mean to him all year after she caught him making a gun shape with his hands in the playground, and he refused to say he was sorry. She had told him that little boys who played with guns would be punished by the State.

But which State did she mean? Tasmania, where he lived, or a different State?

Then, too, there was the green man who said 'shhhhhh' on Sesame Street. Last year Michael was mortally afraid of him, and would hide whenever he came on. He even thought the shhhhhh man might have been the one who had locked Uncle Reg up in prison. He wasn't supposed to know Uncle Reg had been to prison, but he knew. Now, though, at the big school, he wasn't afraid anymore of the wicked shhhhhh man.

Last year he'd been bitten by an inchman, and had howled and howled, and the other kids had *laughed* at him. The kindergarten kids were mean, not like the kids at the big school, who respected him, and listened quietly when he read them a story. They looked up to him because he knew what the answer to twelve times twelve was!

When he grew up, he was going to be a helicopter pilot like his hero Dick Smith. Yes, the great Dick Smith who had flown a helicopter all by himself from Sydney to Bundaberg, the furthest ever. And he would also be an astronaut, a palaeontologist, a mountain climber, and a cook, just like Swedish Chef.

Oh, he had so much to look forward to!

Life was good.

*   *   *

The horror.

Walking down the cold empty corridor to the library.

Having to tell the librarian, Miss Frost, that he had lost the book he'd borrowed. He was always losing things, but this was worse because it *wasn't his*. Now he was scared of telling the librarian, and afraid he would cry.

But even worse than that was knowing that his mother would disapprove. That gave him a cold feeling of dread in the crook of his belly…

The book had been about a black dog, and now he imagined a black dog following him down the hallway, stalking him down the empty passage to the library. It looked like Aunty Sylvie's dog, Menzies – a growling, soft-padding, slavering thing. He loved his Aunty Sylvie, but he hated her dog.

And, there was another terror in his life. The house next door, on the opposite side to Aunty Sylvie and Uncle Reg, long empty, was now inhabited by a silent, solitary old woman who always wore black.

She was even scarier than the shhhhhh man, and perhaps it was *her* dog stalking him down the corridor.

*   *   *

There was a strange man at Uncle Reg's, from a place called the 'University', which was like a school for grown-ups. He had a thick blue jumper with a rolled-up neck, which Aunty Sylvie called a 'turtle neck'. He was arguing with Uncle Reg; Menzies was banished to the back yard.

'My dear Mr. Murchison, I tell you that racism is nothing more than the denial of uniqueness. You should read Alain de Benoist on this topic, and know that...' Uncle Reg snorted, interjecting that he considered himself a racist precisely *because* he recognised uniqueness, ha ha ha.

'Well, perhaps we can call it alterophobia, fear of the other.' (Michael thought: other *what?*). 'But to talk of inferior races is absurd, because no objective reference point exists to measure them by...'

'Civilisation and the rule of Law are *my* reference points, Mr. Holloway.'

'But you deny the unique dynamic energies of different peoples...'

'Dynamic? Demonic, don'cha mean? Ha ha.'

'Different races have a right to be *different.*'

'And from where would that hypothetical 'right' come? From the rule of Law, of course!'

'But what of activist judges like Lionel Murphy, *perverting*

51

the law? And, the current law is…'

'Being used against us, yes…we can agree on that.'

Michael felt warm relief flood through him. Agreement! So much better than bitter arguments of the kind his parents often had. Reinforcing his relief, Aunt Sylvie came in and gave him a hot chocolate.

'I'm a nationalist, like you,' the turtle necked man assured Uncle Reg. 'I'm just opposed to imperialism. And it seems so *clownish* now. Take the recent squabble over a pile of dirt…'

'The Falkland Islands are *not* an uninhabited sheep station,' Uncle Reg assured him gruffly. 'They are an outpost of Britain herself. Although I *did* find it odd that Mrs. Thatcher cared so much about the Falklanders, when she didn't give a damn about the fate of a quarter of a million white Rhodesians.'

'Then I take it you're not happy about the recent suspension of appeals to Privy Council?'

'Ha!'

'I couldn't care less myself. I would be happy to see Australia become a republic.'

'Ha!'

'But not a politicians' republic, 'part of Asia'…no, *our* trading partners would be Chile, Argentina, and others with whom we have a southern affinity.'

'Oh, what ineffable rubbish!'

Uncle Reg was funny. He cared so much about far-off Britain. Michael thought he knew quite a lot about Britain from his Ladybird books, and from the 'United Kingdom' entry in his Junior Encyclopedia. He knew, too, about little Prince William, who had recently been born in a hospital in London. How strange – a prince born in an ordinary hospital!

Uncle Reg didn't like Japan much, though. Japan was another group of islands, like Britain, but on the other side of the big landmass. He knew Uncle Reg didn't like it because Uncle Reg had dared to disparage his new favourite TV show, *The Battle of the Planets*.

'Nip rubbish,' he'd called it, explaining that 'Nip' was

short for 'Nippon', another name for Japan. At first Michael felt hurt, but this quickly gave way to intellectual shock - how could *anyone* not like *The Battle of the Planets*? It wasn't possible!

But then, he reflected, Uncle Reg was what mummy called 'eccentric', and had once been to prison for tipping mud over a bishop and beating him with a cane...so Michael decided he would be tolerant of Uncle Reg's immense cultural ignorance. Besides, how *could* the show be Japanese, when he knew from a playground rhyme that Chinese and Japanese had slanty eyes, while the characters in the show had round eyes like Australians?

The sun, rising from behind the earth as the title music kicked in, was the most beautiful thing he had ever seen!

He loved the way the characters helmets were each a different colour, and he dreamed about protecting Princess, the female member of the team, from attack by mutant space monsters. The weird flashing of 7-Zark-7's computer screens held mysteries he could scarcely fathom, so much more entrancing than daddy's computer which he mustn't ever touch, and which was gathering dust in the basement.

But most of all he loved the team's spaceship, especially when it turned into the Fiery Phoenix!

He took up the organic crayons his aunty had given him, and which he had barely used until now, and wore them to stumps drawing space battles between Saturn and Earth.

He had begun to create his own mythology.

*   *   *

By October he had found a new real-life hero...Dick Smith was forgotten, and a Robert de Castella poster from the *Saturday Evening Mercury* adorned his wall, between blue-tacked space drawings and Weet-Bix cards with pictures of cars and tropical birds.

Castella had come from far behind to win the marathon at the Commonwealth Games in Brisbane, winning glory for

Australia and beating two spindly blacks in the process. Uncle Reg said blacks were 'chaotic', so Michael associated them with Saturn, and Castella with Earth.

The giant kangaroo mascot Matilda was smiling on him, and smiling on everybody, even the blacks...except his parents, perhaps, who had both seemed very withdrawn of late. Once he had heard them whispering about a woman who had killed her baby...or did a dingo do it? But that couldn't be what was troubling them.

He knew that Daddy's type of computer had been 'pulled from the market', which meant he could no longer get spare parts or programs for it, and Daddy said this made him feel old...but that couldn't be what was bothering him either, as Daddy was *already* old. Sometimes it was hard to believe he was actually younger than Uncle Reg...

*   *   *

He was rehearsing for the nativity play. He was playing a sheep, and the costume was a lambswool rug. He liked Sunday school because they gave him colourful stickers. Mummy didn't go to church herself, but picked him up afterwards. Soon she *would* be going, though, to see him in the nativity play.

He was humming a tune he had heard on the car radio, called 'Eye of the Tiger', and imagining *he* was a tiger, eating sheep. And then he imagined he was a sheep again, running from the tiger.

His Sunday school teacher was a nervous lady who had told him that a country called Israel was very important and very wonderful. It was a tiny country, and it had a taken him a while to find it on Daddy's globe.

He was interested in it, because Aunty Sylvie had said it was a naughty country, and the people there had dropped bombs on a city called Beirut as a warning to them not to violate a cease-fire, something which Aunty called a 'breathtaking act of hubris'.

As he rehearsed, he could hear Uncle Reg's guinea fowl screeching next door.

Mummy and Daddy hated the guinea fowl, but Michael liked them, because they were funny and because their noise formed a welcome contrast to the Woman of Black Silence who lived over the *other* fence.

The male guinea fowl made a noise like someone scraping two jagged bits of metal together, and they did it lots and lots, at all hours of the day!

Aunty Sylvie said they were good guard animals (so why didn't she get rid of Menzies?) and also ate the ticks which attacked their regular chooks. Yes, Aunty and Uncle were setting themselves up quite a little farm in their back yard, even though the yard wasn't much bigger than Michael's.

Daddy muttered his disapproval, saying they had set up their incubator shed without approval from the 'local council'. Michael knew that the mean teacher, the one the kids called 'Fuckface McCunt', was a member of this mysterious local council.

Aunty Sylvie called her yard a 'permaculture oasis', but Daddy said it was a 'stupid Felicity Kendall fantasy'.

One day, Mummy came home full of rage because Uncle Reg had asked her to hold one of the male guinea fowl while he did something disgusting to its abdomen, and got something out of it to put in a glass tube; something she had to say in a whisper to Daddy, because Michael was there, but he knew it was something to do with 'fertilising the eggs'.

To add insult to injury, one of the guinea fowl had pecked Mummy's ankle as she left! Michael pretended to be shocked, but really, he thought it was very funny, adding to his opinion of what he thought of as the 'funny birds'.

*   *   *

The mainland was more important than Tasmania, that's

why it was called the *main*land.

But it was also dangerous, hot and full of fire…he had seen it on TV. He didn't ever want to go there.

He wanted to stay by the cool grey Derwent, gathering seashells at Kingston Beach, or looking at the *Australian Women's Weekly Children's Birthday Cake Book*, which made his mouth water. There were cakes like swimming pools, filled with green jelly, surrounded by picket fences made from chocolate logs. There were castle cakes, with turrets and banners, and this year he wanted one of *those*.

It was funny, but the Women's Weekly was now a monthly magazine and they kept on calling it a weekly! Funny, too, was Australia's new prime minister, who was a world champion at beer drinking. Aunty Sylvie called him 'Begin's Best Boy', and 'a Zionist lackey'. His name was Hawke, which was even funnier because the opposition leader was called Peacock…Michael imagined them pecking each other to death in the big parliament building where grown-ups argued about which laws people should follow.

In America, the leader was called 'Ray Gun'. Why did they all have such funny names? In Tasmania there had been Holgate, which sounded like Colgate toothpaste, but he had been replaced by Grey (the colour of the Derwent in autumn as Michael walked along the beach to his secret cave, while Mummy watched from a distance). Another was called 'Good Luck', and there was 'The Mouth of the South'…or was that just Mummy being silly?

Uncle Reg hated all of them, though. He said he would consider voting for the Imperial British Conservative Party, run by someone called The Wizard of New Zealand (was it a real wizard, or just pretending?). But they weren't running any candidates in Tasmania, so he had drawn a picture of a crown and a flaming sword on his ballot paper, and hadn't numbered anyone.

Oh, politics was funny all right!

* * *

Daddy was going away for a while.

He said he needed to 'sort himself out'.

Michael thought it sounded like he was putting himself in a container, but deep down he had an uneasy feeling in his stomach, as if part of the foundation had been knocked from under the house, and it was hanging over a lava pit.

Mummy told him he could visit Daddy every second weekend, in the boarding house in South Hobart where he would be staying. But would it be the same Daddy, or a different person?

Both of them seemed to have changed, subtly, in a way that Michael didn't like.

If he had known that the sense of unease would stay with him for decades, he might have worried more…but he told himself the problem would be resolved, and everything would be as it had been before, all ordered and neat.

Things would be sorted out.

* * *

Now he had been to the cinema! It was amazing, incredible. The dark womb, mealy smell of pop-corn, curtainous backdrop for the film that would haunt his dreams - *The Dark Crystal*.

He wanted his own pet Landstrider, but more than that he longed to embark on a *quest*!

He went next door to tell Aunty Sylvie about the film. She wasn't there, but Uncle Reg let him in. Menzies was safely out the back. Uncle Reg played him a tape of some Rhodesian war songs. It was strange music: grim, yet somehow it made him feel peaceful.

'You won't hear this music in the future, my boy. Mugabe's tightening dictatorship will see to that. But this cassette will preserve it for future generations.' Michael had heard of Rhodesia (which had been renamed 'Zimbabwe'), because the Australian cricket team were being forced to go there by the prime minister, Mr. Hawke, even though it was supposed to be dangerous.

'Uncle Reg?'

'Yes m'boy?'

'Why did you tip mud all over a bishop?'

'Sometimes you have to make a stand, boy…upset the decorum.'

'I thought bishops were good?'

'Not this one. You must learn to distinguish between Christians, lad. Some are good, but others are more like wolves in sheep's clothing. Take these Festival of Light idiots, Fred Nile and his cohorts. They had the nerve to attack my group, the TUL, because we are anti-Zionist. They believe that Jesus won't return until Israel stretches from the Nile to the Euphrates!

'And then there are the *other* mob…the liberation theologists, of whom your bishop is one. He wears his cassock during demonstrations, but in the pulpit he wears shorts and a t-shirt. Ha! What a poseur. The rot inside the church is certainly deep.'

'I'm afraid I didn't understand all that Uncle.'

'You just enjoy your childhood, my boy. It'll end soon enough.'

'Is it true that you hate feet and inches?'

'You have it the wrong way round - it's metres I'm opposed to.'

'Why?'

'It's an artificial measurement. Inorganic, no basis in tradition. The metre was recently defined, you may be interested to know, as the distance light travels in a vacuum in one 299 millionth of a second, or something like that. What rubbish…'

The front door banged, and Aunty Sylvie came in.

To Michael's alarm there was dried blood on her face.

'Aunty, what's the matter?'

She was crying.

Uncle Reg took her to another room to clean her up. Michael couldn't hear everything they said, but it seemed she had been attacked at a protest against the dam.

Michael knew all about the dam. Half the cars in Tasmania were sporting stickers about it, either a green triangle saying 'No Dams' or a red one saying 'Dam It.' A boy at school said his father had told him that without the dam there would be no light. All Tasmania would be without electricity, in total darkness!

But Aunt Sylvie apparently thought differently.

Michael knew she was against the dam for some reason; but as he listened, it became clear the people who attacked her were from the 'No Dams' side, *not* the 'Dam It' side. From the same side as her! What on earth was going on? Was it something to do with Uncle's secret club, the TUL? It made him feel nervous.

As for Uncle Reg, he was angry at Sylvie's attackers, but also angry at her. It seemed he had advised her not to go, but she hadn't listened to him.

'Man is the sense organ of the earth,' she was saying.

'These 'greenies' are just rootless cosmopolitans,' he snorted. 'As soon as it's over they'll move on to Roxby Downs or some other place.'

'I had to try and join two worlds, Reg,' she sobbed.

Grown-ups were even stranger than children, Michael reflected, and not for the first time.

*   *   *

A week later he was playing with his toy soldiers in the back yard, pretending the grass was a vast, hellish jungle, and could hear Uncle and Aunty in their garden, so he decided to spy on them through a hole in the fence.

They were doing something strange, something that looked a bit like a medal ceremony from the Commonwealth Games.

'You understand why I have no choice but to expel you from the Tasmanian Union of Loyalists?'

'Yes.'

'States' Rights are not an issue we can budge on. And the people of Tasmania voted in the referendum for the dam…'

'Yes. But I would happily do it again anyway, in an instant.' She had tears in her eyes. 'And if Tasmanians vote for the dam, then democracy is stupid.'

'The Marxists are using the protests as part of their strategy to centralise power.'

'It doesn't have to be that way.'

'It's the thin end of the wedge. If outside interference is brooked, where will it end? Will Papua New Guinea insist via the UN that cannibalism be tolerated in Australia?' Michael saw, with shock, that Uncle Reg was crying, too. 'And yet, I have hopes that we shall still be fellow travellers in other regards?'

'Oh Reg, I will always be your wife…'

So Uncle Reg had kicked Aunt Sylvie out of his club, but they still loved one another!

Michael loved Aunty Sylvie too, and couldn't bear to see her cry…but he thought that if he ever got married himself, there's no way his wife could be anything other than a loyal member of his own gang.

He had spoken to no one yet of this top secret gang, which he had copied directly from his Aunty and Uncle's…

2

'AVERAGE 80s CHILDHOOD'

School camp meant he would miss three whole episodes of his new favourite show, *Star Blazers*. *The Battle of the Planets* was forgotten as he sat glued to an epic voyage through space to save the Earth from destruction, each hair-raising episode announcing the number of days Earth had left.

But, joy of joys, they were allowed to watch it in the TV room at camp each morning, before filing into the kitchen for Cocoa Pops or Rice Bubbles, far more glamorous than the Weet-Bix of home!

* * *

On the second night, he pissed his sleeping bag. The other kids all knew about it because the teacher reassured him, very loudly, that he had done nothing wrong. Now he would be known as a bedwetter, even though he hadn't wet his bed at home in a long, long time.

* * *

The third night, wrapped in new bedding, a hollow feeling hacked at his guts and the base of his skull.

He had no name for what the dictionary called homesickness, knowing only that it was something he and only he had ever suffered. The void sucked his innards and he wanted to die.

*   *   *

When class resumed next week, he had lost his admired status, and was the butt of frequent teasing, especially from girls.

'The Rivers of Babylon', the tune to learn on recorder that week, was a song he already knew from one of his parents' Boney M albums. Formerly, he would have taken pride in such knowledge, using it to further his reputation as a walking encyclopedia, but as he was now *persona non grata* he kept his mouth shut, wondering idly what 'Zion' meant, and why anyone would weep to remember it.

*   *   *

But next year, grade two, brought a different teacher and mainly different kids. He never regained his walking encyclopedia status, nor wished to, for now it was a suspect thing to be. The world had turned upside down. The kids admired now were the ones with the most *Star Wars* action figures. The world was measured in plastic dolls.

There were *Ghostbusters* dolls, too, but he thought they looked tawdry, and his mother wouldn't let him see the film they were based on. But one kid had a huge Millennium Falcon and he had never wanted anything so badly. He pestered his mother to get him one for Christmas, with a sinking feeling she wouldn't. Maybe he could have a Soda

Stream instead? Then he could make his own fizzy drinks, in a whole rainbow of flavours…

In kindergarten, another kid had scared him by telling about someone called 'Darth Raider'…but he had seen *The Return of the Jedi* last year, and knew *Vader* was really Luke's father. And, it seemed, there were two more Star Wars films…some other boys had seen them. But how could *he* see them when they were gone from the cinema forever? The kids muttered darkly about something called 'video', but he couldn't figure out what this was meant to be.

He could discuss the intricate theology of TV shows at length, however. *The New Adventures of Flash Gordon. Doctor Snuggles* with his wooden rocket made from an old barrel. And *Educating Marmalade,* about a girl so rebellious she was expelled from a new school every single episode. He secretly wanted to be like her. His mother tried to stop him watching it, but Marmalade was his heroine, a female he could empathise with. Females frightened him in general; even his beloved Aunt Sylvie would go to a land he couldn't access.

*　　*　　*

The world was changing. The *Saturday Evening Mercury* had been replaced by the *Sunday Tasmanian* (whoever heard of a newspaper on Sundays?), and dollar notes were now being replaced by a shiny gold coin. It felt like a betrayal, somehow…just like Daddy had betrayed him, by leaving.

But here he was, going to the basketball with Daddy, who had wanted to watch a woodchopping contest, but Michael had insisted on basketball. The Tassie Devils were playing the Adelaide 36ers. He would have loved to see Leapin' Leroy Loggins, but the Brisbane Bullets were only in the Eastern Conference.

How strange that there were black men playing for the Tassie Devils. He had never seen any blacks on the streets of Kingston or Hobart. So where did they live when they weren't playing basketball?

The slide-out seats of the Kingborough Sports Centre were packed, for the only big sports league Tassie had a team in (not counting the Sheffield Shield). The Devils lost, of course, were roundly thrashed…which felt like another betrayal.

His father off in another world taking Michael home, didn't greet his wife, but drove away as his son was knocking on the front door. His mother, distant in a different way, had a prim-tight smile on her usually frowning face.

Grown-ups were strange, and remote.

Michael looked forward to the next meeting of his club, the Nat Sav G, which now had a second member, making it a bigger organisation than his uncle's!

But his friend Sean was leaving at the end of the year, going to another city far away on the mainland, and the Nat Sav G would be reduced to one again.

Nat Sav G was short for 'Nature Saving Gang', for they wanted to save nature from evil polluters, just like Aunty Sylvie did.

They had their last official meeting in the virgilia tree in the back yard, a Rhodesian tree overlooking his aunt's place. They didn't talk much about nature, though, but mainly about the Apple Macintosh computer Sean's parents had recently bought, which was controlled by something called a 'mouse'.

They also talked about Zola Budd, who had run *barefoot* at the Olympics. She had been unjustly accused of cheating, when in fact (Uncle Reg told him) it was *she* who had been cheated against, spiked with someone else's running shoe. Michael wanted a poster of Zola, but couldn't find one in any of the magazines. Oh, why didn't the magazines care about this miscarriage of justice, this unfair tarnishing of her name? Michael wanted to protect her from her lying accusers. Sean gave him a weird look, however, and their talk returned to the familiar topic of *Star Wars*. Now he learned for the first time what a 'video player' really was, and how a 'remote control' worked. You could watch things on 'fast forward'!

His greedy longing for a consumer product had never been so painful.

The meeting broke up early when they noticed the old woman staring at them from behind the fence. Mummy said she was a Greek Orthodox widow, but the boys were convinced she was a sorceress. Why would she stare at them if she weren't some kind of a witch, perhaps casting curses through the 'evil eye'?

Next day at school Sean had gone, even though he wasn't meant to be leaving until the day after tomorrow. That proved it: she *was* a witch, and had done away with his one and only friend…

*   *   *

His mother, always at his throat. There were only two of them in the house, but a wall of oppression existed between them. He only felt calm around Aunty Sylvie.

'Your mother loves you,' Sylvie told him. 'She's just scared for your future.'

He liked to look at Sylvie's paintings, which were strange, with vivid colours mixed in ways he couldn't have imagined coming up with himself. She was painting one of the *Titanic* wreck, which had just been discovered in the Atlantic. She had also painted AUSSAT, making it look evil, a red eye glaring down on earth forever.

She played him strange music, too. One record was called *The Sylvie and Babs Hi-Fi Companion*, a crazy mish-mash of songs, noise and weird talking.

'Did *you* make it, Aunty Sylvie? Who's Babs then?'

She laughed and said she hadn't. He thought it sounded better than the recorder pieces at school or the pop songs aped in the playground, boys singing 'Money for Nothing' and girls singing 'Material Girl', invisible guitars and microphones. But he loved to hear Cyndi Lauper sing 'Time After Time', which sent shivers down his spine.

Sylvie told him of new troubles Uncle Reg had been having, his list of enemies now a mile long. Michael, who hated strife, could barely comprehend such an existence. Two of his new enemies were Dr. Vitale, who regarded himself as a 'Sicilian supremacist', opposed to the 'pale whimperings' of the British-descended in Australia. He was connected somehow to the gangster Robert Trimboli.

Then there was a group called New New Labor, who were alleging that Uncle Reg himself was part of an 'international conspiracy' with ties to the mafia and the dope trade, via the Queen of England. Sylvie described them with a smile and wink as 'real weirdoes'. Uncle Reg's enemies all sounded like villains from a Saturday morning cartoon!

Sometimes, though, Aunty Sylvie went to the place where he couldn't reach her, and then it was worse than being alone, stuck in that room with her. He felt ever more alone at school, too, many lunch hours following his feet around the playground aimlessly, talking to nobody, joining in none of the vicious and innocent games. There was something in him that wasn't in the other kids, something different, a core of loneliness.

At about this time he discovered the Fighting Fantasy series of solo gamebooks in the library, and was snared in a seductive, anarchic realm of Wheelies, Miks, Elvins, Snattacats, Gonchongs, Slime-Eaters and sinister undead. Besides the maze-like structure of the books, he was drawn by the illustrations - thin and spidery, emanating from some cobwebbed cupboard beyond Time.

There were the Cretan Chronicles where one entered a labyrinth; and the mysterious *Starflight Zero*, whose pictures entranced him long hours. The Dungeons and Dragons modules were inaccessible, because he had no friends to play them with, but there *was* a nameless paper board game he took home and tried to grasp the rules of, which took him right *through* the cobwebbed cupboard, not to Narnia but a world where cold sunlight glinted on rime frost...this was the first time he had read the names Odin, Thor, Heimdall, Loki, and Fenris...yet it seemed he had heard them before, immeasurably long ago.

His mother wasn't interested in games, however. He gazed in vain at the colourful boxes in the toy shop of Kingston Town shopping centre - *Scotland Yard*, *Cluedo*, *Game of Life*. The coloured components seemed like entries to a mathemagical Otherworld.

Denied access, he made Fighting Fantasy-style adventures in the back garden. A patch of chives that had gone to seed became 'Mysterious Blue Herb, restores Stamina,' and a Tiger Woman lurked in the trees.

His world in the garden...

A fence protected from Menzies.

The larger garden of his grandfather's house at Ross, where hidden among the bushes might be a true gate to the Otherworld.

Magic in Hobart, in the shoe shop with its labyrinths of shoe boxes, and maze-like cubby-house in the mall.

All held secrets, he was sure, if he could but penetrate the walls.

*   *   *

He learnt a great deal about the world, much information coming from *Australiana* magazine, which he read at his grandfather's house.

A single issue educated him about Australia's Most Haunted House, about UFOs, devil worshippers, and a glamorous rich couple called Donald and Ivana Trump. There were pictures of women who poured drinks behind a bar with their bare bosoms hanging out, and funny cartoons about Abos and Japanese tourists. *Australiana* was far more educational than school!

One issue was devoted to the Rebel Cricket Tour, where an Aussie team had played in South Africa without the cricket board's permission, and Prime Minister Hawke had called them 'traitors'. That was funny, because Michael remembered Mr. Hawke had *forced* another Aussie cricket team to play in Zimbabwe.

He wondered how any of the teams would eat in Africa, where there was said to be no food. Earlier that year his class had been obliged to bring money from home to send to a starving black kid called 'Goitem', and some of the kids had been outraged when 'Goitem' hadn't written back to thank them for the money.

Michael's mother said Goitem's letter might have gotten lost in the post.

Near the end of the year she bought a second-hand upright piano, and signed him up for lessons with an old lady whose fingers smelled of lavender.

*　　*　　*

Halley's Comet came and went and he couldn't see it from Mt. Wellington for the clouds.

The woman in black had gone, too, and a loud family had moved in, blowing away the cobwebs. A mother and no father, just like Michael's house, and a boy around his own age, but from a different school. Michael tried to tell the boy about the Nat Sav G, but Julian thought it stupid.

Julian was funny in other regards, however, and they played rough shoot-'em-up games around the yard. He still had the feeling Miss Quinn was looking over his shoulder, waiting to punish him for playing guns, but he laughed her presence off.

Once they tried to get his father's old computer going, but they couldn't get it to 'boot up'. Adam's mum had a computer, too, with a four-colour screen! She had bought a game for it called 'Space Quest', where you typed in words telling the little man what to do. Michael and Adam spent whole Sunday afternoons playing it, often trying to get the man to do rude or ridiculous things.

But sadness, too, was a big part of his life.

He felt it reading *The Lord of the Rings* in the school library, especially the bits about the Elder Days and ancient starlight…the starlight of Elbereth on the Western Seas, and the 'grey rain-curtain' which 'turned all to silver glass' revealing 'a far green country under a swift sunrise.'

For some reason, this made him think of Sydney, a city he had never set foot in…and piano music floating out from a building that looked like a castle, drifting out across gardens in the rain.

There were sad shows on the ABC, too: *Under the Mountain*, *Chocky*, *Children of the Dog Star*, *The Haunting of Cassie Palmer*. And sad songs on the radio: 'Take My Breath Away', 'Lady in Red', 'The Final Countdown'. His mother turned it off when Samantha Fox came on, however…and wouldn't let him go to the big Dire Straits concert in Glenorchy.

Michael didn't *like* 'Money for Nothing', but he had wanted to go because it was a BIG EVENT.

*   *   *

The world kept changing.

TAA would soon be Australian Airlines, the boat to the mainland was now the 'Abel Tasman', and *Yes Minister* had changed to *Yes Prime Minister*.

Aunty Sylvie was taking him to see Uncle Reg protesting the Federal Labor Party Conference, held that year in Hobart. There would be bad people there, she said. She told him about the things they did, and it was terrible hearing them from the mouth of his gentle aunt, but he must realise it was a harsh world, she said.

She told him of a pale man, coughing and wheezing, who went around Sydney threatening to inject people with something deadly and disgusting called 'aides', though Michael had thought aides were people that helped you.

Worst of all, she told him about necklacing, where Africans would put a tyre filled with petrol round someone's neck, then light it. The victim's throat would catch fire as he inhaled the fumes, and the molten rubber would burn into his skin. It took him twenty minutes to die, while a mob jeered and screamed at him. Family and friends were given water and mockingly invited to rescue their loved one, but no water would ever put the fire out.

An evil witch called Winnie Mandela was behind some of the necklacing, but the newspapers claimed she was *good*. Weird that she had the same name as Winnie-the-Pooh, thought Michael, vowing to never trust a newspaper again.

The papers were full of the story of Barlow and Chambers, two Aussies who were to be hung by the neck until dead in Malaysia. He asked Uncle Reg what he thought about it, and to his surprise Uncle was in favour of hanging them. They had tried to introduce deadly drugs into the Malaysian community, he said, drugs that would kill or enslave many people.

But what if they *weren't* guilty, thought Michael, like Lindy Chamberlain. How could someone be guilty and then not guilty? It didn't make any sense.

He had been surprised to see a picture of a rock star on Uncle Reg's wall recently. It was Angry Anderson from Rose Tattoo, and Uncle had put a typed quote under the picture: 'Multiculturalism is like preparing a meal that's indigestible.'

'Not bad for a half-wog,' commented his uncle wryly.

Michael thought a 'wog' was a virus that kept you home from school, and thus something good.

*　　*　　*

It was cold outside the conference. Good his aunt had made him wear a jumper and parka, otherwise he *would* catch a wog. But still, it was cold. A wind from Antarctica, teeth chattering.

He knew Prime Minister Hawke would be there, as well as the federal treasurer Mr. Keating. Even his mother didn't like

Keating, because he had told a struggling Tasmanian housewife with children that 'Just because you choose to stay at home and watch soap operas in preference to working, that's your problem,' and Mummy was also a housewife (for which Daddy gave her money each month), although she was looking around for a part-time job.

Uncle Reg was round the corner somewhere. Michael was with Sylvie, who would keep him safe. Suddenly there was a shouting and a scuffling, and lots of men grunting, and Uncle Reg came round the corner, being dragged away by three burly policemen.

'Our system represents the collective wisdom and accumulated experience of centuries,' Uncle was screaming. 'The Labor Party used to *support* social credit, under Curtain. The internationalists have taken over it, just as they take over everything...'

'And so, Michael...you see what the system has in store for dissidents,' said his aunt, a strange tightness in her voice.

'Yes,' said Michael, lesson learned. 'But did you *know* he would be taken away, Aunty?'

*   *   *

Two months later a snow fell from heaven, blanketing Tasmania in white.

His mother, furious at what had happened, had forbidden him to see Sylvie and Reg, or talk to them, except at family gatherings where she herself was present. Uncle had only narrowly avoided another prison sentence, Michael knew. He was upset about not seeing his aunt, more upset than he showed, but his mind was also on *other* important things.

With the money Mummy made at her new job, he calculated, she should be able to get him some proper Transformers instead of crappy old Machine Men.

He also wanted He-Man action figures, a skateboard, and a toy space shuttle just like the one that blew up.

71

He would have to wait for birthday and Christmas, but it would be worth it!

3

SCOUT'S HONOUR

Feelings of dirt, worthlessness. Too scared to sneak across the fence to Aunty Sylvie's. Menzies would be there, slavering, slavering. His mother watching always, like an Eye. She worked during school, but perhaps the holidays?

Deprived of his chief source of information on politics, Michael tried to gather arcane knowledge from the newspaper. He wondered idly what a 'yuppie' was, a term the columnists used quite a bit.

Then there was something called an Australia Card - would his uncle and aunt be for it or against it; or would they disagree like with the dam? He decided they would probably *hate* a national ID card. It was like metrification, centralisation: efficient and ludicrous.

The same beer-swilling prime minister who had kicked Uncle Reg out of his conference was now saying in the papers that 'no Australian child will be living in poverty by the year 1990'; Michael could see why politicians were rumoured to be liars!

His interest gradually turned from politics to pop music, a subject of increasing fascination. He'd seen the very last episode of *Countdown*, but now there was a new show called *Rage*, and he got up in the pre-dawn light each Saturday to watch it, ultimately rewarded by seeing a drummer play upside-down in a cage! The song was called 'Wild Side', the band 'Mötley Crüe'. His mum, emerging sleepy from her lair,

73

was asked to buy a cassingle of the song to be played on her old mono tape recorder. She looked, said 'No way!', turned the TV off angrily.

She did buy him Kylie Minogue's 'Loco-Motion', but he scowled and said it was stupid girl's music (though he secretly liked it), and besides, the tape chewed the third time he played it. Stupid old tape player, just like the ones at school…why couldn't mum get a hi-fi? Or a *ghetto blaster* with a graphic EQ (whatever that was)?

Snobby Jenkins, however, thought Mötley Crüe were stupid. Michael didn't like Snobby because he had once said field marshals only control regiments, when Michael knew from his Junior Encyclopedia that field marshal was actually the highest rank of general; and when Michael got a copy of the same book from the library and showed it to him, Snobby actually *refused to look*, then made a mean taunt about Michael being a bedwetter who had been sent to the principal last year for writing bad words on a wall.

Michael hoped people had forgotten about that, as the principal hadn't told his mother, and under no circumstances did he want her to find out. The very idea chilled him to the pit of his stomach.

*   *   *

He had his Scoutcraft badge, now he could start to earn proper badges and cords. This patrol camp would give him a 'patrol activity' stripe.

The Quokka was his patrol. Their arch rivals were the Dibbler Patrol…the other two, Numbat and Bilby, were insignificant. The patrols were named after Western Australian mammals because the leader was from there, but Michael thought they should be changed to Tasmanian ones.

The Leader insisted they call him Macka, not 'sir' or 'skip'. He had sandy hair and a protruding Adam's apple that bulged even more when he shouted - which was frequently, yet not in anger. Michael had only seen him angry once, when one of the boys had flushed his packet of Winnie Reds ('five smokes ahead of the rest') down the bog, though the pack had floated in the bowl and he had been caught when a Dibbler had ratted him out. That boy had scrubbed toilets after the last six weekly meetings as punishment.

Now Macka was taking the Quokkas camping in his Troopy, a Winnie Red dangling from his lips as he drove past the ugly new Sheraton Hotel on Hobart's waterfront. He put a tape into the vehicle's cassette deck, which to Michael's shock was a recording of Australia's rudest country and western singer, Kevin 'Bloody' Wilson.

The boys laughed uproariously to the tunes of 'I Gave Up Wanking', 'The Pubic Hair Song', and 'Born Again Piss Tank'. Michael laughed too, but was mortified. He didn't understand all the references, but the abundance of 'f's' and 'c's', crudest words of the playground, made the bus trip both more and less than real, and he shivered with the sub- and hyper-reality of it.

Then Macka treated them to his own satirical rendition of Midnight Oil's 'Beds Are Burning', which had the boys in stitches. He had Peter Garrett's wonky voice down pat. It seemed he didn't like 'greenies', so Michael kept quiet about Aunty Sylvie, who, his mother said, had gone to Far North Queensland to attend an anti-logging protest. Michael hoped fervently nothing would happen to her as it had in the South-West.

But now Macka was talking about the Grim Reaper ads, which Michael's mother had made him watch, and which had scared him.

'I've news for you boys,' bellowed Macka. 'You're never gonna get AIDS...the ads lied! Normal people *don't* get it. AIDS is a fag disease, and the fags got it from coons in Africa, who got it from screwing monkeys. And now they're asking any old lady who was kissed by a stranger decades ago to get blood tested. Just to make the benders feel better! Fucking unbelievable...'

The boys liked their sandy-haired scoutmaster, they felt he

was treating them as equals by talking to them in this rough, manly way. When they finally reached the camp site, though, he shocked them for real.

'Alright, boys, you'll be right to fend for yourselves a couple of days, eh? I'm off down the pub.'

They thought he was joking, but he was dead serious. Dumping them in isolated bushland, fifty kilometres from the nearest phone box, would make men of them, he said. He waved a cheery goodbye and the Troopy diminished toward distant clumps of pubs and houses, the boys silent and despondent.

The patrol leader, who was twelve and knew how to put a tent up, did so, muttering. The others stood around making nervous jokes.

Michael sat on his bag, from which he pulled the latest Fighting Fantasy and began to read it. It was called 'Beneath Nightmare Castle', and was about—

But one of the other boys looked at him and sniggered. 'What are you reading a *book* for?'

'He's not even reading it properly,' said one of the others. 'Just flicking through the pages.'

'It's a gamebook,' retorted Michael.

'A what?'

'Go get some water, dipshit. The creek's down there…'

Michael, hurt and humiliated, picked up the flung jerry can and ambled towards the sound of running water, trying his best not to appear ruffled.

The creek was further than he thought, and when he had filled the can as best he could, he found he couldn't lift it. He dragged it step by step, nearly half an hour of strenuous effort, vowing silently that he would follow the weight-lifting regimen prescribed by a Maori boxer in *Australiana* magazine as soon as he got home. The Maori claimed he had built his muscles from lifting library books, as he couldn't afford proper weights. Michael resolved to use his dad's old books on computer programming (mouldering in the basement) as props, and soon would be as strong as that Maori!

He expected to be lambasted for taking too long, but

when he finally dragged the jerry can back the others were listening to the patrol leader discourse on 'shredding'. This was something you did with an electric guitar – preferably an Ibanez with something called 'humbuckers'. The leader was waving a cassette called *Surfing With the Alien*, although he had nothing to play it on.

Michael, trying to appear knowledgable, mentioned Mötley Crüe, but the patrol leader didn't approve of them as their guitarist 'couldn't shred'. He proceeded to insult Mötley Crüe, to the laughter of the others.

'But their drummer plays upside down in a cage,' Michael argued.

'Yeah, that's pretty cool,' admitted the patrol leader, making Michael feel popular, the glowing centre of wise attention. 'But they still can't shred for shit, though.' Heart in his feet again.

The tent was up, and now Michael entered a hostile world of matter. The patrol activity which would earn them their stripe was to make a bridge from rope and sticks - a dirty net of splinters, unpredictable weight and entanglement.

The others yelled 'keep it taut, keep it taut,' but he couldn't hold it, couldn't hold it, slipping, painful, edifice in the mud, shame round his ears hotter than the ropeburns. They jeered and sent him to the tent to read his gamebook, but the magic had gone from it. He could hear their dirty jokes, only half understood, about things you do to girls…infused with hostile matter, but deep down another feeling, religious fear in his stomach and groin, yet nothing like the religion of Sunday school.

There was cooking, and he felt it his duty to help…after struggling with shyness an hour he left the false tent but they jeered, tipped water, and pushed him in the mud.

Only when he blubbed did the patrol leader intercede on his behalf, offering a burnt bowl of food, worse than anything ever.

Sitting by the campfire in winter twilight, shivering with the wet of his clothes, too bird-brained for their talk, he stared at shadows while they laughed with voices deeper than his.

When all retired to the tent they made him lie under the dangerous middle bar, a metal pole that could fall during the night and splinter his skull, so they said. Were they only teasing? He held his tears for the night watch. He would be brave like his uncle.

But he needed to piss. Leaving the tent might wake the others, so he lay and considered life up to that point, thinking of himself from 'external' eyes as an other, if that was what the turtle neck man had meant…one *other* others reacted to. He held all night with bladder burned in agony, then finally, in the pre-dawn, could stand it no longer, clambering across the others nearly waking them, unzipping dew-damp tent, stumbling shivering in bushes to relieve. It was dark enough still for Drop Bears to be a menace…like koalas they were, but with razor-sharp claws…they would drop onto your shoulders and slash your throat…

He kept looking over his shoulder.

There was nothing but the soft carpet of buttongrass spread beneath the feet of ghoulish mist-ragged trees, a skeletal army of giant eucalypts marching to god-knows-where.

Dawn bled through a dappled red shot with filaments of black like the inside of his eyelids when he stared at the sun.

He came across the stream again, and this time crossed it.

He knew not whither he headed through damp purple columns of weird spiky plants he'd never learnt the names of, despite having lived in Tasmania always. Or had he? Hadn't he once lived in Sydney? He thought he had…

If he kept going, would he soon be on a cold beach facing the Antarctic?

He shivered in the mist, dampness of time.

Who was he? the thought filled him.

'Michael Glendower' was a way air moved over lips, not him. There was blood, linking him to his family, to Aunty Sylvie. Or was there? Hadn't he once been someone else? Would he be someone again in a far future where smoke-dark rockets edged out past black-blue suns?

He'd once had a club, the Nat Sav G; he was ashamed,

now, as he thought how he had abandoned its ideals, even if those ideals seemed impossible to fulfil. Save nature? He was *in* nature, eerie Gondwana remnants. Did the spiked guardians need 'saving', or did *he* need saving from them? Why couldn't he retain the courage of Uncle Reg?

Was he going to hell, to the empty, trackless Antarctic? Would the boys scream in the distance when they realised he'd gone…or would they track him down and beat him up?

Some kind of creature, standing on a peninsula jutting into a small tarn. It tensed as if wanting to skip and twirl, but didn't move.

It looked the business.

Was it real or not? It didn't look human. Was it mocking him? It had a sympathetic look, not like a demon from hell…yet was shadow, completely opaque. No third dimension, yet nor like a silhouette. It was nothing but something, like a pimple or blemish, purple shade blent into darkening shadow.

It wasn't real, he decided…just his imagination reading tricks into the shadows.

Then it moved.

It turned and walked into the forest beyond the tarn.

As it did so it seemed to stoop down and pick something up…then disappeared, as if into the space behind things.

Staring at the tarn and its backdrop, he knew that there was nothing there…Nothing at all.

4

CELEBRATION

Dragon were singing, telling them to *celebrate good times,* come on.

Sylvie whispered that the song was originally by blacks, winking as Uncle drummed along with his knife, twirling pasta on a fork unknowing in this airy seafood restaurant near the docks, with sunlight the colour of white wine illuminating the Tallships majestic in the harbour.

Uncle worried that he'd left the Scouts.

'You should stick at it, my boy. Don't you want to be a patrol leader?'

'I don't think the others would want it.'

'What…not the Michael who used to read stories to his prep class?' winked Sylvie again. 'A natural leader!'

'What grade will you be in this year, boy?'

'Six, uncle.'

'Six, eh? You should be learning Latin, boy…it gives you a good insight into grammar, which will help you phrase arguments against your enemies.'

'Why did they throw black balls at Pat Cash, uncle?'

'Eh, boy?'

'At the Aussie Open…'

Mum kicked him under the table. She didn't want any talk about politics, and Michael knew it had something to do with South Africa. Dad gave him a sip of white wine to shut him up…it was delicious, much better than the cheap cask wine they gave him at communion with a soft unnourishing wafer. He'd worked diligently at his confirmation classes, with the sole aim of having access to the communion wine, and what a disappointment it had been...but this restaurant wine was great, even better than the brandy he sometimes surreptitiously nipped from his grandfather's liquor cabinet at Ross. Grandfather was with them now, having travelled to Hobart for the first time in years...but Michael noticed he wasn't touching his wine.

Dad was sipping and smiling. He had lost his job (fired or quit? it wasn't to be spoken of apparently) at the insurance office, but had managed to get part-time work as a sales assistant at the local nursery.

Michael had been in there and seen him on his knees among the potted plants, wry self-effacing smile showing that his psyche hadn't dipped completely below the horizon. He was doing his best, thought Michael. But there was no denying that money was tight.

His mother's part-time job hadn't prevented her getting him Machine Men *again* for Christmas, though he was too old for them now anyway. What he wanted above all else was a proper stereo to replace Mum's antiquated mono tape player. It would probably have to wait til he was grown up, he realised. Yet, worth the wait!

Mother's work as a typist at the State Treasury office seemed to have made her more fidgety and neurotic. She couldn't take the slightest hint of argument or dissension on his part, which didn't bode well for the future. Sometimes when he looked her in the eye he noticed her odd manner of staring. Her mouth would move strangely and adopt a strained expression of joylessness.

But all that was absent today as they basked in the social glow of Australia's impending 200th birthday, even Mum and Dad exulting and radiant.

Soon the Tallships would leave Hobart, racing for Sydney for the magical date of Australia Day, when Sydney Harbour would be magically ruffled with zephyrous air, playful breath from godlike realms; but now Hobart was blessed with their presence. Michael's official Tallships Book had been stamped by sailors from various countries, South American ones, even the Soviet Union. All came to honour Australia with their presence on this laid-backest of holy occasions.

A Russian sailor had joked with him, patted him on the back, friendly feelings, *glasnost*.

Tasmanian crowds happy, feelings blessed...

Michael in his bones knew no subsequent summer would top this one for excitement and potency. He felt somehow he was awakening. This summer of waking dream and mystic nationalism, bound somehow with sunlight, the terrible godhead of the Sun.

Yet the ships looked more at home *here* than he imagined they would on Sydney Harbour.

Hobart, maritime city of hills facing the mystery of the Southern Ocean and the unknown Antarctic beyond. Tallships with the romance of Exploration behind them, even in an age when Earth had been mapped to the bottom of the Mariana.

The grown-up talk turned to politics, regardless of intent, though for once they weren't arguing.

'I see that that mendacious expat John Pilger has been bawling forth his lies again,' slurred tipsy Uncle Reg. 'No doubt he's heard another whispering in his heart.'

'They say Hawkey didn't want the Tall Ships to be part of the celebrations...but he was forced to in the light of public opinion!'

'Oh, surely *no one* would have a problem with the *tall ships*,' slurred Michael's mother, also tipsy after a single glass.

'You'll note none of the Aboriginal protestors have been fullbloods.'

'Isn't Michael Mansell supposed to be storming Circular Quay with ten thousand armed warriors,' laughed Sylive, 'to throw the whites in the sea?'

She was lovely when she laughed, thought Michael. He imagined himself fighting Mansell in a loincloth and barbed spear, face painted with ochre in a barren, tribal-style ritual.

Oh, everyone agreed that the Aboriginal protests were in

bad taste, like a turd on the shimmering, glistening harbour!

'The absurdity of Mansell's claims, when he's mainly white himself and wouldn't exist if it wasn't for the First Fleet!' Sylvie muttered with mock-serious indignation.

"I thought you were giving up on politics after your experiences in Queensland,' slurred Mum with just a faint edge of frost.

'She is,' said Uncle Reg, 'but *I'm* not. I'll keep going til I drop. My new project is a non-partisan alliance to compel people-iniated referenda. Currently only the government may call a referendum…which means they treat public opinion with contempt.'

'And I expect you want a referendum on the topic of immigration,' said his mother, 'and there I fear we must change the subject lest we all die of boredom.'

Murchison wasn't offended, however…and the talk turned to recent Soviet developments, of *glasnost* and *perestroika*, and Michael got the impression the world was somehow thawing in the sun. It was a day of fun and joy, a happy time he tried later in vain to recapture. The warmest emotions, bound up with family, and also with country and island. A reconciling between the adults in his life, between his two parents, and between them, Sylvie and Reg.

But Sylvie still wasn't pregnant, and she must be approaching the age where she couldn't get pregnant anymore. Michael knew that Reg wanted a son. He had a grown-up daughter whom Michael had met once, and who seemed nice, but that wasn't enough for him.

Michael knew a little of the facts of life now. So why hadn't Sylvie had a baby after ten years of trying?

*   *   *

Expo '88 opened in Brisbane, the queen opened the expensive new parliament building in Canberra that looked like a rocket, and now his class were having a Mock Election.

Kids in the years below would vote, while Michael's grade six class divided into two parties to present their case to the voters. Just like the real parties - one moderately left-wing and the other even more moderately left-wing.

But one kid rebelled and demanded a New Party!

It wasn't Michael, it was Josh Hayes, the class clown. It was no prank, though…he seemed genuinely ticked about the lack of choice, and Michael with a wavering voice seconded him. Mr. Lewis glared then acquiesced, knowing Josh's popularity.

'But no more,' he said firmly. 'A third party like the Democrats, then *no more*.'

'What about the Greenies?' someone snickered.

'C'mon, no one votes for *them*.'

In the coming weeks Michael found he was actually popular. It almost took him back to prep days when he would read to the class…but not quite, as he was nothing more than second fiddle to the charismatic Josh in a party regarded as a joke party, resented but admired by sensible, prudish girls.

So far, all the impetus had come from Josh. He had wanted them to have mobile phones to communicate their plans at all times (walkie talkies didn't have a big enough range), but found they cost $5000. A uniform was essential, though - acid wash jeans and basketball boots were all the rage at the moment, so Michael went to his mother.

'Now I'm a politician I need you to acid wash my jeans. Also, I need some Nike Airs, or Reeboks.'

She thought he was mad, so he asked his father next time he took him on an outing. Dad was pleased he was part of a Democrats-style third party, so he bought him some boots…only they were a cheaper, less modish brand, to Josh's disgust. His mother finally acquiesced in acid-washing his jeans, but she did it in such a cack-handed way that they looked like clown pants. Josh was pissed off, and Michael was a laughing stock.

Mr. Lewis, the only male teacher in the school, hadn't originally wanted to observe any bicentennial activities, saying it was his legal right to abstain, backed up by the

Federal Union of Teachers, but eventually had at least agreed to a Mock Election.

Mr. Lewis often told them that Australia would be under water by the year 2000, then all the water would boil because of the ozone hole caused by the hairspray everyone used, both girls and boys....but 2000 was so unimaginably far away that no one cared, not even Michael who generally tried (unsuccessfully) to see things *sub specie aeternitatis*.

Mr. Lewis thought himself witty, but the kids found him dull. He was always fiddling with his trousers. He read to them from *Spycatcher*, which all the grown-ups were reading at the time (a British secret agent had moved to Tasmania and written a tell-all book, and Mrs. Thatcher had threatened to jail him for if he ever returned to the UK), but the kids found it very dry and disappointing; they preferred Roald Dahl's new book 'Matilda'. Sometimes Michael felt a bit like Matilda: he should be in a higher class, but at the same time was awkward and socially dumb.

He wanted to be cool, like the kids on *Degrassi Junior High*, his new favourite show, or like Kylie Mole from *The Comedy Company*. Actually he preferred Kylie Minogue, sipping champagne in a bubble bath in the video to *I Should Be So Lucky*. She looked so lovely...

He followed the pop charts on *Rage* religiously every Saturday morning and his mother couldn't stop him now, not even Samantha Fox (though nothing of hers was currently in the charts).

He made a list of his favourite songs:

INXS - Never Tear Us Apart
The Church - Under the Milky Way
Kim Wilde - You Keep Me Hangin' On
Belinda Carlisle - Heaven is a Place on Earth
Rick Astley - Never Gonna Give You Up
Cheap Trick - The Flame

He decided it wasn't long enough, and added:

Whitesnake - Is This Love
Tiffany - I Think We're Alone Now
New Order - Blue Monday '88
Tracy Chapman - Fast Car
Underworld - Underneath the Radar
The Choirboys - Run to Paradise
Crowded House - Better Be Home Soon
Transvision Vamp - I Want Your Love
Poison - Fallen Angel
Guns N' Roses - Sweet Child O' Mine

He had saved his pocket money to buy GNR's *Appetite for Destruction* on cassette, a very daring album because it had the 'F' word in it, because the music was dark and mysterious. An undercurrent of grim sadness beneath the aggression matched how he sometimes felt. The artwork inside showed a robot raping a woman, but about to be destroyed by a bigger robot. The picture haunted him, and he spent a long time staring at it, getting lost in it. He knew quite a lot about sex now, as a woman from the education department had given them a week-long course of 'Health and Society' lessons, but this painting wasn't about sex – it was about love. He wanted to *save* the woman from the robots, then she would love him *forever and ever*, and never be distant from him...she would be his queen in an apocalyptic future.

He was interested in other artwork. In the newsagent, he leafed through heavy metal magazines, his eyes lingering on t-shirt ads for bands with names like Sabbat, Tankard, Helloween and Voivod. They reminded him of artwork in the Fighting Fantasy books, and he was extremely curious what the music would sound like.

Josh, his political partner, gave him a tape of some rap music, but he found it boring, not funny like 'Stutter Rap', just pompous and angry for no discernable reason. One song was called 'Raising Hell', another was 'Miuzi Weighs a Ton'. He thought 'Miuzi' might be the name of a gorilla at the zoo.

But he told Josh he liked it, disgusted at himself and for the first time uncomfortably aware of a reliance on what others thought of him.

He woke one morning all steeled to be assertive. He would bring ideas like Uncle Reg's into the Party. He wanted to ask Uncle about a range of issues, but still wasn't allowed to see him outside of family occasions.

Did Uncle Reg believe in democracy, Michael wondered? To a degree, perhaps, because he believed in the sound instincts of ordinary people. But if the people's instinct failed them, then he, Uncle Reg, would no doubt believe in 'guiding' them.

Very well.

Michael doubted the instincts of the kids at school with their acid wash jeans and puffy white basketball boots. Clothes *weren't* important. Only *policy* was important. He drafted a policy paper, a whole A4 pad page worth.

He presented it at the next debate, without consulting his party leader. The grade four and five kids were bored and puzzled as he read it out to them. Some of it was borrowed from the opposition leader, John Howard, whose One Australia paper was concerned with non-white immigration, just like Uncle Reg was. Asian countries didn't accept white immigrants, so why shouldn't the reverse apply, too? Apparently this flew in the face of what other Liberal party bigwigs wanted. But if it was an important issue then why shouldn't it be debated?

The girls representing the two big parties didn't want to debate it, however. One said she didn't even understand it.

The leaders gave their speeches. Josh Hayes advocated free icy poles at the tuck shop once a week. *That* got a set of applause.

And Michael arrived at school next day to find he had been ousted from the Party. Josh had kicked him out because his speech had been unpopular with the girls.

'You'll lose me the election you stupid wanker,' he growled through gritted contemptuous teeth.

Michael appealed to Mr. Lewis to be allowed to start a fourth party, but was sternly told off.

'You had your chance, Michael. You'll just have to sit the

election out as an impartial observer. After what Mrs Creighton tells me you said at the debate yesterday, you've no place in politics anyway. You're not related to some old duffer called Reginald Murchison, are you?' Michael, red to his eartips, felt a hot flush in his chest. Was it embarrassment or pride?

Then it happened. Alicia Hughes pressed a note in his hand. She wanted to know if he would 'go' with her, be her boyfriend. So, his integrity had gained him an admirer after all!

'Yes...I'll go with you,' he told her shyly.

'Alright. And now...you're dumped!' she shrieked, and the class exploded with laughter. Two other girls threatened to beat him up.

How could these weak conformists reduce him to stuttering, helpless stupidity? These self-assured, lanky girls, gabbling their steady vacuity to the empty air. And the teacher, a font of bitter drabness.

Michael couldn't wait for high school to begin. Surely it would be better?

5

INTO THE LABYRINTH

The labyrinth of D'Entrecasteaux High held many forking paths. Each led to a different hive of learning, a different branch of the ant nest.

The school was abandoned factory, carpeted theatre, structured encyclopedia...Michael was mystified, enchanted and afraid. Part of the ant nest four years...the things he would learn...science, maths, woodwork, metalwork, cooking, foreign languages, broiling and steam-cleaning, mystic strains of future in green-glowing computer labs!

It was too good to be true.

But two forces struggled for control, one subtle and occult - the school itself, embodied in the vast building and the secret tunnels he knew must link different parts of the school. He was sure they existed, and was told off more than once for prying into stationary cupboards and alcoves. He was convinced the secret links were inaccessible, even to the teachers, and only he could find them.

The second force was the school principal, Mr. Hendriksen - a potency of nature in his own right.

But the sides were unequal - the school knew Hendriksen, but Hendriksen didn't know the school. He was unaware of the dark secret maze threading dimly-lit classrooms together between and behind walls and unused storerooms. No, Hendriksen didn't know his nemesis, and his nemesis would ultimately win, Michael was sure.

Hendriksen's rule of the school was a bold experiment. He brought select principals from other Tasmanian schools for 'wine afternoons' to see how he ran D'Entrecasteaux, including the previous headmaster, whom he disparaged as having let the school go to seed, fights breaking out every lunchtime and general slatternliness. Belittling his predecessor in front of the others, he had brought him to tears. Hendriksen had an important ally in the Department of Education (some said the Minister himself), and none would gainsay him, certainly not the PTA. He held the staff together by terror of gaze. (Michael would learn much later that a fearless glance can change the world, and he who has to *work* at such a glance is more powerful yet.)

Hendriksen made examples of students at assemblies. Show trials. He gave lectures on the dangers of 'populism', and Michael knew instinctively he would hate Uncle Reg. His vision seemed to revolve around rooting out the last remnants of 'non-rational thought'. He gave one weird speech claiming science would light up other worlds, worlds we don't know about, and claim those other worlds back from the populists.

The word 'educate' came from 'ducere' (to lead) he reminded them. Same root as 'duke'. Teaching was a matter for teachers, *not* parents or politicians. Peer pressure must be crushed ruthlessly, because it interfered with what teachers wanted for their students. The teacher must prepare the student for a career, which is life. *All* students must have a career trajectory mapped before finishing year ten. Computers would aid in this. There must be no exceptions, or the school would not be performing its proper function.

Michael admired Hendriksen in some ways, but also feared him. Discipline can be a creative impetus…but what the principal called 'science' was not what Michael understood by science. For Michael, 'science' meant rock pools, sea anemones and the iron grey Derwent; it also meant gentle, earnest and forthright people, middle class in the best sense.

*　　*　　*

The librarian, on the other hand, had no personality at all, yet a vast array of knowledge was at her command. Mechanically stamping books and saying nothing was just her charm.

The Satanic Verses by Salman Rushdie was on prominent display. Everyone on TV was talking about it, but leafing through the novel Michael thought it looked boring.

There were Fighting Fantasies here, too, but not the ones he knew. *Dead of Night. Portal of Evil. Vault of the Vampire*; morbid, not classics - the glory days of Allansia and Khakabad would never come again. His childhood was over and wouldn't return - he was now almost a teenager.

Pop music was dreary, the charts full of music that depressed or sent him to sleep - he must discover something new! He had pestered his mother to get him Bon Jovi's *New Jersey*, but found that he only liked one song ('Blood on Blood', about loyalty, far better than the tacky single 'Bad Medicine').

But a poster of ABBA had been found in the basement, perhaps once his mother's, and appropriated without asking. The two female singers wore tight blue satin jumpsuits, and he was fascinated by the void between their legs…a nothing that seemed electrically charged.

He also dreamt of Debbie Harry in the 'Heart of Glass' video, only seen twice but haunted by it, eyes that *looked*. He became defensive, protective in fantasies. He thought of her as 'Heart of Glass Debbie' in Snow White's glass coffin, but Snow White had dark hair, so Debbie became a light/dark duo just like ABBA… heaven and hell, interchangeable, each in each.

He decided he would have *two* wives when he grew up, one brunette and one blonde. The blonde would look like Wendy James from Transvision Vamp, but the brunette would be sensible and wise.

His first wet dream surprised him, and had nothing to do with girls. He dreamt of a cold, grassy sports field, completely deserted, then a warm spring breeze came, and something exploded out of him. He scrubbed his pyjamas with a sponge before putting them in the wash, embarrassed, shaken to the core. So the things taught in 'Health and Society' lessons were true…

He longed to express his feelings in music, but his mother had sold the piano and cancelled his lessons because his teacher had complained about his lack of effort. He didn't miss the lessons, but missed improvising. He would take every opportunity to improvise in the music room at school, despite being called out on it by 'shredders', who were here, too, trying to ape Yngwie J. Malmsteen and Michael Angelo. Michael's own improvisations on the nylon-stringed Yamahas sounded nothing whatsoever like shredding. They didn't really sound like anything he had ever heard before.

Mr. Travis, the music teacher, hated shredding and gave detentions to anyone caught doing it. He said they had to learn to crawl before they could walk. He made the sullen class listen to the Surfaris, and Dick Dale and his Deltones. Michael liked these, but was embarrassed to admit it as no one liked Mr. Travis.

The teacher once cocked an ear at Michael's guitar-noodlings, then snapped from trance and dismissed them as half-baked.

*   *   *

Dog was silent when teased, always playing a silence game. This annoyed everyone, including Michael, who had lately come to love sound, meaningless noise. At least Dog didn't blub like Prime Minister Hawke, though. Hawkey was always blubbering, an international embarrassment, this time about Tiananmen Square. A few months earlier he'd blubbed because he had cheated on his wife. Michael, feeling wound up and vicious, wanted to beat the prime minister up.

He had started a band, and for once in his life was going to be boss.

His band was called The Mutineers and would be the best, for he had a shred guitarist called Leighton Owen. Leighton could shred in numerous scales, and more importantly *over* Michael's noodling, fitting scales to the chords, or more accurately half-formed proto-chords. Michael had written lyrics over these sketchy designs, and actual songs were born! Leighton, who had transferred from a mainland school in term two, was most welcome, and Michael regarded him as almost-equal to himself in the grand scheme of the band, although of course it was he, as lyricist, frontman and rhythm guitarist, who would garner the most adulation, indeed, would be remembered as a genius for generations to come.

He was particularly pleased with his song 'Royal Commission'.

Royal Commission

I make it my mission
To beat to submission
The master magicians
And scheming morticians
To send to perdition
All phoney musicians
And mathematicians (a reference to the maths teacher, Mr. Willoughby)
With no inhibitions
At all!

[first guitar solo]

Gonna start a royal commission
Gonna start a royal commission
[repeat 22 times]

[second guitar solo]

[fade out]

Dorry 'Dog' Wendle, the bassist, was a worry though. Always with a look like you were leading him into a labyrinth, like he was *your* responsibility. Fluffed hair and softly chiselled face like soapstone which didn't fit with the posters Michael envisioned of the band. But he was the only bass player in year seven. Ordinary students could only play Yamahas (unless they owned their own guitar), but somehow Dog had been given permission to play the school's electric bass.

Dog had a terrible homelife, they said, father gone like Michael's, mother played mindgames. But something about him smelt like sour milk. Michael wanted him gone eventually, but kept him for now because everyone said you *needed* a bassist. A band called Metallica had apparently 'mixed down the bass' (whatever that meant) on their last album, Leighton had told him, and it had suffered as a result.

The drummer, Hayden Burn, was an aggressive buck-toothed son of a bitch who had been held back a grade, but again, the only year seven allowed to use the school drum kit due to some previous private lessons, so Michael had no choice. Hayden could play a straight-eight beat and that was it, but Michael hoped he would expand his repertoire before conflict ensued, because even though *he* was band leader, Hayden was bigger and angrier than him.

Hayden was working on learning drum fills, which was promising. Leighton made sarcastic remarks behind his back, but Michael stuck by his buck-toothed drummer, believing God, fate or providence had put him in D'Entrecasteaux High for the purpose of furnishing Michael with a fully developed rhythm section.

But Michael's hopes suffered premature burial.

When Travis heard Leighton shredding in the music room he banished the nascent group to a small soundproof sideroom usually used by trombonists. Michael seethed with resentment, and the others couldn't understand why he was quite so angry.

Then (sensing that banishment had in no way daunted the 'lunatics' as he called them) Mr. Travis exiled them to a darker room, essentially a mouldy cupboard, and forbade them to play during school hours. That meant they were limited to the time between 3:15 when school got out and 3:45 when the music department was locked up.

Michael begged and pleaded with with his mother to get her to pick him up a half hour later in order that they might practice on the one day a week when all four members could manage it.

She had almost given in, but Dog blew it, telling the teacher, for some reason, that Michael was planning to audition as opening act for Mötley Crüe, at the newly opened Derwent Entertainment Centre. Mr. Travis knew full well that this was a lie, that Mötley Crüe weren't playing in Hobart (Dire Straits excepted, overseas bands never did), and declared that Michael was misleading his classmates in Pied Piper fashion with the aim of Leading Them Astray. He declared The Mutineers invalid under rules never cited and banned them outright from playing on school premises. Just like that, with a click of the fingers.

It must be nice to have that sort of power, Michael thought.

*　　*　　*

They gathered huddled one lunchtime near the entrance to the gym to discuss their options. None of the others seemed to care much whether the band lived or died. They were more inclined to be angry about what Michael had told them about Mötley Crüe.

'I never said they were *definitely* playing, it was just a rumour.'

'You didn't *say* it was a rumour, you said you were booking us to audition as support act. Deadbeat!' snarled

Hayden. 'This band's a crock of shit, anyway,' he said, and stumped off for a half-cigarette behind the cricket nets.

Michael was so enraged by this desertion, this *mutiny*, that he turned and punched Dog in the face, and Leighton had to drag him off of him. Pugnacious, frowning, as if listening to an inner voice, Dog was earnest, too earnest, a face that commanded you to tell the truth about him, but that also seemed wilfully obtuse.

Dog fled in terror, while Leighton remonstrated with Michael, who was in tears.

'He *narked* on me. I can't forgive it.'

'You take things too seriously, man...just fucken forget it...the band was never gonna happen, anyway.'

Michael had spent all his pocket money on hairspray so the band could look like Mötley Crüe, and had even invested in a tube of lipstick, which all the big bands wore. Cinderella, Whitesnake, all of them. It was 'Sex on the Beach' brand, sure to attract girls. The only band he respected that *didn't* wear lipstick was Iron Maiden, but he had only heard one song by them, and was more interested in their album covers than their music.

Dreams shattered, Michael returned to an empty house, dominated by the unseen presence of his increasingly neurotic mother, and an uncle next door he couldn't decide whether to admire or revile.

At church they had given him a pamphlet that denounced Reginald Murchison as an evil man. *That's my uncle!* he had wanted to shout, but he had a feeling that the minister, Rev. Paine, already knew it. 'Wolf in Sheeps' Clothing', the brochure roared.

'The TUL is neither Christian nor conservative, but *radically and dangerously authoritarian!*'

Michael veered dizzily between hating his uncle and hating the church. He despised conservatives deep in his guts, because they didn't believe in the future, he thought...but he was unsure if his uncle really was one.

The conservative premier of Tasmania, Robin Grey, had just been ousted, and he was glad of that. The director of a timber company called Gunns had tried to bribe a Labor MP to cross the floor if Gray's government had a no-confidence motion moved against it, thus keeping them in power. But he had been caught and now the Greens held the balance of power.

Michael wasn't sure if he liked them, either.

But he felt good about a new TV show called Media Watch, which was supposed to put dishonest journalists in their place. Surely the man who hosted a show like that must be honest, he thought.

Altogether, he was having a lot of trouble figuring out who to trust.

6

VALEDICTION

He lay sleepless late one night when he heard a sound like a car backfiring, followed by anguished bellowing, and buried his head in warm womb blankets like a turtle sensing wrongness, hairs on neck every fibre on edge.

It seemed minutes before Menzies barking drew him out again, one cocked ear at least. He realised with shock his mother was out on the street, flapping like a headless duck, shrieking things he couldn't understand, his uncle's replies wavered muted, sound of sobbing. She came back in then out again, three times. Had there been an accident...yes, a terrible accident, Michael was convinced. Now his mother was next door, in Sylvie and Reg's house. He couldn't hear what was going on. It was a dark, muffled mystery. Perhaps he dreamt it. He tried to convince himself that he had dreamt it. Yes, now he could go back to sleep, scrub the fear from his belly.

There was no mistaking the sirens yowling in from the distance, but they would bypass his quiet, quiet street, surely and softly...home wasn't part of the world, it was where you retreated *from* the world.

The sirens reached their peak and stopped...right outside his house. This was happening, actually happening. He peeked between the curtains, saw two cops entering his aunt and uncle's house while another stood guard on the footpath. More sirens. Another cop car, then an ambulance. A universe of bright, artificial light descending on the quiet suburban street.

He saw the paramedics go in, and out again. They were carrying something, a long humped stretcher. Mother and uncle fretful behind them, cops remonstrating with Uncle.

Michael couldn't stand it anymore, he snuck outside in his pyjamas and slippers, out into the garden, and hid behind the row of plants he used to think contained a tunnel to another world, and perhaps still did.

The ambulance pulled away, and Michael watched through lupins. The trees above him in the dark looked *tired*, no longer gentle protectors. Reg's voice shook, he had wanted to go with the ambulance, but cops insisted they take him in for questioning. They were gentle but firm, despite his protests that his arm might be broken. As his anger built they were forced to cuff his hands, making him yell in pain.

Had Reg and Sylvie had a row? *Had Reg shot Sylvie?* He was immediately ashamed of himself, and let out an involuntary sob. Reg would *never* do anything like that…but the sob was heard.

Michael found a giant towering over him, a metal monster from *The Battle of the Planets*, forgotten years ago but suddenly immersed in, giant sweating ribcage, breathing flesh-and-hair cloaked 'robot' standing above. Michael shut his eyes and in a brief series of images prayed he would return to this world in stronger, more perfected form.

His mother screamed 'No!' as she recognised him, Michael prised heavy lids apart to see a jittering cop, legs wide. 'You'd better come out of there, young one, I nearly shot you!' trying to put cheerful face on mother's hysteria. She hugged him, stroked his head gently, but it was for show, Michael could feel her distraction, confusion, amplified signals, directionless compass.

The cops moved off to do their own thing. Two walking up the street with torches, peering into gardens.

Mum ushered him into the house, took him by the shoulders, telling him slowly and carefully, as if he were deaf, to *stay home while she went to the hospital in the car.*

'What's wrong with Aunty Sylvie?' his voice trembled.

'Someone hit her over the head with a blunt implement. A burglar.'

'Will she be all right?'

His mother sobbed 'I don't know, that's why I have to get to the hospital.'

'What was the gunshot?'

'Your uncle shot the burglar, but it only grazed his arm I think, and he escaped.'

'What if the burglar's still out there?'

'I'll lock the door, you'll be fine. The police are in the street outside. Phone your father as soon as I leave and tell him to come straight round. I have to go to the hospital to see my sister.' Her breast was heaving. 'I know we haven't always gotten along, but…'

'Can't I come too?'

'No. It's not a place for children.'

'I'm not a kid anymore.'

'Michael! Just do as I say,' she snapped fiercely, and there was no gainsaying her tone. But he couldn't get through to his father, and the phone rang out.

Having the run of the house gave him no joy. He put all lights on, turned them off again. Would lights attract the burglar or scare him away? He couldn't decide.

It seemed the police were leaving.

He turned the lights on again, then cowered beneath the blankets, terrified. He trembled for what seemed like hours before sleep came, a sick feeling in his stomach. *Please let Aunty Sylvie be okay…*

In the early hours of the morning he was woken by his mother unlocking the front door. She was moaning, moaning terribly.

Sylvie had died in hospital.

*   *   *

The funeral was at the Anglican church at Ross. Sylvie's father looked bad, pale and papery, shaken, ashen. He didn't say much, but Michael would have liked to ask him such a lot.

The minister's eulogy seemed written from notes provided by Michael's mum, nothing about Sylvie's actual good points, just sterile platitudes. While he loved the hymn 'Amazing Grace', the eulogy itself left him colder than the ground which received his aunt's bruised and battered body.

Michael couldn't believe she was really being lowered into cold worm-riddled clay.

But it wasn't her.

'What' was her? 'Where' was her?

Death was a terrible mystery. He wished he could hold Sylvie's hand and tell it was okay, wherever she was. He had decided he didn't believe in heaven because it was static, and 'pleasure neverending' would be pleasure no more; he disbelieved in eternal hell for the same reason. Eternity and consciousness were mutually exclusive, he had decided.

But death couldn't be the end of the soul. He felt intuitively he had lived before, and so had Sylvie...and both would walk the earth again, refreshed. He knew this only in vague images, not refined into words, even in his head.

And when next she entered the world, perhaps he would be *her* protector. But for now she was lost to him. Perhaps their paths would never cross again.

*　　*　　*

The snacks afterwards, fairy bread for him, crunchy hundreds and thousands, lots of party snacks. Uncle Reg had put on a rock song that Sylvie had liked - 'The Passenger' by Iggy Pop. It seemed to create a bad feeling in the room, but Reg was impervious.

Reg had been quiet through the service; Michael had

never seen him so quiet. A couple of his friends were there, old war veterans, and they were as quiet as he was.

Michael liked the song and asked Reg to play it again, which he did, with a soft smile, lost in the world of memory.

Michael wondered what Sylvie had been like when young, tried to imagine her and his mother as sisters in the same household, but couldn't. He saw a void, a blank; nor could he see the visions Iggy Pop sang of. He hoped Sylvie could see the stars made for her tonight.

His father was sitting in a corner mumbling to himself, and how did Sylvie's death affect *him?* Michael long suspected him of disliking her due to certain silences around her name in conversation, yet his father spoke so little anyway it was hard to tell. Last time Michael had seen him he had the air of a flabby jellyfish, now he was more like a shark, with an aura that would brook no shit. Accordingly, few spoke to him, but…what an astonishing change.

Michael had briefly considered him on his list of suspects - his brain had been working overtime, inner detective work to find the killer. But he had ruled his Dad out when it emerged he had an alibi – seeing his new girlfriend that night, which was why his phone had gone unanswered. Convenient - but what if she was in on it too?

Then there was Reg…the cops had wanted his story checked further, before blood (not his) had vindicated him. But why didn't Reg chase the man? Michael realised he was concerned about Sylvie, and had to attend to her. But Michael was angry at everyone, not just the killer; even Menzies, who hadn't barked until it was too late. All those years of being scared of him, and a real villain had no reason to fear him - *but did that mean the attacker was someone known to him?*

Also, what if his uncle thought *he* did it because a cop had discovered him in the bushes?

* * *

Now Reg stepped forth to deliver his own eulogy.

'I think for those who truly loved Sylvie...perhaps you might consider a few dollars for a cause she believed in...the Wilderness Society...or an anti-ANC group in South Africa. Please remember...Nelson Mandela is a terrorist who tried to overthrow the government...his group killed women and children...' His voice shook, like it was about to give out. 'If he'd done those things in a Marxist country he would have been shot. And the sanctions he called for hurt blacks more than whites...'

There were mutterings such talk was inappropriate.

'Come on Reg, give it a rest.'

'What else would Sylvie have wanted? You think you even knew her? Well, sod the bloody lot of you!' Michael had never heard Reg swear before...he must be really angry. He stumped out of the room, and to Michael's surprise no one called him back or apologised. The silence, and the shabby treatment of Sylvie's husband, whom Michael now felt sure did *not* kill her, were embarrassing. Probably (as his mother and everyone else believed) the blow was aimed at Reg and caught his sleeping wife by mistake. Or was it? *Was the killer present in this very room?*

Michael remembered the necklacing his aunty had told him about...but the cool kids at school who listened to interesting music all thought that Mandela was God.

His mother stepped up to give a terse speech. She claimed Sylvie had died for someone else's sins, and it was obvious who she meant, no longer present to defend his honour. Michael suddenly disliked her intensely. Was it *wrong* to dislike his own mother? Surely it must be. Uncle Reg, whose TUL wanted Tasmanian independence, wished to unite the intellect and the soul, and thus make an unbreakable union by means of which the white race could carry out its destiny. That was what Sylvie had said, but Michael was unsure what it actually meant.

Reg's current obsession was opposing the Multifunction Polis, a futuristic city the Japanese were trying to build in Australia. Uncle Reg said the Japanese banks were part of something called the 'Trilateral Commission', which apparently wanted a single government for the entire planet or something. If a government got too bad, you could always go live in another country, he thought. But a world government there was no escape from. But what if it was a *good* world government? Or would a good one turn bad at some point, then there was no way out?

Michael liked the idea of a futuristic city with robots on Australian soil (it was rumoured to be built at Surfer's Paradise, which was a fake city anyway).

He remembered Jap cartoons he'd watched when little; his computing teacher had said that in the future, computers would be 100 times smaller than what they were, and they would *all* be made in Japan.

He wanted to fight monsters in outer space for the memory of Sylvie...

But she was in the ground, and he started to doubt whether she would return. He felt a deep sense of meaninglessness and formless disquiet.

*   *   *

A rough steel comb and insecticidal shampoo. The school nurse, old battleaxe, true to type, something of a sadist, nicknamed from her own mouth 'Twisted Sister'. She was relatively gentle to him, though, perhaps because she knew there had been a bereavement in the family. Just get the nits and lice out of my hair, he thought, stop the others from teasing, at least a while.

The comb dragged words out of him, nervous. He told of his hopes for the future now the Berlin Wall was down and millions had their freedom. Ceau escu and his wife executed by firing squad...he hoped a green tree could grow from their lapping blood. President Bush spoke of a 'new world order', but Michael didn't trust him, there was something about him...he didn't want *him* controlling the direction of this new order.

'You talk too much, young man.'

'Everyone says I don't talk enough.'

'Who says?'

'My old scoutmaster.'

'They're letting girls into Scouts now. Won't that be nice?'

'But they're not letting boys into Guides.'

'Of course not. That would be the end of civilisation as we know it.' Michael laughed, though he thought it unfair and stupid. He craved consistency. Either let both into both, or segregate both.

'There are female priests now, too. You'd better get used to it young man.'

'Shouldn't they be called priestesses, like in ancient Greece?' He hated girls, at least the ones in his grade, because they laughed at him, or worse, were hideously aloof. He wanted them to be his friends and companions…weren't they made of carbon and water like him?

He had been teased a lot recently, not solely because of headlice. Rob Weed, a big, tall kid in the grade above, called him 'Nitwit' and 'Downie,' which the girls in his own grade thought hilarious. Weed told Abo jokes that weren't very funny, and which Michael suspected he had stolen from some comedian, perhaps Rodney Rude; but he was strong and Michael was rather scared of him.

Weed did have a decent electric guitar, could play it well, and could even shred a bit, but he couldn't *thrash out*, Michael's current concern after someone had taped him Kreator's *Pleasure to Kill*, Slayer's *Reign in Blood*, and the new Megadeth album *Rust in Peace*. Now that was the stuff for him!

He had read of youth subcultures in the paper - alternatives, punk-alternatives, pseudo-gothics and skegs - and wanted to found his own culture that would be better than all of them. More than anything, he wants to be a vigilante, like Darkman, or Casey Jones from *Teenage Mutant Ninja Turtles*.

Although Snobby Jenkins said Jones was supposed to be a pisstake of vigilantes, Michael thought he was real and admirable. Michael knew what he wanted to do when he left school – he would be a touring musician who also practiced vigilantism, killing criminals by night in each city he visited. He would cut a swathe of improvement through the world. And most of all, he would butcher the person who had killed his aunt.

The title track from Kreator's *Pleasure to Kill* would be the soundtrack to these nocturnal missions. So vicious and brutal, so much more serious than the glam rock he was now embarrassed to have liked only months earlier. Poison had disgraced themselves with *Unskinny Bop*, and Warrant's *Cherry Pie* was also shit; he would listen to nothing softer than Iron Maiden now, and while he still liked ABBA and Kylie Minogue, it was for reasons other than their music.

In his dark blue backpack was a copy of *Metal Hammer* magazine bought with his pocket money, keenly perused in maths today, but nonplussed by some of the bands included. Sepultura sounded interesting, especially when they said they wanted to tour with Slayer, so that the audience would have to be carried out on stretchers (how he longed to give a concert like that!).

But who the hell were 'Lard'…'Sisters of Mercy'…'Jane's Addiction'…'Soundgarden'? It was disappointing - these didn't sound like real metal bands, not grim like Megadeth and Slayer. Some weirdoes called 'Nirvana' (Buddhists?) had just released a single called 'Silver' or was it 'Sliver' (the magazine couldn't make up its mind which way to spell it). And 'Primus' - wasn't that a kind of stove? A band should have a name like *L.A. Bitch* or *Cocksure Aggressor* Michael thought savagely.

When he listened to Megadeth's wonderful 'Tornado of Souls' he wondered if his band would have made it anyway…could he ever write anything that good? He *was* writing songs, though, with his voice and no instruments, and wanted to cover 'The Passsenger', but a more aggressive version. It was the *90s* now, like science fiction, and the future was open. Why didn't Uncle Reg share his futurist feelings? The school had gotten rid of its BBC computers, now it was all IBMs, with green and black screens. It was the best computer lab in any Tasmanian high school, as long as you didn't get in trouble for starting the computers without inserting a system disk, or disconnecting the mouse while the computer was turned on, which could damage it.

Now the nurse started washing out the foul-smelling shampoo, like she was washing away all the filth of his unmeshed life, leading him into a new labyrinth, but hopefully with less wool over his eyes.

7

NO PEACE

Michael and Leighton were smoking in the toilets one recess when the principal strode in and struck them both in the face.

Too shocked to speak, Michael shook visibly as Hendriksen put the butts out in the sink, grabbed Leighton by the scruff of the neck and roughed him about, snarling and spitting about what a filthy habit smoking was, stunting one's growth. When Michael coughed nervously, Hendriken clipped him around the ear. This was illegal, of course, but it was doubtful whether any pupil in the school would have the courage to report *Hendriksen* to the authorities. In fact, they had trouble imagining an authority higher.

Both were made to stand in the hall outside the office, Michael hoping desperately that Hendriksen didn't inform his mother. He could hear the office ladies snidely complain about the stink of tobacco smoke, which they probably did several times a day. Hendriksen had been very active in his anti-smoking crusade lately.

The boys were relieved they had the cigarettes however, as they had distracted Hendriksen from the real reason they had been conferring in the toilets – a small bag of marijuana to be divided between them. Michael had given Leighton $12.50, saved from pocket money, for his half of the juicy, resinous buds, which he couldn't wait to smoke. He had been stoned twice now, but never in the familiar surroundings of home, and wondered what it would be like. What if Hendriksen found the sachet of dope in his pocket, along with the small hash pipe he had bought from a tobacconist in the Cat and Fiddle Arcade in Hobart? Would he be sent to juvenile detention? Girls might respect him then, he thought, because girls always respected criminals, even if they claimed they didn't.

'Fucking Hendriksen,' snarled Leighton softly. 'He's on a self pity rampage because of CRESAP...been sabotaging everything because he says the government is going to do it anyway.'

'I know...he's shutting down the yearbook, and activities week.'

'Fucker should smoke some weed...he's a big ball of stress.' They laughed, but not for long...the principal blazed round the corner like ball lightning, screamed in their faces again. They were a disgrace to the school, and if it *ever* happened again they would be out on their ear, to a lesser school run by a less interested principal, and how would they cope then?

'Now go home, the both of you. Get out. You're suspended for the rest of the week.'

Had Hendriksen forgotten it was Friday? A half day suspension didn't seem so bad, and Michael's mother would be at work anyway, so would never find out. For an authoritarian, Hendriksen rarely if ever did things by the book...he was always ad libbing.

They left school through the top car park, wandering the nearby shopping street in a daze, parting finally with a laconic wave. Neither knew what to say after the surreal ordeal, which they now found faintly embarrassing.

Walking two kilometres home through lower middle class streets with beautiful well-made front gardens, Michael entered his empty house, nervously fantasising about the contents of his pocket. What hidden world would the weird Asian plant unlock for him this time?

He pulled the school books from his bag and placed them neatly on his desk. Two hours ago, in Social Science, he had written the following lines:

'I am no greenie, and I don't like the yuppie university students who prance around thinking conservation is 'trendy', but I don't like the way the trees are being cut down, either. Too many! One football oval per second.'

Now, though, politics was the last thing on his mind.

He pulled the bag of weed from his pocket, packed the tiny pipe and sucked the bite into his lungs, head out the open window so his mother couldn't smell it.

A cassette Leighton's older brother Kirk taped him went into the tape deck. Side one was *Cause of Death* by Obituary, side two Morbid Angel's *Altars of Madness*. Just the black hole vortex needed after his trying morning at school. After the killing of his aunt, he thought he had better make friends with Death before it came for someone else.

The music became more than music, a vault of inexhaustible mystery. But deep down he suspected *any* music would affect him similarly under the influence of the resinous weed. Was something missing in himself that he couldn't listen this way except under influence of the drug?

When it began to wear off his head felt leaden, and all he wanted to do was eat. He made a sandwich and ate in front of the old colour TV, still without a VCR to his annoyance, watching green Gulf War flashes, Scuds aimed at Israel and American missiles intercepting them. 100,000 Iraqis had died, Uncle Reg had told him…all to protect the Emir of Kuwait who cared more about his chandeliers than about his people. A rich, corrupt despot, said Uncle Reg (who was opposed to the war). And the chief beneficiary was Israel, he said, though Michael wondered how this was so when the news showed missiles reigning down upon that tiny but seemingly influential country.

Uncle Reg had been a shadow of himself since his wife's death, anyway, and scarcely seemed to care…Michael felt bad for him.

*   *   *

His father's new girlfriend Conny was tall and thin and (Michael thought) rather flaky. But his dad, too, was slipping into some kind of zone beyond the world of ambition, so she seemed a lamp of sanity, the needed thing. And her flakiness gave Michael a sense of superiority, making him feel at ease around her. It was weird how he could babble on for hours to some people, and to others could barely speak a word.

Then there was Dorry - whom he had once been easy around, but whose eyes he couldn't now meet for guilt. Since Michael had roughed him up two years ago his shyness and nervousness had increased, and he had become that most hated of things, a loner.

Last year Michael would see him pacing the schoolyard by himself or reading in the library, but this year he had fallen into a new circle, a group of favoured boys who hung out with the dance teacher, Mr. Yost, at lunch and recess. Michael thought there was something unwholesome about this circle, although Snobby Jenkins had loudly made clear that anyone claiming that all dance teachers were gays and lesbians was a 'bigot', whatever that meant (it reminded Michael of running shoes for some reason). Deep down he wanted to tell Dorry they could be friends again, that he didn't have to hang out with the vaguely repellent Mr. Yost, but he couldn't figure how to phrase it without sounding like a gay himself. Homosexuality (or suspicion thereof) at D'Entrecasteaux High was a serious matter - one could be beaten up, and worse, ostracised socially. While Michael didn't like many of his peers on a personal level, he still wanted to impress them.

He also wanted to impress his father's girlfriend Connie and adopted a jaunty air around her completely out of keeping with the way he usually behaved around his family.

She made the mistake of asking him what kinds of music he liked. Michael grinned like a shark, preparing to wow her with his arcane knowledge.

He took a deep breath and began to talk.

'Mainly death and doom, still, you know, the better thrash

bands like Slayer and Kreator…but seriously, there's more extreme bands who are leaving those guys *way* behind.

'Death, and doom?' Her smile vanished.

'Yeah, and a bit of industrial…Godflesh, Lifeswallower. My favourite doom band is Candlemass…like horsemen galloping over darkened plains, like in *The Lord of the Rings* you know.' He pulled a home-recorded BASF tape from his pocket. 'These bands are doomy, too.'

She took it, stiff-faced. '*Gothic* by Paradise Lost.' She strained to read the pseudo-Old English lettering that Leighton's brother had scrawled on the tape cover.

'Yeah, it's got a proud feel, like a lost poet who knows he's damned but doesn't care. His agony gives him this kind of vision that others can't see. And side B is 'Soulside Journey' by Darkthrone… they're from Sweden or Norway or somewhere like that. It's even colder and spacier than Paradise Lost. When I listen to 'Sunrise Over Locus Mortis' it's like being on the moon, really cold, frozen landscapes, you know? Or like being on the damp floor of an ancient forest, with the ruins of some ancient watchtower in the background. It's fucking great,' he grinned.

She handed the tape back, too embarrassed to respond. She looked at his shirt collar with a slightly giddy bug-eyed smile.

'I'm doing Business Studies this year, and I'm planning to open a shop in Kingston called 'Metal Implement'. It will only sell metal tapes and t-shirts. And maybe a bit of punk to make ends meet.'

'Oh, punk. I remember that…the Sex Pistols.'

'Yeah, I don't like them very much.' (In point of fact he hadn't heard them). 'I like Nocturnus, though…they're kind of futuristic metal, really intricate and brilliant. I really think one day there will be planets covered with whole cities like rabbit warrens. But the Japanese economy has crashed, so we'll just have to do it ourselves.'

To her relief, Paul Glendower reentered the room.

'You're not terrorising her with that Guns N'Roses rubbish I hope, Michael.'

His son rolled his eyes.

'You must be thinking of someone else, Dad...I don't listen to that kind of pansy-arsed stuff.' Why did his father insist on being two years behind the times?

If Michael had been more concerned with truth than appearance he might have mentioned how the Guns N' Roses song 'Estranged' have moved him immensely, it's apocalyptic musings combining in his mind with the nuclear holocaust scene from *Terminator 2*, which he had seen on the big screen, making him half afraid such a holocaust could actually occur, threatening his views of a labyrinthine yet orderly future, reducing everything to a level of primitivism he found appealing, yet appalling.

He fervently hoped his dad's girlfriend wouldn't think he was a Metallica fan, however - for he had finally heard them recently, the self-titled album, and wondered where their reputation came from, as they scarcely seemed heavier than Bon Jovi.

*   *   *

Michael was in the Eataway playing an arcade game. When his coins ran out he sat and stared at the wall. Anything was better than home, though, where the atmosphere had gotten so much worse since Sylvie's death.

His mother was dating again, too – a bland, bland, bland businessman, a non-entity in Michael's view, yet whom he sensed instinctively would turn authoritarian if he moved in with them.

He felt he would rather die than submit to such a vapid authority.

Additionally, his mother had been feuding with Uncle Reg (who had scarcely noticed the passing away of Sir John Kerr in March, so out of sorts was he) over possession of Sylvie's stuff. Her journals, specifically, were now in a box in the basement between his mum's new exercise bike and the dust-coated 1970s computer.

Michael read them, of course, and was astounded by some of things he read there. Initially Sylvie had been anti-racist, but at some point became more racist than Uncle Reg! How did that happen?

Michael believed himself to be anti-racist, because he'd come to associate racism with people like Rob Weed, whom he regarded as a buffoon.

He was interested to read of the circumstances in which the now grumpy, elderly and nearly-placid Menzies had been acquired – to guard Sylvie against something called the 'Sunshine Club' (sounded sinister) when Uncle Reg had been in prison for tipping mud over a bishop. Could *they* have been the ones who killed her?

Michael suddenly felt warmer towards his old nemesis, who was getting long in the tooth – but why hadn't he barked the night of Sylvie's death?

It seemed his aunt had listened to a lot of alternative music back in the day. He wondered what she would think of his current favourite bands? Would they fulfil her dream of a sound like 'a thousand steam engines all hissing at once'? Michael thought, with a fond smile, that perhaps they would not be extreme enough for her! It was weird reading about himself as a toddler…the polyester tracksuit still tucked away in one of his drawers along with his other toddler clothes, a sad marker of the passage of time in the meaningless suburb he lived in.

He was torn from his reveries by Leighton entering the Eataway. They sat at the table furthest from the counter and traded their ill-gotten goods – Leighton giving Michael a half-bag of pot and three dexies, receiving in return a whole box of chocolate bars Michael had stolen from the canteen of his old primary school, which he had broken into the night before with a kid with a broken thumb called Jason.

'Don't use both at the same time…they'll just cancel each other out,' Leighton opined, and Michael half-believed him.

Later that day under the teeth-grinding influence of the pills that made him want to talk and talk and talk, but with no one to talk to, he made the bold decision to investigate the rental property next door. He had fallen under the spell of *Twin Peaks*, and wanted to emulate his hero, Agent Cooper.

Michael could scarcely believe such a show existed, in fact was viewed and discussed by all the normal girls in his grade, the same ones who watched *Neighbours* and *Home and Away*. It was more than a show, however, it was a window into another world.

Like Cooper, he would use partly-rational, partly-occult methods, to find out - what?

Who was the man next door and what secrets was he hiding?

Once upon a time an old Greek lady had lived there, then his friend Adam, then the various quiet non-entities who had occupied it since.

Now, though, it was someone fucked-up and smelly.

The bum had moved in only a month ago, so couldn't have murdered Sylvie - or could he? Was it a ruse to disperse suspicion, as no one would expect a killer to move in two doors down from the house of his victim? *Or was he hiding something else?*

Emboldened by dexies Michael jumped the fence. The wreck-of-a-car was gone so he must be out. He tried the back door…open! He ducked in with a swagger.

The man was sitting at his table (the same room where Adam used to play 'Space Quest'), drinking a can of Cascade Draught.

'*Yes*, mate? Can I help you?'

'Uh…I'm with Neighbourhood Watch…your car was gone so I came by to see if someone stole it.' *Shit…what a dumb thing to say.*

'It was repossessed.'

'Ah…fine then. I'll just go.'

The man stood up, holding a pool cue. Michael had never been confronted with a weapon before.

He would talk his way out, he told himself quickly, dexies sure giving him the urge to talk – he pretended to be a vagrant himself who wandered in off the street. 'Why do you leave the doors unlocked? Don't you know this is a bad neighbourhood? My aunt was murdered...'

'The world is my home. I don't have a home. THERE IS NO HOME. NO PEACE.'

What could Michael say? Deep down he already suspected there was no peace...and now this nutty man had confirmed it! Or maybe he was more sane than anyone. Michael looked at his draggled beard and matted hair, eyes just slightly out of focus. He backed out the door, and the man made no move to follow. He jumped the fence, locked his door and retreated to bed with the covers over his head, vowing to never use amphetamines again.

He felt more like the Log Lady than Agent Cooper.

His street was safe but there were holes in it.

Did he have to go poking his head into them?

8

THE REBEL

'So what exactly do you want to do with your life, uh, Michael? Work Experience Week is coming up, as you no doubt know.'

The career guidance officer was typing into a computer. It wasn't one of the school's green screens, but something called a 'laptop' where the screen folded up from a typewriter-sized underbox…Michael couldn't see any place a disk went in.

'Is that a VGA display?'

'Yes, I believe so.'

'Wow. Does it really have 256 colours?'

'I think so, yes. Could you please answer my question, though…what do you want to *be?*'

'I want to be a musician.'

'Uh huh.' He typed something into the amazing machine. 'And what music studies have you made?'

'I do what you would call noodling. You kind of go into a trance and let your subconscious take over, then play guitar. Like Leonardo. The painter, not the ninja turtle. He'd look at a patch of mould on the wall and get marvellous ideas from it.'

'So, no formal studies?'

'I had some piano lessons as a kid. I remember a few of the scales, I think.'

The career guidance officer looked irritated. *Let* him despise me, thought Michael, but at all costs I will be a

117

professional musician…Leighton asked if he had heard 'this new band Nirvana, kind of psychedelic music'. Michael had read about them in *Metal Hammer*, but never heard…then suddenly 'Smells Like Teen Spirit' was everywhere, even on the street from a ghetto blaster one day in the summer holidays, and he was stunned by it…not the music but the phenomenon…how could a song mushroom like that, out of the blue? It would happen to him, too, he decided…it *must* happen to him.

Leighton had played him the album it was off, and he did like one of the songs, 'In Bloom'. It was a pisstake of dumbcunts like Rob Weed. The band seemed to be positioning themselves as the anti-Guns N' Roses.

Michael read recently of Axl diving into a crowd to bash someone who was videoing him for a bootleg…the idea that someone with millions of dollars and his choice of thousands of women would throw a tantrum over a camera! Michael hung a poster of Axl upside down on the basement wall to spit on.

Lately he had been listening to Helmet and Fugazi, and liked the latter's anti-materialist approach to concerts - $5 tickets and underage shows.

Dorry with whom he had been on speaking terms again of late he taped him a spoken word album called 'No More Cocoons', by a weird mask-faced punk singer with the even weirder name of Jello Biafra. Michael found his anti-censorship beliefs appealing, but couldn't help noticing how a caller critical of Biafra had been selectively edited to appear more insane - a form of censorship, and a deceptive one. Biafra was something of a hypocrite, it seemed. If he truly didn't believe in censorship he should let the opposition speak, in free and open debate.

'Jello would hate *you*,' he thought, looking at the career guidance officer. But what would Jello think of Uncle Reg?

He hadn't seen much of his uncle lately, but knew he had been writing letters to politicians opposing a new law which would require people to have a license, like a driver's license, to buy a gun.

'My uncle is a famous political provocateur, Mr. Reginald Murchison.'

The career guidance officer frowned. 'I've heard of him.'

'Perhaps *I* could be a political provocateur.'

'I don't think that's a viable career option.'

'My politics are different to my uncle's, though...free speech is my thing. I hate the fascist system.' Michael knew deep down that he would be a dilettante at politics...what he really wanted was to make music that would haunt people's dreams.

'So, have you found me anything yet?'

'The computer seems to be stuck, or something.' More and more computers had 'hard disks', with capacities of 20 megabytes or more. Mr. Stillwell, the computing teacher, said that one day personal computers would store *gigabytes* and *terabytes*. It seemed like science fiction. CD-ROMs were said to be the way of the future...they could store a whole encyclopedia set on one disk.

'Okay, the computer has found you something, Michael.'

'What is it?'

'A week's work experience at the Dover salmon farm, processing fish guts for use in cosmetic products.'

'Perfect!'

*   *   *

'You will be pleased to know that my long fight to replace all our blackboards with whiteboards has finally borne fruit, in the form of a special white board grant, awarded to this school only.' Hendriksen's face glowed with inner triumph.

But the lack of student response, even a single cheer, pushed his inner pendulum towards a barely repressed anger. Michael would owe to that silence his life taking the course it did, and more than once he later thanked his gods for the impartiality of the student body re: the whole chalk vs. marker wars (markers were later to take on a more sinister

119

role in this assembly, but none of the assembled knew that).

Hendriksen had been pushing for this a long time…now it was finally happening…the school would be transformed…the best state school in Tasmania, and one of the best in the country. But nothing from the student body. Michael wondered idly if he was deranged, and if others wondered the same. It was at this point that he noticed Hayden Burn, his old drummer, holding a snare drum and sticks. This was Hendriksen's new way of announcing suspensions. A fortnight ago someone had been drummed out of the assembly for swearing violently at a teacher. Michael, feeling nothing but contempt for Hayden in his new role as a lackey of the system, wondered who was for the high jump this time.

Then the show trial began. Michael was surprised to find *himself* called to the front, and despite his surface insouciance felt fear…fear of the unknown.

On his way to the front he made eye contact with Sally Hemingway, a girl in the year below him. He knew she looked up to him. They had made friends in the library where he would read at lunch times (last year his obsession had been Sven Hassel, this year he had burned through *1984* and *Fahrenheit 451*).

Leighton had asked if she was his girlfriend, but they were only friends. She was a funny looking thing, slender-faced, freckles and a protruding bottom lip…should have made her ugly, but Michael didn't think so. She was different to the other girls, and he admired that. Now she smiled at him nervously as sauntered to the front.

The principal made him stand to one side, as he thundered to the student body about a vile vandal who had scrawled on his office door a week ago with a permanent marker, two slogans.

DEATH TO THE FASCIST PRINCIPAL!
and
DOWN WITH BIG BROTHER!
Now Johnny Taxpayer must pay to clean the damage.
But the culprit has been found!

Michael wondered who had grassed on him…he had told no one, not even Leighton, not even Sally.

'*Exactly* the same slogans and handwriting can be seen on Michael Glendower's homework diary, as observed this morning by Mr. Willoughby.'

The maths teacher…his old nemesis. Why had he even *kept* the homework diary he had ceased to write in after Week Three, Term One?

The juggernaut swung towards him.

'What was going through his mind when you wrote the mindless slogans, you insolent thug?'

Thoughts pulsed in Michael's head.

His father was reading a new book called *The End of History* (the Cold War having been officially declared over in February), and if history was ending he wanted to make his mark *now*. Plus, Michael's reading of 1984 and Fahrenheit 451 and Ministry's 'New World Order' clip on 'Rage' had convinced him that unless he fought, the future would bring him under the iron heel of the Fascist State.

He had told Snobby Jenkins he was an anarchist, to impress him; Snobby had sneered and mocked him, just as he mocked everyone, except the teachers. But Michael didn't feel like an anarchist. The State itself had come from anarchy originally. Australia came from The United Kingdom, which had developed from Anglo-Saxon kingdoms - ultimately based on looting. But if the State had its roots in anarchy, it wasn't an ongoing anarchy.

Could the State be a living entity, independent of the parts (people and land) that seemingly made it up? If so, was there a reason for its existence? Did it have a purpose which would give it a legitimacy?

But was there even a purpose for the individual? Did he, Michael, have a purpose, or was it that he just *was?* Was he a work in progress, only visible as a whole at the end of his life? Were nations like that too? He thought of the Romans he had studied in Social Science last year. They were gone, and he could see Rome as a pattern laid out from beginning to end, an organic entity, from Romulus to Romulus

Augustulus…but what purpose did the pattern serve, if any? But, if no pattern, then anarchy, and what purpose did anarchy serve? The introduction of a new State?

He wanted to express these complex thoughts to principal, but couldn't.

So he shoved him, hard, in the chest.

In the uproar that ensued, he was drummed not just out of assembly, but out of school quite literally. The rat Hayden followed out into the car park, drumming him out, while Hendriksen urged him on.

What would have been a two week suspension had become a permanent expulsion from the school, only two months before graduation.

*   *   *

Clive, his soon-to-be stepfather, was berating him in a very pompous manner, partly because he hadn't done his homework, partly because he smelt like marijuana, but chiefly because his smug expression indicated he wouldn't accept discipline from the limp suit who was berating him.

Michael, finishing grade ten by homeschooling as it was too late in the year to enrol in another school, had no interest in his work. Nor did it console him that Hendriksen had been placed on indefinite leave two days after expelling him, and was rumoured to be recuperating in a mental hospital on the mainland, where he wouldn't be pressing assault charges against Michael as he had threatened.

As soon as his 'father substitute' left the room he would start packing his bag to run away.

He was missing the leaver's dinner at the Yacht Club around now, or was it tomorrow night? Anyway, tonight he would sleep in a Vinnie's bin. It would be warm and comfortable from the second-hand clothes dumped in it. And it would give him the aura of a real rebel, an iconoclast. Wait until he told Leighton about it! That, coupled with his expulsion for shoving the principal, would ensure his legendary status at D'Entrecasteaux High for generations to come, he believed. He would get a flat and find musicians to make the best band in the world…

He had heard a new Darkthrone song called 'Where Cold Winds Blow' on the metal show on the community radio station which had made the hairs on the back of his neck stand up. He wanted to make music like *that*. There was a melody *under* the melody, or so it seemed…it was eerie.

In a magazine of Leighton's he had read an interview with the group's drummer, now renamed 'Fenriz' (which brought back memories of the Norse mythology game he had played in grade four). 'Fenriz' had announced the band's next three albums in advance, and each would be more extreme and anti-musical than the last. Their fourth album 'Transilvanian Hunger' would only be for 'total perverts', Fenriz said. Although Michael didn't think of himself as a pervert, he couldn't wait to hear it, and was jealous. The ante had been upped – Michael's band would have to make even more extreme and grandiose anti-commercial statements to outdo Darkthrone!

He listened to Clive blabbering in front of him, but none of what he said made sense. It was like a duck quacking in his face.

'What would you know,' he thought with smug inner grin. 'Working nine to five each day may be admirable but it doesn't make you a father to *me.*'

*   *   *

The Vinnie's bin was empty, the metal cold with neither blanket nor pillow. Getting in had been easy but he couldn't manage to get out again without anything to stand on. He would have to wait for morning and call for help from a passing suit…the indignity! He wondered if he would go to Sally's house tomorrow, and call his mother from there. He wasn't on very good terms with his father, having offended Conny somehow-or-other.

He curled up and tried to get some sleep. He was lonely and felt like crying.

He wondered if he would ever see Uncle Reg again. Reg had told him directly that he thought his act of defiance against the principal was spirited, but misguided - it didn't serve a purpose like Reg's stunts had. Michael told himself this was sour grapes, and hated him for it, but deep down knew his uncle was right.

Yet Reg knew little about the principal and assumed he was a 'legitimate authority'. Who is to define legitimate, thought Michael. Tradition? Hendriksen was 'progressive', so how could 'tradition' authoritate its nemesis?

His final thought before going to sleep was that authoritarianism was *good*, because without it, there would be nothing to rebel against.

9

MUSIC MAN

'And so there's no chance of your moving in with your father?'

'Uh, no.'

'Has he said you can't, or do you just not want to?'

Michael frowned, and words came forth unbidden.

'My father...do I even have a father? Mum said he retreated into his shell at a certain point, and never reemerged. What drove him in there? Was it me? Maybe I'm to blame! I don't exactly know how, though. He's got a girlfriend now and they don't want me there. He told me so, not in those words...he just looked fidgety and uncomfortable and talked about how they needed time to sort out their issues around each other or something...and so that relationship must be carking it, too! Then he'll probably just crawl into a hole and burrow underground. I *hate* him.'

The mediator, always calm, seemed ever so slightly taken aback at the vehemence of the last three words.

'So...it seems that moving back with mum would be the most sensible and realistic choice?'

Michael, who was trying to grow a beard with little success, would often rub his chin to stimulate growth, and he rubbed it now as he listened to this man whose services his mother had paid for as a prerequisite to moving back with her and the one she soullessly called her 'life partner'. The 'partnership' mainly involved Clive taking orders from her, so no wonder Mr. Dopey , as Michael thought of him, was wont to take an authoritarian tone with Michael which he never would with the erstwhile Mrs. Glendower (the divorce having gone through a month ago).

His thoughts roved back to his home of the last two months, the weatherboard house at Kingston Beach where Sally lived with her mother, her father being conveniently deceased. Michael had been given the spare room, his board taken out of the income Mrs. Hemingway gave him for helping her fill orders for her mail-order crystal business. It was easy work, and while it didn't pay much, the board was so minimal he had plenty left over for cigarettes and cassettes. Benson and Hedges was 'his' brand of smoke…so much classier than workhorse brands like Peter Jackson or Winfield, but not as snooty as the European import brands. The gold packet was shiny, solid and just right. The smell of tobacco as he opened it was delightful.

Sally's dad had left his barbell behind when he died, and Michael was blessed with the chance to use proper weights for the first time. How his arms and chest ached after the first few sessions! But it passed, and he was starting to feel tougher, more confident of his future destiny.

The paradisiacal idyll came to an end, however, when Mrs. Hemingway offered him a massage (her main line of business, the crystals being a side project). The light of a dozen candles, full earth mother works. But when he looked up, relaxed and buzzing, she had removed her blouse and was inviting him to touch her 'big floppy dumplings'. This was not how he had envisioned his first taste of female flesh.

Even now he felt embarrassed and slightly nauseated when he thought of it (although part of him regretted not squeezing the 'dumplings'). His relations with his employer were now strained as a result of his refusal, Michael had been politely asked to leave, and Sally herself was puzzled by it all. He had refused to discuss it when asked point blank, hoping she wouldn't imagine he was somehow to blame for her mother's actions. She seemed sad, but hadn't begged him to stay, and a slight coldness had come between them. His vanity had imagined her hopelessly in love with him, now he wondered if she would even consider him a friend. Now was to move back in with his mother and her 'partner'. The dumplings had a lot to answer for.

'Do you have a problem with female authority figures?' the mediator was saying. 'Or just authority in general? Because your mother said…'

'Well, I don't like the royal family very much.'

'Mm hm. And why is that?'

'They're supposed to be figureheads…role models…but they behave like trashbags. Not just Fergie and Di, but even Charles. Fuck knows why my uncle respects them so much.'

In point of fact Michael had no idea what his Uncle Reg thought of the leaked remarks by the Prince of Wales, desiring reincarnation as a tampon, but doubted it would anywise diminish his respect for the institution of royalty.

'Ah, yes…your uncle. Your mother seems to think that he's a bad influence on you.'

'I hardly even see him.'

'Well, perhaps you should keep it that way.'

'Why's that?'

The mediator looked uncomfortable.

'Well…'

'He's been more of a father to me in some ways than my real father, you know,' said Michael, suddenly angry. 'So you can stick it up your arse, mate. Reg is all right.'

'There's no need to be rude.'

'Sylvie should have been my mother. *They* should have been my parents.'

'I'm sure you don't mean that.'

'You're sure about a lot on things, aren't you? But you don't understand much. It's Reg that I have to rebel against, not my real father. My real father is a jellyfish, there's nothing to rebel against. But Reg, Reg is like an iron warlord.'

'Are you jealous of him?' the mediator said, looking suddenly shrewd.

'Are *you* jealous of *me?*' sneered Michael insouciantly.

'Not at all.'

'You know I'll be a big music star at some point, with bitches throwing themselves at me, but I won't touch any of them because it's sexist. I'll *teach* them not to make sex objects of themselves. It's so degrading.'

'Then why do you want them to throw themselves at you?'

'I don't, that's just what chicks do to rock stars. But I'm going to be an anti-rockstar, like Fugazi, only better. Maybe more like Darkthrone.'

'You're a interesting young man, Michael, but all I can say is…'

'And what if I *am* jealous of my uncle, anyway? It gives me something to strive towards.'

'What?'

'To better him!

*   *   *

'So, in *Falling Down*, we have a truly egregious example of the 'backlash film' Hollywood has been pushing upon the people of late.' The youth pushed his glasses up his nose and brushed his lank wavy hair from his eyes. 'Just when pop music is starting to see the decline of sexist, racist white boys like Guns N' Roses, then Tinseltown takes up the torch of reaction. We badly need a reaction *against* the reaction!' Michael stifled a yawn. Why would anyone care about stuff like this?

His eyes returned magnetically to the slender, intelligent looking girl directly opposite him, at her silver skirt, black top, long dark hair, then looked to the floor again in case she saw his looking as sexist. That wouldn't be good at a meeting of Youth Revolt, whose renowned weekly paper *Red-Green Alternative* was sold by dedicated volunteers on busy streets across the country. Michael admired them because they did it for no pay, and in the face of hostility from the public.

'You know, Daniel, I actually disagree that *Falling Down* is a backlash film,' she said, looking extremely serious. 'The guy is messed up, but he isn't a Nazi or a bigot, and he has this kind of unspoken link to that black man who was dragged away by the cops…no, I think in many ways this is actually a *good* film. It will get people thinking about the injustices of capitalism, practiced on those who aren't 'economically viable'. If you want to talk about backlash films, they're out there, but this isn't one of them.' Michael loved the way she brushed the hair out of her eyes, so chic, so serious and serene. He adored those silver eyelashes, and wanted to lift up her skirt and…

Even Daniel, who clearly disagreed with what she said and fancied himself something of an intellectual, deferred to her grudgingly with much umming and ahhing and tripping around words, trying to emerge from the hole of backlashism he had dug for himself.

Michael tensed, ready to pounce with some witty, incisive comment, but was forced agonisingly to wait for the meeting turned to a topic, any topic, he knew about…movies, unlike music, were not his forte. Soon he had his chance, as talk turned to the 'unwinnable election' that the lizard of Oz, Paul Keating, had just somehow managed to win. Michael said what he thought they would want to hear him say (since he felt there was no point him being at the meeting at all if he didn't back up their worldview somehow), yet put his own touch on it.

'Well it was a near thing those good-for-nothing Liberals didn't get back in! And I was pleased to see that my father's party, the Australian Democrats, performed dismally in both houses. Instead of keeping the bastards honest, maybe now they'll look to keeping themselves honest, ha ha.'

No one knew what to make of this remark. They smiled tautly at him, the 'newbie' not expected to know much about dialectical materialism.

He needed to fill the patronising silence. Worried about a comment he had read in a magazine of his uncle's regarding the failure of Ross Perot's presidential campaign, he blabbered his fears into the void.

'Is there at this very moment an American Caesar, sitting in some great estate, contemplating these things?' he quoted, sans explanation. 'If history is a guide, we can most certainly respond in the affirmative!'

'What on earth are you talking about,' asked the silver-eyelashed vixen with a puzzled frown.

'Iggy Pop, one of my aunt's favourite singers, just put out a new album called *American Caesar*. Could it be him?'

'Could *what* be him?'

'The coming dictator of America.'

Suspicious looks were directed at him for the rest of the meeting, especially from long-haired Daniel.

He contributed nothing more, and was relieved when it was time for them to hit the streets selling *Red-Green Alternative*.

Trooping down to Salamanca a dead-serious gang of middle-class serfs who had discovered a more exotic brand of serfdom. All looked excited and engaged except Daniel, hands in pockets, ginger frown on his crown. He wasn't looking anymore but Michael could sense he was onto him. Did he glean that Michael wasn't fully committed to the ideals of Marxism, which admittedly he didn't understand too well. He had only skimmed their newspaper, liking the radical look of it but only registering its content in the haziest way.

They reached the Salamanca Market and were given a dozen copies each from an older balding comrade who looked like a mainlander…too old to be an official member of Youth Revolt. Michael's intention had been to stand near the silver girl, but she slipped off through the crowd before he'd been given his papers to sell.

So he ended up opposite Daniel.

He stood, feeling like a fool, with his papers and the pocket full of change, ten dollars or so, they had given him, feebly croaking 'Red-Green Alternative! Red-Green Alternative!' ignored by tourists and locals alike, except for one old lady who demanded to know if the paper contained a cryptic crossword. Told no, she put her hands up and fled as if he were the devil.

Michael noticed that the man who had given them the

papers had returned to his van and driven off...why wasn't *he* selling too? Was he some honcho too 'important' for the troops? Well fuck him! Michael would show them *he* could sell!

Some weird nihilistic part of his psyche swung in, a voidal point he had felt before but never given in to in this manner.

'Come and get your papers, you braindead sheep!' he hollered.

Daniel stared at him eyes straining to crack the skull that held them, then bounded over to take him in hand. One of the other sellers too had rushed up. They were dragging him away as he laughed and roared and shouted.

'Mate, you can't do this...are you a fascist plant?' Michael assured him he wasn't. 'Then you must need psychiatric help. Please, go and get it, and don't come selling papers until you're cured!'

They released their grip on his arms at the top end of the market and he headed off down Davey Street in a manic haze, wondering what it was that triggered him off so.

He realised he still had their ten dollars change and in light of their rudeness (as he saw it) decided to buy a six-pack of beer to calm himself down.

*   *   *

Fugazi were playing the Hellenic Hall in North Hobart. International acts *never* came to Tassie, not since Dire Straits in the 80s. And *Fugazi*, how utterly thrilling! They were promoting their new album, *In on the Kill Taker*, which Michael liked very much. The crisp guitar sound pleased him, the intensity jarred him.

Leighton and a couple of others were smoking buckets before the gig, plunging a sawn-off plastic bottle into stinking tar water, pushing the smoke deep into their lungs...it can't be healthy Michael thought, declining to puzzlement and shrugs. It felt inappropriate for a straight edge act, he told them. He felt apprehensive, in any case, that the Youth Revolt people might be there. He hadn't paid back their ten dollars and it weighed on his mind. Stealing from a political group…wasn't it as bad as the street kid he knew who had scooped up money from the cancer charity fountain in the foyer of the police station to spend on drugs?

Michael had moved out again, into a dump of a share house on Goulburn Street where he worked by candlelight on his lyrics, fingering notes on a battered ukulele bought for two dollars in a Barrack Street op shop. He had a job sweeping the floor of a cafe at the end of each day, but most of his money came from unemployment benefits, much to his mother's disgust (her vision of the welfare state didn't extend to members of her own family).

Michael stood up the back in shadows, hoping not to be seen by Daniel or Silverlashes, waiting patiently through the sets of local support acts Mouth and Little Ugly Girls. He liked the Mouth guitarist's shitty looking guitar, which he had heard didn't have the right amount of strings, but he disliked the lyrics to 'Homophobia' because they reminded him of what had happened to Dorry, rumoured to be in some really bad circles right now. Once more felt a knife-twist of guilt and repressed it. Was he really responsible for someone because of one unfair beating? He couldn't shake the guilt, a dirty clouding shadow, and focussed on the crowd to try and forget.

Half of them phoneys, he thought, feeling a surge of disgust at seeing Rob Weed moshing in the front row. Had Weed even *heard* Fugazi? Surely he was just here to see 'the American band'.

Some of the punks were no better, though. Michael spotted one with a Nirvana *Nevermind* t-shirt with a track list on the back; he had crossed every song title on the back with a permanent marker and substituted the track names from *Bleach*, their lesser known first album! What a poseur, snickered Michael, praying silently he would never indulge in such affectation himself. He had decided that his band would play with plain, drab Soviet-style clothing, and turn their backs to the audience - or perhaps be hidden behind a screen so the audience would focus purely on the music.

Fugazi came on finally, and Michael watched them with interest. People worshipped them...what was going through their minds? Did they feel a proper sense of responsibility, being rock stars? Not to morality, of course, but to art. How many in the audience understood them, and how many were merely seduced by image?

Two songs in, the band began schoolmarming the audience about dancing too violently, and Michael was amused. Personally he couldn't care less if the trendies trampled each other en masse.

He stood hypnotised until the set ended, then saw Leighton across the room and went to ask what he thought of the set. Leighton was talking to someone he had never seen before, with a chubby, inscrutable face and pointed goatee. He quickly realised that this was Music Man, whom Leighton and others had spoken of frequently, and became quietly respectful, as if suddenly in the presence of a bigger celebrity than Fugazi themselves. For Music Man was a Sage. Too saturnine to be a Buddha, he was said to smoke tobacco in a strange pipe with a bubbling water chamber (when not attending straight edge gigs...though it was rumoured that Fugazi had their own problems with that movement).

Leighton saw a girl he knew and Michael was suddenly alone with the bearded demigod.

'You like Fugazi?' he attempted, flustered by the serene stare.

'Mmmm. I incline more towards their self-titled EP than later efforts. But I don't listen to mainstream stuff like this much as a rule.'

'You've got to respect them because they refused big offers from all the major labels. If you sign to a major, you're an employee of the label, and you can kiss your creative control goodbye.'

Ian MacKaye walked within spitting distance of Michael as he said it, and he wondered if he should talk to him, ask his advice.

'Yes, a sad facet of the record business,' said Music Man.

'I heard you have the biggest record collection in Tasmania, maybe Australia.'

'Perhaps.' Very relaxed, nothing would impress him. 'What sort of bands do *you* like?'

'You mean local bands? I like Rare, these two girls that played at Hobart College a few months back. I have the hots for them a bit.'

'International bands?'

'Well, uh, I've been listening to Tumour Circus, and *The Untidy Suicides of Your Degenerate Children* by Alice Donut.'

'What else?'

'Sepultura's new one, *Chaos A.D.*, which I don't like much.'

'Why not?'

'It's affected, not as lean and hungry as their old shit. And Darkthrone…do you know, they dedicated *Under a Funeral Moon* to the Brazilian Death Squads! That's a bit fascist, eh? Still, I like that one of the songs is in their native language, Norwegian.'

'How would you like to be co-DJ on my new radio show on 92 FM? I was going to ask Leighton, but he seems to have fucked off.'

Michael, with visions of money, power and girls like sugarplum fairies, accepted instantly.

10

MADAME SOSOSTRIS

He was stepping into the unknown. Hasty, trembling fingers fumbled the dial, not remembering that Tasmanian phone numbers had just been extended to eight digits. He tried again. Plucking up courage, listening for a Rhodesian accent on the other end of the line. No one answered, just a silence of consciousness. Only his crude, dead ego, ticking like the clock, weighing everything down, heavying the room.

He replaced the receiver. It would have been too good to be true.

Then it rang, bell feeling in his spine. He snatched, breathed 'Hello?'

But it was Music Man.

More complaints about Michael's solo show last week, when Music Man was sick. Not the swear word he had accidentally let drop, but his political rant, when he had ripped into Paul Keating's comments about Australia being the 'arse end of the world' (leaked by Hawke as revenge for ousting him as PM), mocking his own call for a Republic with Australian head of state. Michael may have despised the royal family, but he wanted *consistency*. But this was 'party political' on a station meant to be community.

'I hate the Liberals as well, though.'

'Doesn't matter. Just leave politics out of it, okay? If it happens again, they may shut the show down.'

'All right. '

'Just a friendly warning.'

135

Replacing the receiver again. Awaiting more silence.

*   *   *

In the supermarket he ran into Sally, his ex-friend wth the dumpling mum. It seemed she wanted to talk, but his heart was closed, he didn't trust her. She wouldn't believe him, he knew, he knew. His eyes focussed narrowly above her head, but she wasn't cold, just hurt. Why? Why would she be hurt? It's an illusion, a charade, he thought. Don't be deceived, don't be deceived….

A rustle at his elbow and the big-titted matriarch was there.

'Hello, Michael.' Nonchalant.

Wreaths of inactive steam swirled about her, Michael's vision blurring. A vision of motherliness, but not for Michael. He had to get out of there. Walking away without another word left them both surprised.

*   *   *

A girl at a party, saying 'Anyone who doesn't like Kurt is a *wanker*.'

Kurt Cobain was hot property now he was dead. Michael had followed the story with vague interest, enjoying seeing someone give fame and wealth a smack in the mouth like that. It was funny how the note ended in a different-looking scrawl, though. Anyway, Kurt was in thrall to *girls*. Most of his lyrics were about *relationships*, something Michael as yet had no experience of so felt at liberty to sneer at.

'About A Girl'. 'On A Plain'.

Friends. 'Just friends.'

Friends with a *girl*. Ha ha.

You *couldn't* be friends with a girl. Something more,

something less, but not friends.

Michael put this particular female specimen down witheringly.

'Kurt *was* a wanker,' he said coldly, just because he could. Some pussy-worshipping jock stood up for her and threatened to punch him, but Michael held his ground, braced for the blow and jabbing back. But it never came, the jock spitting and walking off crookedly, like Rob Weed...'In Bloom' written about him, but impossible he would ever realise. So what was the point of the song?

He would *always* be alone. He was resigned to it. Who needed bitches anyway?

*   *   *

Anika was his torment, his yearning, he couldn't wait to see her each day.

Annihilation of opposites, the Orphic Egg, circumpolar ring of light. She liked ABBA, Queen and New Order, and introduced him to Bowie's better stuff (*Station to Station* and *Low*). She seemed to belong to another age, that of Sylvie; yet op shop clothes fixed her to the 90s, blonde hair dyed red. Her personality morphed into a pack of cards.

Each girl in Hobart had one in those days, and the more precocious had Aleister Crowley's 'Thoth'. Michael leafed through the accompanying book and thought Crowley had warped the meanings of the cards artificially, to fit something called 'Kabbalah', yet the artwork fascinated him, and he began to play the game common to novices where he would associate certain cards with people, colours, jagged angles, vortexes, rays of light. He had no interested in alleged divinatory functions because he already knew he was destined for greatness.

Even more than what was under her skirt, he liked the patchwork fabric itself, soft and velveteen, fading to something good. Oh, how he wished he could love Sally, who he heard was now going out with a man of means, who actually owned a car. Michael would have far more prestige than a mere car would bestow, it was only a matter of time. He *willed* it. Yes, that was something Crowley was right about. You *could* will things.

He didn't like that his new Rhodesian girlfriend (*girlfriend*, he had to keep reminding himself of that, he had an actual *girlfriend*) worked each fortnight as a life drawing model, stripped bare for an entire room to ogle. Had he fallen in love with a whore? But you can't fall in love with a whore he told himself, so she can't *be* a whore, simple as that.

Yes, better times were ahead, the soft skirt a nest, a point around which he could accelerate like a comet spouting around the sun. He even enjoyed watching TV with her, something he officially despised. *The X-Files* was their favourite; it was goofy, but they both agreed that UFOs were probably real.

* * *

On a tight-lipped visit his mother informed him that Menzies, his fear-inducing childhood nemesis, had passed (aged ancient sixteen) to the Kennels Beyond, perhaps to the Dog Star itself. Had slobbered his last.

Most of his teeth had fallen out and Reg had been forced to make him a meaty paste each day, but now Reg had an electronic alarm system to guard him from enemies like the ones who killed Sylvie.

Michael wondered what had happened to the dog's teeth, and if he could persuade his uncle to give him one as a souvenir, perhaps to make into a necklace. Another link to the faraway world of childhood was gone, and he was truly entering a dizzying new world.

His mother was outraged that he was cohabiting with a *girl*, one whose tattered velveteen skirts littered the living room.

Michael got angry and told her at least he wasn't divorced.

'No, and you're not likely to be as you'll never be able to afford to get married! How can you afford the rent here on unemployment benefits?'

'I work part time at a cafe. And there's my radio show.' He didn't tell her it was volunteer, but it sounded important. 'And Anika works...' He stopped. He didn't dare say she was an 'undraped mannequin', although he longed to shock his mother.

'Works as what? A gypsy fortune teller? Look at these ridiculous garments.'

'So? Look at the crap the Beatles wore on your Sergeant Pepper's album.'

'That was the sixties.'

She left, leaving him some homemade casserole in a plastic ice-cream tub. She hadn't completely given up on him.

But with the death of Menzies (whom he now quixotically developed a soft spot for), he felt his life was entering a new phase, unfettered by the past. He would make himself afresh. First a cult following on 92 FM, then syndication to the mainland and (somehow) overseas. It would happen, he could feel it. He was destined to achieve success in the USA, first as a DJ, then as a musician himself. And his career trajectory started tonight, for Music Man was sick again, and he had the show to himself a second time, on the promise of no political rants.

But Music Man hadn't said anything about sociological rants.

Michael had developed a passionate hatred for Rage Against the Machine, the phoney, manufactured 'anti-corporate rebel' band who just happened to be promoted by Sony, a gigantic corporation. He knew Rob Weed and Hayden Burn were heavily into them, and in part his barb was to be aimed at them, if they were listening. He would deliver a rant tonight about fake rebels, sponsored by the system itself as a safety valve to defuse *real* rebellion.

Such stale comforts would be gotten rid of, under the

future system that would derive from his music. Things were darkest before the dawn. But a leader, or group of leaders, would come, and transform society, and Michael would be their prophet, or perhaps they his. His music would inform the very laws the populace would be ruled by, and Michael would be revered as a culture hero, poet, sage. This was far in a dim future, probably beyond the year 2000, but it *would* happen, he'd no fears on that score.

*   *   *

His speech had fallen flat, not a single angry call, but he no longer cared. Were the masses beyond reaching? As long as he was in *her* skirt he didn't care. Backing into a corner, but so small the rest didn't listen.

He needed inward withdrawal to counter-balance the aggressive tendrils he had thrust into a docile and uncaring world.

Anika and his mother *hadn't* gotten along, though he had desperately hoped they would have.

Sometimes his mother felt like a black, dry shadow always hovering about his throat. He wanted to tear it away but it would have ripped his breath out.

But, sometimes, sometimes, when he was with Anika he felt he was being lulled into a false sense of comfort.

Was what *he* wanted important? Wouldn't she be the same being with him or without him? That was the question that assessed his worth, for if she needed him as much as he felt he needed her his future Work would come about, and if not…

Already he had started to doubt himself. He cursed her, drank her honey at the same time…wild dark honey from bitter bees, dripping from Roman aqueducts.

She made him hope.

She made him fear.

Sometimes she made him the core of a bright, shining light of simplicity.

Morphine? He compared it to a siren and rejected it, worse than cigarettes, yet when he saw her inject it once a week (when finances permitted) he didn't flinch. He even kissed the track marks on her inner arm.

*   *   *

Next week Music Man and he went on a rant *together*. It was weird to hear that placid man get worked up.

The topic was Mötley Crüe's grunge moves. Belatedly sensing prevailing winds, the boys had put out an album aping Soundgarden, hiding their party-wog ambience under a bushel. Michael was disgusted they would change to fit the times (Guns N' Roses' 'punk' album *The Spaghetti Incident* was a similar feint). Why couldn't they respect their *own* traditions? They had invalidated their back catalogue for legions of fans, etc. etc. It was quite an extended sermon the two of them gave. They also discussed a major publisher who had put out a new novel on two floppy disks, billing it as 'the world's first electronic novel'. Would music, too, one day be released on floppy disk? Music Man, who was a vinyl purist, fervently hoped not.

'So now let's see what you've blown the budget I gave you…out of my own pocket…on this week, young Michael. What kind of rubbish are you foisting on our listeners?' Music Man lived on the interest from an inheritance, and by Michael's standards was loaded.

'Well, Music Man, I finally got to hear Burzum, the solo project of Count Grishnackh, who killed the head of the Black Circle in Norway.' Michael had been electrified by pictures of 'The Count' posing aggressively with his medieval mace, and equally impressed to hear 'Tomhet', which, far from being extreme metal, was a cold and haunting synthesiser track.

'And this is *Caravans to Empire Algol*, by Neptune Towers…its purpose is to help you escape the earth. Both courtesy of Pig Records in Elizabeth Street. And finally Beherit's *H418ov21.C*, which is another dark ambient synth album.'

'Bah! Pushing your worthless synth crap on me…at least it's not more lame heavy metal, though.' The banter between them usually went something like this.

'I think the anti-commercial nature of this music is more extreme than, say, Fugazi, and it's more interesting artistically too.'

'Hmmm, well, we'll see about that. Put it on, then.'

Michael had wanted to play the odd mainstream song, like Kylie Minogue's 'Confide in Me', which he found eerie and haunting, and 'Zombie' by the Cranberries, but Music Man wouldn't let him, and for now Michael let it alone, not wanting to fall out with his benefactor.

Music Man also didn't like Kurt Cobain for some reason and wouldn't mention him on the show. He showed rare emotion and his jowls wobbled when asked about it.

11

COCKY LITTLE BASTARD

He stood awkwardly at the door of the Youth Revolt meeting. Entirely new faces, none from the meeting two years ago. Was their turnover so high? The upper age limit was 25, there should have been at least a face or two from before.

The chairgirl turned quizzically.

'I took money from you two years ago and didn't pay it back. It was about ten bucks. I think you'll find it's all here.' He handed her a crisp note. Some silence.

'And, what made you decide to pay it...now?' Smiles, or smirks?

'I find honesty best...not out of some kind of goodness or phoney morality...on the contrary, because it sets a higher standard for *me*.'

Someday he must get round to reading that Nietzsche fellow so many of the metal bands were quoting. The girl's confused smile.

'Come in then, and thanks for your honesty, whatever the motive. Would you like some Nicaraguan coffee?'

'No. I don't hold with your goody-two-shoes brand of socialism. 90% of people belong in death camps, and some day I will achieve it.'

Their shock was more at his relaxed delivery than content...he had tried to put on a Norwegian or Eastern European accent, but somehow it had come out sounding Jamaican. A Jamaican neo-Nazi, with matted hairs.

Embarrassed, he turned on his heel and stalked out, throwing back an imaginary long cloak he wore.

He was at the height of his Black Metal phase, and wanted to convey what he saw as the power and mystery of this music in his very gestures and movements. He wanted to be like The Count, whose real name he now knew was Vikernes, and whose medieval war club he was attempting to replicate in his share house by hammering nails through a sawn-off axe handle.

He had read an interview with The Count in Australia's second biggest metal magazine, *Metal Masters*, stating that he hailed all who loved their race, 'like the proud homogenous Japanese.' Michael approved this because it showed objectivity, and aristocratic largesse. Vikernes' claim to be a worshipper of Odin reminded him of the board game he had played in primary school, and now the feeling of immense icy distances somehow linked with blood came back to him like a familiar scent, just as if it had been a real memory linked to a smell, like his grandfather's house in Ross, but somehow beyond it.

He had been listening a lot to the Polish band Graveland, particularly their *Thousand Swords* album, which made Immortal's *Pure Holocaust* sound like a dry old biscuit in comparison. Graveland's singer Rob Darken looked forward to 'to the coming era of a new war, a new holocaust and a new Führer who will lead the strong and powerful youth educated in pagan traditions,' and Michael wanted to be that Führer.

'In Poland, black metal is a sacred, religious music. Those who profane it are afraid of the black metal underground because we will not let them get away with it. Kill all fucking pigs who want to make business out of black metal!'

Michael approved mightily of all this. He wasn't sure what to make of Darken's views on Jews, who he claimed were bent on absorbing Black Metal into a musical machine and making it a 'new fashionable alternative to Death Metal.' Michael no longer liked Death Metal, in any case, as it had been largely taken over by bands with commercial motives.

Michael had worn out his childhood, but no initiation ritual existed to pass him into adulthood, so he sought strength where he could find it, and Norway music gave him that feeling.

*   *   *

After Youth Revolt he decided to visit Dorry, who according to Leighton was living in a squat on Goulburn Street. He passed the library, where a week ago he had used the much-vaunted new 'World Wide Web' for the first time, attempting to find information on Swedish bands Deutsch Nepal and Raison d'Etre. There were discographies under square grey buttons, but zines were a far better source of information on the underworld of music Michael imagined fuelled his essence.

The Web had two 'browsers', as they were called, Mosaic and Netscape. Just as there were two political parties, two colas, two of everything…the illusion of choice. How long before they merged and became monopolies? Would people then realise perhaps there weren't any real choices?

Half a block past the library he passed a young man with long blond hair who called to his turned back: 'Hey!'

Michael spun warily to face him.

'Yeah?'

'What's the definition of pain?'

'What?'

'The definition of *pain*.'

'What?'

'Masturbating with a cheese grater, ha ha.' Without trace of smile, the youth spun on his heel walking rapidly along Bathurst Street while his unfunny joke hovered in the air.

Too many weirdoes in Hobart, thought Michael. Surely the city can't hold this many this long?

Keenly aware there were those who thought he fell into the 'weirdo' category himself, confirmed by the distant sight of Cover Band Man, Rob Weed, getting into his panel van. Weed now ruled the roost of the Hobart pub scene, proclaiming his anti-racism in the post-grunge era, but Michael remembered a very different figure at D'Entrecasteux High. Like Crüe he had changed with the times, craven submission to Popgeist. Weed considered himself a genuine Rock Legend, and looked down upon Michael accordingly, indeed had publicly snubbed him twice, but *who would have the last laugh?* Michael had the Norway energy, while Weed had recycled Stone Temple Pilots riffs.

Feeling smug, he knocked on the door of Dorry's squat, dimly aware that he was subconsciously going there to lord it over him, cheap power boost coming from perceived elevation above one weaker than him, not yet realising true power refers to no other soul.

Dorry opened the door, surprised to see him, and Michael didn't waste time with small talk.

'Hi Dog, are you still angry with me? You were, I think, but I can't remember why.' Feigning nonchalance, Dorry eyebrows raised.

'No, I'm not angry with you.' Shaky, hand on the door frame tremouring slightly.

'Oh…good.'

'You're such a c-c-cocky little bastard, though, that it wouldn't matter if I was.' Ouch. Though Michael kind of liked 'cocky little bastard', and had heard that Cover Band Man had once used a similar description behind his back.

Cockiness was better than Uriah Heepism, anyhow. Michael stared at left-wing graffiti smattering the hall walls, and got to the point of his visit. He knew Dorry had been homeless…did he know if there was truth to the rumours circulating in the city's homeless shelters about something called the Order of Sion, a shadowy group aimed at trying to take over the government of Tasmania? Michael, who aimed to be Tasmanian dictator himself, felt resentful of such a group were it real. To his surprise (but not relief), Dorry claimed to have heard nothing, indeed seemed to think he had made it up to mock him. He now became hostile, accusing him of being not only cocky but cold and arrogant, with nothing to merit such.

Michael denied it. 'I'm humble,' he said.

Then someone disgusting walked in, and Michael was turned away.

*   *   *

Reg, on the other hand, was warmer than expected at their reunion.

He had sent Michael a letter asking him to come around on this date because he wanted an unbiased witness, and had heard Michael was something of a philosopher these days. Michael couldn't work out if this was meant to be ironic, but was interested to witness his uncle's latest escapade. Now that he himself had attained a small cult following locally, with far greater prospects ahead, he felt less eaten up with jealousy at Reg's notoriety. He even brought Anika along, because he thought her Rhodesian background would please the old man.

Reg, well into his seventies now, walked less steadily, and Michael noted for the first time a subtle frailty and crack in his voice that hadn't been there on their last meeting.

'I've heard that radio show of yours, boy. Young man, I should say.'

Michael felt a cold shock. He had no idea his elderly uncle listened to the show, which thrust the most extreme and outlandish music imaginable onto the airwaves.

'I don't understand a lot of your gibberish, or the noise you call music. A cliched line, but in this case true. Most of it sounded like a constipated witch being tortured and strangled during a thunderstorm. Anyway, I wanted to say I appreciated your comments on that squalid little rat Keating. If you would put your nihilism aside, my boy, you'd make an excellent political commentator.'

'I've been banned from making political comments on the

show.'

'What's the point of the show, then? Politics is life.'

'*Art* is life.'

'Politics can *be* art. It depends how you go about it. As you're about to see.'

'Really? I still remember that Labor party conference, waiting outside with Aunty Sylvie while you were arrested and dragged away…'

'Ha ha. Good times, my boy, good times!'

They shared a laugh, and Michael felt an uncomfortable and unaccustomed warmth, drained temporarily of looking at his uncle (and people in general) through the lens of rivalry, suddenly comrades against an enemy caste of slimy, cartoonish and goblinesque sub-men, encapsulated by the Australian Labor Party of the 1990s.

'How are your guinea fowl?'

'Only one left. Haven't bothered getting new ones when they die off. I'm winding things down. Your mother will be taking care of Boudicca for a while, actually.'

'Boudicca?'

'The last guinea fowl.'

'Oh. You're going away somewhere?' A faint chill piercing feigned coolness.

'You can't witness evil and not make a stand, my boy.'

'I'm beyond good and evil, Uncle.'

'Nonsense, my boy.' He turned to Anika. 'Is Michael beyond good and evil? If so, how does he manage it?'

She faltered, unnerved by his glittering eye. 'Every man and every woman is a star…' she muttered.

'Not so…only those who burn internally could be called stars…and there are large areas of void and lifeless dust between them.'

Michael couldn't have this, Reg showing him up again. He thought of the Nat Sav G, his old gang. And his band, The Mutineers - what were they mutinying against? He had been expelled from high school, admittedly, and moved out of home young (Anika admired this). He had dabbled with Youth Revolt, created controversies with the radio show.

But Reginald Murchison still seemed somehow the better rebel. His jealousy returned.

'Let's get in the car, then,' he said shortly. 'We'll see what you have planned this time. Something significant I hope.' His uncle bowed ironically, opening one of the car's back doors for them.

Ever the rhetorician, Reg regaled them on the way with talk of the Demidenko affair, of which Michael had only vaguely heard. It appeared that a young authoress, not much older than Michael, had depicted four or five ethnic groups unflatteringly in her novel, of which just one had complained and created 'controversy' around the book. Michael didn't like special pleading from minority groups, Jewish or otherwise, but regarded himself as an equal opportunity misanthrope and tried to differentiate himself from his uncle by this fact.

'Anti-vilification legislation' aimed largely at silencing one Reginald Murchison had recently been spruiked by federal opposition leader Alexander Downer...then Downer had been ousted by John Howard, who had to walk back his own previous anti-immigration remarks, remarks that has influenced Michael's primary school speech (seven years ago now) when he had tried to emulate his uncle. Would he ever emerge from Reg's shadow?

'Your accent, young lady...are you South African or...'

'From Zimbabwe.'

'Rhodesia,' Reg corrected. 'Do you remember much about it?'

'I was only eight when we left. I remember the sunlight, which is different to here. And the sounds and smells of the bush. I remember some blacks shot in a pile further down the valley from where our farm was, and I heard about missionaries being slaughtered nearby.'

'You can thank the World Council of Churches for that,' muttered Reg.

'The blacks thought that no death is accidental, even if it seems to be...it must be sorcery. But these deaths were deliberate by any standard, and I guess they *were* a kind of evil sorcery.'

'Did you mix with the blacks much?' asked Michael curiously.

'There were some workers on our farm but I wasn't allowed to talk to them. I stayed in the house. We had a housekeeper but she was from Finland. It seems like a dream, now, I can scarcely believe I lived there. Sometimes it seems that everything passes like a dream, and one day this will seem like one as well.'

'Remember it as well as you can, then,' said Reg. 'Sear it into your memory.' Michael noticed a tear on the old man's cheek, yet his eyes seemed dry.

'Here we are,' he murmured, pulling into the stronghold of his enemies.

12

ROO HUNT

As they got out and stretched their legs, Reg was retrieving something from the boot. Something large and fuzzy, which he began to pull on over his clothing.

'Give me a hand zipping this up at the front.' To their astonishment it was a kangaroo suit, hired for the occasion from a theatre company. It was only semi-convincing, and he realised it. Michael was too proud to ask what he had on his mind. Some epic stunt, no doubt, which he himself would never dare attempt. He bit his lip.

A fresh breeze blew. Michael remembered his grade six trip here, in the Bicentennial year of 1988. He had enjoyed dressing up in colonial clothes as the ship's doctor. But now Risdon Cove was to be shut off by people claiming Aboriginality, but with a majority of white blood. Did they hate seven eighths (or more) of themselves? It really got one thinking about identity.

'Wait here,' instructed Reg. 'I only need witnesses in case things go awry. Which they no doubt will.' He hopped away, actually hopped, aged as he was. It was surreal. Did he think he could creep up on them and they wouldn't notice? Kangaroos were rare this close to Hobart, and they were sure to glance at him, especially as he had a rolled-up sheet of paper in his paw.

Michael could see a group of Aborigines (if that's what they were) conversing with someone he thought he recognised

151

from TV, a well-known politician. There was a flash little weaselly Abo on crutches, all swagger, Rossi boots with jangly bits at the back, short to long haircut, silver crucifix around his neck (what meaning could it have when both they and Murchison claimed inspiration from the same sign?). An AC/DC shirt made Michael sympathise with him a bit, for that band (while rich) never changed their style to commercialise…but the Abo was too arrogant, cocky like Michael now thought himself to be, but minus the self-reflection that was his own saving grace.

Then a cluster of elders and lumpy aunts. There was a feeling of hostility in the air, a very unwelcoming atmosphere for outsiders. Anika could sense it too and shivered. What were they doing to this place, which belonged eternally to the bright year 1988, did they wish to shut out the sun? Muttonbirding and stringing shells were the traditions they claimed to uphold…couldn't they do those things elsewhere?

Reg Murchison hopped up to them and began reading from the paper in his paw. Michael couldn't hear what he was saying. The Aborigines looked understandably startled.

'We can't really be accurate witnesses from this distance.'

'I don't know…I don't like the look of that ferret-faced guy.'

'Aren't you dying to know what he's saying to them, though?'

'Well…maybe. I don't understand your uncle. What's he going to achieve by all this?'

'I think he's creating a kind of cultural artefact…it's performance art.'

As they drew nearer, the blur of raised voices separated. Reg was taking them to task over what he considered their 'fake reconstructed culture', and they were laughing in his face.

'*British* culture is your culture,' Reg mocked. 'You can't escape it or subvert it, try as you might. Give it up. Give up now!'

But if they reconstruct their culture, however fakely, thought Michael, then it gives nationalism legitimacy, and

Reg is a nationalist...or is he? But if he wants imperialism doesn't the fakeness legitimate them being subject peoples? Reg should be more proud of his empire's conquests...

'When did Furneaux Islanders, Moonbirders, suddenly become 'Aborigines'?' Reg bellowed. 'Oh yes, in the '70s, with Whitlam's money...I remember it like it was yesterday.'

'Bullshit,' the young ferret sneered. 'We were *coerced* into rejecting our identity by government agencies. And what would you know about it you old white bigot?'

'Nah, he's a kangaroo,' one of the aunties pointed out, cackling. 'His fur is *brown*.'

'It's that Murchison idiot.'

'You, young man, are descended from the very worst of the whites, the sealers who beat, rape and enslaved Aboriginal women. So perhaps you should pay your own reparations, ha ha ha.'

Ouch...that must have hurt. But Michael did envy the Abos their unity of purpose. Unity? A large woman sidled across from the periphery.

'I represent the Lia Pootah people, and...'

'Oh, fuck off you old bat,' said Ferret-Face.

A three-way argument now ensued, with the newcomer, belonging to a faction unrecognised by those holding the flag ceremony, berating both Reginald and Ferret. The politician looked on, crestfallen at all the upstaging, ignored by all whose blood was in any way circulating.

Suddenly Reg grabbed the Aboriginal flag (which was the colour of mainland deserts, not temperate Tasmania) and made a mad hopping dash across the park.

'Stop him,' bellowed an aunt, and they waddled after him, the ferret on crutches hobbling behind bellowing obscenities, a game of catch the flag.

'C'mon,' Michael prodded.

'I can't run...my asthma,' she hissed.

'Can you walk fast?'

'Okay.'

'Let's go, we'll soon catch up.'

'Do we *have* to?'

'We're supposed to be witnesses, remember.'

So Uncle Reg had made a neo-imperialist attack on a nationalist culture, however trite. Would his Empire, unchecked, keep growing until it swallowed every last nation in its vast shadow?

Michael felt that shadow, its weight...he had to emerge from under it, lest it suffocate him. His uncle's frontier mentality, the White Man's Burden, his need for imperial control must keep him in constant tension – was that the very source of his greatness? Must Michael be an imperialist, too, for such tension to occur? He couldn't stand the British royals, so it must be a *new* empire, an empire of the soul. A pagan empire, such as Rob Darken has prophesied on.

Yet couldn't there be a patchwork of equal nations? Would such a nation-patchwork destroy itself *without* imperial intervention? The Abos, forever in tribal wars...and where empire withdraws, chaos, butchery, barbarism. Reg wished to avoid that. He was a good man, good at heart. Better than me, Michael thought ashamedly.

And there he was, in the distance, hopping up the East Derwent Highway with the waddlers in pursuit.

Was the history of humanity nothing but an eternal vicious cycle, empire building up and breaking down? An alternative was the name of that book his father had read, *The End of History*. Was such a thing possible and was it really happening? But what would Time be, or mean, without history?

As for nationalism, was it mere mob rule? How did Reg reconcile his nationalism with his imperialism? The British Empire had commercial roots, not lofty moral ones...he had heard that from Reg's own mouth. India had only been acquired reluctantly from the East India Company. And yet the British Empire was also bound up with specific places like London, the atmospheric labyrinth of a city Michael hoped one day to visit. Were zoos, universities, museums imperialism?

No doubt the Abos were better off materially since the British, but what about culturally? Was there any objective standard to judge by? Reg would have said his own will or instinct - he was a 'star', and not everyone was. He would probably say it reflected cosmic order. The concept Michael had heard him talk about, Natural Law. Yes, Reg respected the law, but refused to obey it – spirit not the letter – but this only meant he thought his instincts put him above the herd. Was he a secret Nietzschean? Was his belief in God even real? Was God the same thing as Natural Law?

The nationalist response would be the 'right to difference'. Michael had heard of the idea of autarchy. It seemed genuine…look at the fate of the Japanese, a commercial empire yet their star was in decline…in the '80s everyone had thought they would take over the world. But perhaps there was a future for nations who *despised* trade and commerce, as Michael affected to despise it. Sole 'trade' allowed would be art, and the artefacts of art….Michael's band, for instance, which he hadn't given up on, would be mandatory for all nations to purchase in bulk. The music would cleanse the souls of all who heard it. He had been trying to convince Anika to be female vocalist, but she couldn't be persuaded, her voice was too cracked, she thought. He would have to find someone else, he would…

As they walked past the turnoff to the Bowen Bridge, Michael realised he could remember (just) when it was built, replacing the bailey bridge that had served when the Tasman had been smashed apart by a ship. That was before he was born, but he remembered his parents talking about it, and wondered what had happened to his father, who had apparently disappeared, and…

Uncle Reg had managed to hop nearly a kilometre up the highway, not bad for a senior citizen. Anika, meanwhile, was lagging behind, and Michael could barely restrain his impatience.

The Abos were hot on Reg's tail, Michael could see. Would they, too, be imperialists if they amassed more power? Michael felt sure they would…human nature was such. But now they had passed out of sight again.

Up ahead was the wreck of the *Otago*, a ship the writer

Joseph Conrad had once commanded.

He caught sight of the aunts once more.

But what were they staring at?

*   *   *

The corpse was blue, skin as dry as paper even waterlogged, kangaroo skin drenched. What was this mystery, what did it mean?

Reg had hopped into the wreck of the *Otago*, a foot had stuck in its rusted ribs, tripped and hit his head, and drowned...a symbolic statement? Michael, shaking, couldn't figure out what it meant, he hadn't read any of Conrad's books. Would he find a clue there in years to come?

Had Reg *meant* to die?

As with his aunt, now a leafedged echoing memory, the mystery was the perpetrator...but here the victim himself was the chief suspect.

Or was it accident? But why had he hopped there in the first place? It seemed a funny way to make a final stand against those he considered treasonous.

When Michael and Anika arrived, the Abos were trying to pull Reg out. Had *they* killed him? Looking at their faces, panicked concern, Michael thought not. Had Reg's heart given out (he liked his imitation claret), or had the unresolved tension between Nation and Empire now resolved itself in Reg's death?

Michael wished to resolve it both intellectually and practically, thrusting down into the caves and up into the stars. But perhaps that would never happen.

All he felt was anger...anger beyond belief that his uncle wouldn't live to see him become more famous than himself. That was tragedy beyond words, tragedy beyond tragedy itself...

PART TWO

THE THRESHER

13

BURNIE

Picking carrots, dirt, dirt, dirt...flakes of carrot cutting under his fingernails, dirt in cuts, tetanus shots? Farmer yelling, but better than Rob Weed and Hayden Burn in fish factory. Tasmania's Northwest, so-called Bible Belt, sifting rich volcanic soil for tuberous roots. The farmer, crusty old devil, in old times slave driver with niggerslaves, but Michael had learnt to ignore his aggressive whining, not cowed by it like some of the other pickers, cute German girl next to him reduced to tears at one point, but Michael didn't care, wasn't going to fall for feminine nonsense. Michael was Übermensch, beyond romanticism. Besides, at $15 per crate, he didn't have time to listen to sobbing of prettygirl stranded halfway round world.

He slept on the floor of a scruffy acquaintance in Burnie, and hitchhiked to the farm each day, the dreary, monotonous farm, devoid of the Art which he worshipped.

Hobart felt dead to him, leaden, since Reg's death. Management at 92 FM had forced Music Man to remove him from the show after some loony's repeated calls to the station threatening acid attacks on employees if they didn't let him go. Michael hated the gutless Committee far more than the terrorist, whoever it was (probably Dorry or one of his worthless friends), all the more because prior to being kicked off he had discovered an English label or distro called World

159

Serpent whose albums were utterly fascinating but *expensive*, and now there was no money from Music Man to buy records by Current 93, Death In June, The Moon Lay Hidden Beneath a Cloud, and others he just *had* to have.

So, he would just have to earn the money by the sweat of his brow.

But mustn't become bourgeois like his father, who had disappeared along with Conny after talking of moving away from Tasmania, but why hadn't he told his son or ex-wife where he was going? Typical bourgeois selfishness…

There had been an unpleasant confrontation between Michael and his mother, which ended with her accusing him of being an alienated freak and good-for-nothing, and he snapped back no wonder he was alienated when he wasn't breastfed as a baby (something his father had let slip a couple of years ago and had been rankling him ever since), and he felt like punching her for damaging his health, and he knew she had inherited some of Reg (and Sylvie's) money, so why not give him a loan to buy musical equipment for his non-existent band, what kind of low philistine wouldn't patronise musical genius, given the chance?

That did it – she said he was in danger of turning into another Reg. A dangerous autocrat! She wouldn't talk to him anymore, she sobbed – like most women's blubbing half put on, he sneered.

Autocrat, he thought storming out, what nonsense, because I will have thousands of mourners, not like Reg's funeral at Ross, a rainy springtime affair with none save himself, his mother, Aunty Noela and her family, and a single one of Reg's dour elderly military comrades, wordlessly shaken.

The press were waiting outside the gates, though, filthy vultures. He told them, 'You should interview my mother as to why Reg had to be buried on the other side of the cemetery from Sylvie. Why was the plot given instead to my grandfather who died a year ago, when he could have had the side plot? The one next to Sylvie should have gone to Reg! And by the way, go fuck yourselves.'

They hadn't printed this in the paper, to his disappointment, merely alluding to 'family squabbles' in their hit piece on Reg. *Those vermin will write my obituary one day,* thought Michael, *unless I manage to cleanse their kind from the earth. And if they do, they won't find the words come so easy as they have with Reg.*

He had succumbed finally to Anika's request he sit for a tarot reading, only on condition she didn't talk of the future, merely stare deeper into his own soul. She obliged with a little-used spread, designed for gleaning not contingency. A star-shaped pattern, and to Michael's surprise the Star was at its centre.

'You live in a world that seems real only to you, you're extremely sensitive also. You're a serious idealist but you often lack touch with reality. You're inclined to the esoteric. You have intense feelings and a need for attachment, but also independence. Which means your ideal girlfriend would be an obedient slave, ha ha. What you need above all is *peace*.'

'No, what I want is *war*, war on the degenerate Hobart scene above all.'

'Well, you know best, darling.' But did he really want war for *peace?*

And here he was, in a peaceful field of yellow carrots and dry, dead shallots, the companion he had come up here with having fucked off after day one, couldn't hack it. Anika wouldn't be able to hack it, either, he thought. But he would make the best of it, and when finished get more rural work. So hard on the back, though.

Perhaps he could sell the music collection he had amassed (mainly thanks to Music Man) and use the money to buy instruments – wouldn't that be the *genuine* thing to do? But he must, he *must*, get the latest Moon Lay Hidden album…oh shit, what was he to do?

*   *   *

Saturday night, and they had Sunday off.

He told the German girl, with feigned reluctance, where he was staying…in Shorewell, a housing commission area. She asked if she could stay there too, as her caravan park had an agreement with the farm and took rent (too high, she thought) directly out of her wages.

Michael was reluctant…he hadn't known Karen at all before coming up here, and their mutual friend had gone back to Hobart. She was a scruffy, hippyish pot dealer on the cusp of middle age, and Michael slept on a mattress in her spare room with a ragged sheet for a blanket.

Michael asked, very apologetic…but the German girl started blubbing again, and Karen fussed over her, giving her the clean fold-out couch, not a dirty beer-smelling mattress like Michael's.

He half-listened to their kitchen babble as he lay trying to read an Icelandic saga he had found in a Burnie op shop.

Someone with a deep, gravelly voice dropped around to ask Karen if she knew where so-and-so was. Michael had received a suspicious look last night when someone came to buy weed off her, so he wasn't inclined to be sociable tonight. Deep Voice stayed for a Tooheys Red, and picked up a battered acoustic guitar in the lounge that Michael had been playing last night…and played it.

Simple and direct, certainly different. Michael, impressed by the energy, crept into the lounge. He saw a tall person his own age with broad shoulders, short-to-long haircut (the kind that in later years would be called a 'mullet'), flannelette shirt (not an expensive 'grunge' one like Rob Weed's cover band wore).

He nodded at Michael, gave him the thumbs up, and commenced to sing. He was good at that, too. He had two modes: a guttural, primal growl and a haunting, melodic croon. He beat the guitar like a beast, but somehow it worked, and somehow the strings didn't snap.

After a while he stopped and offered Michael a beer.

'That was great. Was it original?'

'Ah, some of it. Some was covers. That last one was

'Lonely Man of Spandau' by Angelic Upstarts. My own weird version.'

'I never heard that.'

'You like punk?'

'No, metal mostly.'

Deep Voice, it turned out, was into what he called 'true punk.' Sham 69, The Exploited, GBH, and a 'Scottish Aryan punk band' called The Skids. Michael had heard none of it, but was interested because what he played had such an intensity.

'I thought punk was crap like Green Day.' Michael remembered that he used to like the Dead Kennedys, but that seemed an age ago.

'Mate! I fucken near flattened someone in a pub one night for calling Green Day a punk band. That shit's so bad, it makes me want to puke my guts up. Did you ever hear Amebix?'

'No.'

'That's *real* punk. Skrewdriver are alright too. I found their *Blood & Honour* album in a shop in Melbourne.'

Ah, Melbourne, the land of culture, where Michael half wished to go. On an impulse he began to talk of his own favourites, of the World Serpent bands he had recently discovered, and was surprised to find his new acquaintance interested, particularly in Sol Invictus.

'He had this old band called Above the Ruins, but he's disowned it now due to the 'politically incorrect' lyrics. It's been reissued on CD as a bootleg, but I haven't managed to get it.'

'So it embarrasses him?'

'Right.'

'It's probably better than his new stuff then. His old self would punch out his new self, maybe.'

'Ha ha, yeah.' Michael *really* wanted to get hold of Above the Ruins.

The singer went to get them another beer, but something delayed him. Michael sat patiently in the lounge listening to the German girl laugh at something, then something else.

The singer showed no sign of coming back, and it appeared he had found a maid to seduce. Twenty minutes later Michael was in the kitchen drinking a Tooheys Red with Karen, trying to block out the exaggerated sex noises coming from the spare room. He was banging her on Michael's mattress…and to Michael's jealousy, wishing *he* had comforted the wench. He had snubbed her from misanthropy, but thought of Anika between the grunting and the groans.

'So what do you think of Shiv?'

'Is that his real name?'

'I dunno. He comes from a *terrible* background, his mother was a complete junkie lowlife whore. He's lucky to be alive, to be honest.'

'He's a good guitarist…simple, but powerful.'

'He's descended from convicts.'

'So's half of Tasmania. I've got some.'

'His father fucked off before he was born.'

'My father disappeared, too,' said Michael self-importantly.

'When you were a baby?'

'No, last year. I think his girlfriend kidnapped him or something.'

'Really? Did you report him as missing?'

'No. He might still turn up.'

'What if he's dead?'

'I hope not…I need him to see me get famous. My real parents are gone, there's no one else.' Did the grunting and banging in the other room herald a change in his fortunes…or just more of the same crap?

'Well anyway, Shiv has these casual outbursts sometimes which polarise people. His presence alone has been known to cause friendships to dissolve. Just thought I'd give you a heads up. He won't mind me saying so.'

'Thanks for the warning.'

'It was nothing.'

She left the room. Michael drifted asleep, drifted awake, and now could hear Karen in there being loudly serviced by

Shiv - had the German gone, or was she watching? Michael shook his head tolerantly at the stupid rutting animals; he didn't care at all, because he had Anika, Anika, Anika…

*   *   *

It was Sunday…Michael slept on the couch, she in squalor, had he won or lost?

As if to show there were no hard feelings, Shiv asked him on a walk. Because it was Michael's first trip to Burnie he offered to take him to what he considered the 'special place' of the city (Michael didn't know this was an honour Shiv had accorded to no one before).

'It's where I saw some UFOs once. But I haven't told many people about that."

An old abandoned ruin on a windswept scrubland between faded pale blue weatherboard houses, rusted water tank and abandoned crane to the right. On the slope of the hill above was a dark line of pines where Shiv indicated he had seen the UFOs coming out from behind - red orbs moving strangely, like no known vehicle. Michael kept his mind in neutral, not wishing to consider the admitted possibility that Shiv was speaking truth. Certainly there was no trace of a lie in his voice, which was discomforting. Michael didn't quiz him – he had been uncharacteristically nervous of the topic since a discussion Anika and he had once had about 'cold chariots from the abyssal sky.'

Michael would have liked to show Shiv the 'special places' of Hobart, but knew his stories wouldn't be as good. Already he was wondering how he use this strange character in a band; the band to end all bands. Problem was, Michael had always envisioned *himself* as singer/guitarist. Could the band have alternating singers, like Fugazi? But the 'punk' stuff would have to be augmented with an overlay of something better. It could work, a hybrid that broke the vat, more than the sum of its parts.

But another hurdle arose when he learnt with some surprise that Shiv was a Christian. This was a direct affront to Michael's desire for a Pagan Empire with a wise, powerful Führer (himself, with Shiv perhaps Caesar to his Augustus). His imperialist, nihilist side had recently won out in its struggle against nationalism and autarchy, or so he thought. But Christianity was tainted with equality, egalitarianism – and he had learnt from Youth Revolt that that kind of thing wasn't for him. His shallow part wanted to quote some aphorism from Nietzsche, but a deeper part sensed he should refrain from this; he respected Shiv enough to overlook what was surely a small hindrance.

As they talked, it emerged that Shiv's vision of Christ was based largely on Aslan, the lion in the Narnia books, which Michael found strangely touching, remembering the role *The Lord of the Rings* had played in his own spiritual development.

Shiv wasn't ignorant of actual religious history, though – he spoke of the ancient theologian Origen, and now it was Michael who felt ignorant. Origen taught that God had created a vast number of spiritual intelligences, most of whose love for Him had cooled, with those who cooled the most becoming demons. Only Christ remained fully devoted.

'So does it *hurt* God when the intelligences don't love enough?' Michael tested.

'Dunno. I don't think God can be hurt.'

Shiv was far from orthodox – he stated baldly that he disliked the Old Testament, besides believing in reincarnation and UFOs.

Yet, his activities the night before.

'Hey, I don't always live up to my beliefs. But I will, at some point.'

Shiv also claimed to be an anarchist, if a lapsed one.

'Freemasons run this town,' he growled. 'Look at the size of the fucking lodge.'

Shiv's project, his great love, was something called 'The Thresher' he had been building for the past month in an abandoned warehouse where he was sleeping ('I won't show you, not yet…but I s'pose if you're serious about this band thing…' 'Yeah…' 'I'll have to take it apart and bring it down to Hobart in a horse float or something, then put it back together.')

The Thresher, it turned out, was a car-sized 'vehicle' made of skateboards bought from op shops all up the North-West coast, and meant to look like an old abandoned grain thresher once seen in a paddock that has struck Shiv as exemplifying Tasmania's haunted past. The point of Shiv's 'Thresher' was that, unlike a normal skateboard, you could drive it on a public road, and the cops couldn't stop you…or so he imagined.

'Legally it could be classed as a bicycle. But it's the size of a fucking four wheel drive.'

Michael, impressed, gave him his phone number.

'I'll come down soon, and we'll jam. So see what kind of equipment you can get together, huh?'

Michael left Burnie in high excitement, dreams of everlasting fame biting at his guts.

14

POSSESSED TO SKATE

His head ached immeasurably.

She had left him, Anika had left him.

For the first three days he had stared at the wall, too vain to suicide in earnest. Now he sat writing poem after poem. In the grey dawn it all came out wrong from his shrunken tired head.

For some reason he had expected her to be loyal. The signs, he had misread the signs. Her increased assertiveness, he had thought, had meant she was *happy*. Now she was with someone *else*, the thing that gave him torture…the thought of someone else's member inside her…moths in the stomach, *severe* nausea, tears. He wanted to puke but couldn't, wanted to sleep but couldn't, wanted oblivion but for the feel of some fibre inside him, bigger than the pied Anika, bigger than himself, connected inexplicably with years and sadness yet unknown…*a rainy day in Sydney, a garden in the rain*…and a deeper sadness which would not come to fruit without him. Airports sensed only with the unconscious. For his fore-mind was filled with Anika, the pied cloud of flickering femininity cut off from him *forever*. He didn't believe in Eternal Return, had argued about it at length in his head with his fallen idol Nietzsche, his erstwhile narrow-minded teacher whom no one had yet replaced. Far greater than the stunted ones of D'Entrecasteux…yet Nietzsche had no message to impart to him now. Michael was utterly alone. Oh, this was *real* this bloodcurdled pain, and no one had ever experienced what he was experiencing before, nor ever would again, not before Time ended and curled up in a ball, spitting him out.

*   *   *

With the morning post came a letter.

Michael,

It distresses me to think that you are suffering so terribly.
Please know that I am still thinking of you...
Empty platitudes aren't what you need right now, but nevertheless being cast aside may be good for your spiritual development.
You need to find yourself.
I wish you full convalescence and healing.

Your friend,
Anika

Michael, trembling, read it and exploded. *The arrogance!* He rose from the musty orange armchair and tore the letter up, then strode to the wall and punched a hole in the plaster, kicking several more holes. He unscrewed a leg from the kitchen table and set to all around him, jarring tendons and ligaments, and plaster dust was flying. He trashed the flat like a rock star but it didn't fill the awful angry hole that had opened in his stomach.

Had he *mourned* her? He vowed *never* to let a woman make him feel like that again.

He found the dreary Syd Barrett albums and tarot deck she had given him and threw them out the window. All those cards had taught her not a whit of wisdom or she would realise that *he* was her rightful lord and protector. As the archetypes scattered, his action stuck him as blasphemous somehow…pathetic, too, as archetypes can morph but can't be destroyed. No, he would find out where she lived, find the washing line, drag her velvety skirts through the mud…she would *worship* him and if not, fear him as a force majeure…his life was a sinking ship and he wanted to desert it…for real this time?

A knock saved him from thoughts. Leighton…astonished when he saw the damage to the flat.

'Hey, man, don't go off the rails…I've been through this, too…everyone has…' Michael took Leighton's very casualness as proof that *no one's* suffering could compare to his own, and Leighton, annoyed at his arrogance, changed the subject abruptly.

'You should see this crazy fuck who rocked up at my brother's place from out of town…he was asking random people in a pub if they knew of any local 'squats', and someone gave him Kirk's address. He bought them a slab of beer, and he's kind of polite, in a weird way, so they let him stay.'

'Whatever, Leighton. I want to be left alone.'

'I haven't told you the best of it yet. He was driving a removal truck he claimed to have stolen from a Burnie rapist. Weren't *you* just in Burnie?'

'Do I look like a fucking rapist?'

'Just a joke. Anyway, this tall prick with a bogan haircut, short-to-long, gives me a lift to Northgate where I had some stocktaking work….in his stolen truck.'

'Did you say short-to-long?'

'That's what I said. So, he gives me a lift, but on the way we pass some cops, who swerve and do a U-ey. Next I know he's tearing through the back streets of 'Norchy trying to outdrive the cops…in a fucking removal truck…I nearly shat myself. Thought I'd be arrested as an accessory. But somehow…fuck knows how…he evaded them. We got onto Kalang, ended up hiding out in Lenah Valley for an hour. So I missed work, and there's no more coming up. He apologised but said he was hiding something very, very special in the truck, which was why he couldn't just dump it…but he wouldn't say what it was. 'All will be revealed in the fullness of time,' he said…crazy bastard.'

'I think I know the guy.'

'Then he took me to Perfect Prints in Collins Street to get a photo so he could make a fake drivers license, so he said. There was some black guy in there getting ID done…must have wandered down from the mainland…anyway, he walks out and this Shiv guy…'

'Yeah…'

'…said, and I quote…'Why would a nigger bother getting a passport photo…you could just draw a black blob and put in a couple of white bits for eyes."

Michael laughed, for the first time since Anika had left him.

'Michael,' muttered Leighton, disapprovingly, 'it's not *funny.*'

*   *   *

'So, you get Above the Ruins yet?'

The question was an unexpected punch, exposing the insincerity of his commitment to world-changing Art.

'I had a feeling I might run into you down here. Shoulda got in touch, matey.'

'I lost your number.'

'We gonna jam or what?'

'Sure.' Was this rough beast an ally? *Against* a Hobart Michael felt increasingly at war with…or would Shiv, too, be sucked into spiritless depths of profane stupidity, leaving Michael fully alone before lights went out? Didn't dare trust, but wary acceptance couldn't hurt, couldn't hurt. A bass riff popped into his head from nowhere, creative nothing. *Something happening.* Excitement in the pit of his guts, forgetting Anika. Well, not forgetting. In his mind's eye, music-weapons trained on her, worlds to win. She would regret casting him aside!

'But first there's something I have to finish,' said Shiv, 'something special.'

'What is it?'

'You'll see soon, matey. Everyone will see it soon…'

*   *   *

Michael took Shiv to the 'special place of Hobart', for him currently the Female Factory, ruins of an old convict women's prison in South Hobart where he often went at night to think. You could feel the sadness there.

Always deserted, lonely spirit unvanquished by tourist displays like Port Arthur's, where 35 people had been killed a fortnight earlier.

Michael had been shocked to see the photo splashed across *The Mercury*, Hobart's Murdoch gutter rag. Holy shit, it was the 'masturbating with a cheese grater' guy – there was no mistaking that face – Michael had been face to face with the killer! Or *was* he the killer? *How had they gotten the photo?*

And the headline, unethical, probably illegal: *THIS IS THE MAN*.

Michael's opinion of journalists, lowered by their treatment of his uncle, fell further. Media Watch's Stuart Littlemore was, as far as he knew, the lone voice of skepticism.

Now Prime Minister John Howard was rushing through gun control laws with obscene energy, which Miss Quinn, Michael's kindergarten teacher, would no doubt approve of.

Shiv had his own theory on who had 'done' the massacre, but even here in the silent ruins of the Female Factory wouldn't tell Michael what it was. Michael didn't press him. *Had* he been face to face with a killer?

A false note here, faintly nauseous.

Sadness and isolation, not just the baggage of the past.

Power at play here, a power struggle. Was power all there was in this world? The thought depressed him.

*   *   *

Finally, Michael was initiated into the secret of the truck, parked in the grounds of a small, disused warehouse in North Hobart.

'Remember, the guy I stole this truck from is a dirty rapist, though it was never proven against him in court.'

The truck contained a machine – a beast – the infernal engine known as The Thresher. A toppling structure built from old skateboards and thin crossbeams of wood. Made of sticks and blood, or that was what it looked like. A spindle surrounded by furze, become relentless, a locomotive of silent concentration.

It was named for a piece of farm equipment, a Victorian era threshing machine he had seen on a farm in the Tasmanian midlands, whose shape it resembled, and so it was in fact The Thresher Mark II.

'Got most of the skateboards from different tips. Burnie, Ulverstone, Smithton. Been collecting for two years now.' Michael helped Shiv wheel it from the truck. On the sides of its baroque structure were two longer boards, which the two of them stood on, using their legs to scoot slowly and ponderously around the grounds of the warehouse.

'She's not too fast.' The thing was also hard to steer, and was weighted to the right because Shiv was so tall and gangly, with broad shoulders…Michael thought that if Shiv ever took up body building he would be the proverbial brick shithouse.

'And what's the actual purpose of this creation? Wouldn't a single skateboard be more convenient?'

'Convenient?! C'mon Michael, you're better than that. But the purpose of The Thresher, to be precise, is that I can now legally ride a skateboard on the streets. It must surely count as a car, due to the size of it. I think so, anyway. So the nine-to-fivers will have to get out of my way, and there's not a damn thing the cops can do about it, ha ha. And *you* have the honour of being the first co-driver.'

Michael, feeling awkward yet strangely exhilarated, helped turn-kick the thing out into backstreets, then onto Elizabeth where heads turned like sunflowers as they made their painful progress towards the CBD. Only twice did real cars honk at them, and Shiv gave them the finger. As they passed through the intersection of Elizabeth and Warwick, Michael noticed Snobby Jenkins crossing the street, an all-too-sensible frown on his prematurely aged face. Michael laughed and gave *him* the finger. Snobby looked quickly away, and Michael was unsure if he had recognised him.

Their steady downhill journey lasted only another few blocks, for there was a flashing light behind them, another from round the corner, and they were surrounded by four sardonically amused cops.

'Now, what is *this?*'

'You can't skate on the road, boys.'

'It's a car, not a skateboard,' snarled Shiv. 'Road's the only place for it. It can't go on the footpath, can it?'

'I dunno,' grinned one cop. 'Maybe you could get away with calling it a bike. But in that case, where's your helmet?'

'C'mon…how we gonna pick up chicks with bike helmets on?'

'Not a bike,' said the senior of the four cops, shaking his head, 'and not a skateboard. But not a car, either. It isn't a roadworthy vehicle of any description, so we're going to have to impound it.'

'But I spent *ages* building this. It's a work of art, for crying out loud.'

'It's impressive, I admit.' Two of the cops sniggered. 'But it'll still have to be impounded. You might get it back in a few months if you fill out the appropriate paperwork.'

Michael wondered which of the good citizens of Hobart had snitched on their harmless endeavour…Snobby Jenkins, from a payphone? In any case, it was the end of The Thresher's first incarnation.

* * *

174

Shiv's new flat, almost bare, where he lived like a warrior monk, was the setting for a meeting on what to include in their new zine. They had decided on a zine instead of the band for now, as they had no money for musical equipment. If bands were the artillery of the '90s Kulturkampf, then zines were its infantry and snipers. The paper vehicle was to be called The Thresher Mark III, in memory of the wheeled vehicle. For Michael, it was a chance to get his propaganda out to the world. Or to Hobart, at least, which would serve as a testing ground.

Shiv asked Michael if he had access to a computer.

'Just an old '70s one in my mother's basement that probably doesn't work. It doesn't even have a word processor.' He did go down and look for his father's old typewriter, which was nowhere to be found, but they found another cheap at an op shop, with just the 'k' and the number 8 missing. The ribbon still usable, surprisingly. After cutting and pasting, photocopying would be at the homeless resource place where Michael's mail was now directed, after his eviction for damages from the flat he'd once shared with Anika.

He was staying on various different couches and spare rooms, including Shiv's, and now he was entering the zine wars. *Will zines define our time* he pondered idly, then kicked himself for the cliché.

Michael was handling most of the music reviews, being better at these than Shiv, who was mainly doing articles on esoteric or political topics.

Music Man had given them a small grant, a one-off donation for buying albums with, but had declined further involvement. Comments made to Michael hinted at a dislike of Shiv, whom he referred to with uncharacteristic warmth as a 'great lummock', irritating Michael, who replied: 'No…he's a great fountain of energy.' Each privately questioned the other's judgement, and they were never to collaborate in any way again. But the grant was welcome, meaning the latest offerings of Veles, Aura Noir, Dødheimsgard, Current 93, Allerseelen and others could be purchased, scrutinised and culturally assessed, lending further weight to the zine's articles, which the current meeting's purpose was to plan.

They sat cross-legged on the floor, as the only chair was covered in papers. (Shiv had one of everything - one chair, one spoon, one fork, one plate, one towel, one change of clothes …the minimalism helped keep him focussed, he said.)

Shiv would give an account of their brief adventure with The Thresher Mark II.

He had also drafted an article on the Sex Pistols, prompted by their recent twentieth anniversary reunion tour. The article would discuss whether they were genuine, and what they achieved if anything.

The Pistols were formed the year he was born, Michael realised, but he preferred The Pogues when it comes to foul-mouthed Irish singers based in London. Punk in general bored him shitless, and also made him think of Dorry, which nauseated him.

'Meanwhile, let's talk about *real* music. I've been delighted to trace the origins of Black Metal to Tacitus' *Germania*, section 3. The ancient Germans had a chant, to kindle their courage. A harsh tone and a hoarse murmur, to inspire terror in the enemy. They used their shields as microphones and the sound echoed off them.'

'Cool.'

'I think part of the zine should be devoted to Odinism, even if, as a Christian, you don't agree with it. It was our ancestors' religion before the universalist Church took over.'

'All right, wait a minute.' Shiv took his one bowl from the kitchen cupboard and filled it with water. He washed his face, then spat in it and blew his nose in it. He held it out to Michael.

'Huh?'

'I heard the Vikings used to blow snot in their communal washing water before meals. Thought you'd like to revive an ancient tradition.'

Michael was offended but bit it down, considering coldly how he could use Shiv to attain fame and notoriety.

'You'd prefer to bring back the dietary requirements of

Deuteronomy or one of those fucked up books?' he shot back.

'I already told you, I'm not interested in the Old Testament.'

'We *need* the Viking spirit to colonise the galaxy, with space ships instead of dragon ships.'

'But someone's already colonising it...UFOs, like I told you.'

'Oh yeah, maybe you should do an article about them. The truth is out there.'

'You can take the piss, but they're real. I'll be writing something about parallel universes and crop circles. Yeah, and I'm also putting in a piece about Milli Vanilli.'

'Eh? The lip-synchers?'

'One of the members, Rob Pilatus, is on the skids. He's been stealing cars. He tried stealing one with someone in it, and the guy got out and beat him with a baseball bat.'

'Really? Ha ha.'

'So the theme of the piece is on how making soulless, formulaic music turns you into a criminal and lands you in hospital. As opposed to me, who was beaten frequently as a child, and who *was* a car thief, but who's now making soulful, meaningful music, which, as soon as we steal some equipment, I'm going to record *without* lip-synching. It's the same trajectory in reverse. I am the anti-Milli Vanilli.'

'I like it,' enthused Michael, partly to hide embarrassment that Shiv had mentioned his deprived childhood for the first time, making his own middle class upbringing seem sterile. From sterility was nothing born...still, he was making up for it now with his bohemian existence...here he was in a flat with only one of everything, for crying out loud. But that, too, was Shiv's doing.

'I'm doing a piece on the American so-called alternative scene,' he announced. 'Have to call it mainstream now, because it is. Lollapalooza and that kind of shit.'

'There can't be anything good in it in the first place if the system can co-opt it that easy,' opined Shiv.

'Yeah. But I'm focussing on the so-called tribalism. These phonies with their dreadlocks and piercings. What *is* their tribe? Because the vast majority of them are white. So wouldn't tribalism for them mean being more like my late uncle, working for the interests of white political structures?'

'Maybe they mean they want to emulate third world tribes in having less possessions?'

'But that's appropriating the culture of the third worlders, whoever they are. It's stealing, because they have no instinct left to immerse themselves in their own culture. Besides, I hate these dreadlocked types on a visceral, personal level. I want to put pictures of lots of dead, dreadlocked hypocrites throughout the zine, to stir up controversy.

'Collage of butchered dreadlocked trendies?' roared Shiv. 'Now you're talking! Revelation 3:16.'

'Huh?'

'God hateth the lukewarm, neither one nor the other...He will spew them out of His mouth.'

'You should be a preacher, you Christian freak.'

'I am one. As are you...'

*　　*　　*

They were also trying their hand at investigative journalism, just for a laugh. A group calling itself the Order of the Holy Knights of Sion and the New Temple had recently been exposed by the tabloids as aiming to take over Tasmania and make it into a mystical, monarchical state, inspired by the book 'Holy Blood, Holy Grail'. Although not taking them seriously for a minute, Michael and Shiv wanted to find out what their *actual* beliefs and aims were, not what the Murdoch press said they were. Their leader was supposedly a mercenary who had killed Iraqis in 1991. They knew the house because it has crosses all over the front. There was no answer when they knocked. They went down the laneway at the side, peeped in a window in silence through a gap in the curtains, and were startled to see blood on the walls.

They could see nothing more, nor the source of the spattered blood.

'Call the cops?' whispered Michael.

'Dunno,' muttered Shiv, the anarchist, none too fond of police.

'What if someone *killed* them?'

'Let's get out of here…we'll decide what to do later.'

They scarpered up the laneway onto the street. Mr. Hendriksen, of all people, was walking down the footpath. He had grown a beard, but Michael would have recognised him anywhere. The remembrance was mutual.

'Michael Glendower, you little ratbag. Skulking in gutters and alleyways, just as I would have expected.'

'Who the fuck was *that?*' panted Shiv down the block.

'My old principal. What on earth was *he* doing here? I thought he stayed on the mainland after they released him from the loony bin.'

'Ha ha, what kind of school did you go to? No wonder you're so crazy.' Shiv looked at him with new respect. Michael could feel no pride however, for Hendriksen's reappearance had filled him with a raft of disheartening memories. What drama queens of the grunge scene would have called 'demons'.

They ran down the rivulet track past the tannery to Shiv's flat in South Hobart to work more on the zine, agreeing not to talk or write of what they had seen tonight…yet.

It was weird at night, the rivulet track – you could feel the breath of Old Hobart, and you never knew what might be out there, the willows a liminal zone between known region…South Hobart a convict loneliness, and beyond the tree line West Hobart, but that a mere blip before the wilderness. And further down, the mysterious hill behind Cascade Gardens…where did *it* lead? A limb of great hills, no town or hovel to be seen before the west coast, empty southern expanse of darkening ocean. No lights of Rivendell, nothing human or comforting. Altogether a nothing. And Michael thought, for the first time in ages, of the creature or apparition he had seen as a child, and tried to broach the topic now with Shiv, but found he couldn't do it. So he asked Shiv to tell him more about the UFOs he had seen. But Shiv didn't want to talk either, giving merely a 'some things can't be put in words' and turned-out silence, arms folded walking.

Then Michael tried talking to him of Reg for the first time, wondering how those great forces would have regarded each other, but to his dismay Shiv didn't seem to listen much, or realise the import. He had heard of Reg once in a newspaper, but knew little of his beliefs. He was more concerned with the blood they had seen tonight. Was Reg's greatness a secret only Michael could behold now? And Sylvie…he didn't even try to talk about her. Being related to Reg, albeit not by blood, gave his life a grandeur he had so far not attained by himself, but this in itself depressed him. How could he carry on Reg's legacy, but not his stuck-in-the-past beliefs, without betraying his own individuality and soul? It was a riddle, and his great fear was paltriness, paltriness in all things. Would Hobart suck him into the earth, another of its crawling minions? *Never*. He would never let that happen. That alone would be his salvation.

* * *

Next day they were hard at work on the zine again. There was nothing in the paper about a killing.

Michael was writing music reviews. He had largely ignored Black Metal for fear of being associated with a 'scene', not even the biggest releases: Satyricon's *Nemesis Divina*, Dissection's *Storm of the Light's Bane*, and Burzum's long awaited *Filosofem*. He had even ignored Veles' *Black Hateful Metal* (which he did push-ups to every day). He loved the feeling BM gave of being a wolf among sheep, who seeks solace in high and lonely places, rather than suffocating amidst the masses. But was this, too, a degenerate impulse?

Although he could never be Christian (in Michael's future empire, peoples would be forced to adopt their original native religions), he had come to dislike the cheap histrionic blasphemy Black Metal bands routinely engaged in, feeling it didn't advance the cause. Motivated no doubt by rebellion against the stifling left-wing conformity of the Norwegian State Church - but that didn't explain the horde of bands in Poland, where Catholicism had been suppressed for decades. Although religiously, it mattered not a whit, as the true God could not be blasphemed anyway, being the answer to the question 'Why is there something rather than nothing?', a question that could not be thought about deeply without having your mind blown and apprehending God. But that had nothing to do with Christianity. Michael had explained this to Shiv when the latter had accused him of being irreligious, and Shiv had respected his answer. People respected Michael when he explained things, explained himself - too bad he hated explanations.

They had limited themselves to albums released in the last year or so. Above the Ruins' 'Songs of the Wolf', while 80s, made it as it had just been put out on CD for the first time. It was given the prime review, Album of the Issue, the only one with a picture of the cover art. 'Will be remembered as Tony Wakeford's most important album.' They both liked the album *a lot* (though they argued over the meaning of 'Make Us Strong'), wanted to punch its author for dismissing his own best work, and vowed they would be influenced by it themselves (though not too much) when they started their band, which would surely be very soon now. 'Roses', a haunting piece about the First World War, was the album's finest moment, but 'Progress' and 'Hundred Flags', the latter inspired by Yann Fouéré''s *L'Europe aux Cent Drapeaux*, mirrored Michael's own vision of an empire-patchwork of local regions, each with distinct identity (the opposite of homogenising Brussels' bureaucrat goals), and showed you could make intelligent political songs that, while angry, weren't tacky.

Einstürzende Neubauten's *Ende Neu* was also reviewed favourably, but Michael was heartily sick of Tool's *Ænima*, dedicated to a very dull and unfunny comedian called Bill

Hicks, which Leighton and his friends had been playing incessantly, venerating it with near religious intensity as they smoked their stinking herb (Michael now officially looked down on marijuana). While he admitted 'Eulogy' had its moments, he preferred Ministry's *Filth Pig* as a bleak, sardonic attack on consumerism.

Michael's reviews were short and to the point...atmosphere was what he craved above all else.

Inade - *Aldebaran*
(Cold Spring)
Many would write this off as a Lustmord rip-off, but it far outclasses Lustmord, listening while drifting to sleep unfolding a voyage through infinite vastness to the Black Sun of secret knowledge, whence universal spirituality is said to emanate. This is the sound of journeying Home. Arcane star charts and outlandish alphabets hold the key to secrets long buried in unconsciousness. Hissing and rasping of cold space melds with the deep throb and rumble of warp-drive engines, filling the abyss with all-engulfing echo of mankind's approaching Renewal. Highly recommended.

Neurosis - *Through Silver in Blood*
(Relapse Records)
Heavy in a way few bands have come close to, but even behind this crushing wall of apocalypse is a fragile hint of rebirth. Does anything ever really end? Songs start in miniature and build like tributaries feeding into a great river, or capillaries into an enormous beating heart. What could have been a vision of all living things connected in a hellish matrix of biomechanical totality under the mindless glare of a blood red sun becomes instead something pulsing, holistic, irrational, powered by rhythms *within* rhythms, amazingly organic, a vast twisted tree with neither beginning nor end.

Future Sound of London - *Dead Cities*
(Astralwerks)
This age too shall pass, everything shall pass. An ancient

city, a million years in the future. Despite sordid beats, brings you face to face with the ceaseless, unending Heraclitean cold fire.

Allerseelen - *Sturmlieder*
(Ahnstern)
Holy fire of ages past breathes storms to come.

Penitent - *Melancholia*
(Cold Meat Industry)
A depression that leads to strength, a sparkling embrace of death. The centrepiece, 'Dance of Demons', is white man's soul music, grim and rainbeaten.

Shiv's only solo review was a largely positive one of Pantera's *The Great Southern Trendkill*, but two albums they trashed together in joint reviews; one was *Dusk and Her Embrace* by Cradle of Filth (absolute gaylords), the other was Sepultura's *Roots*, which they attacked savagely, laughing at the middle class Brazilian white boys trying to be 'ghetto' by adopting a black identity, comparing it unfavourably to Penitent's 'Dance of Demons', where the poet had embraced his own heritage and not someone else's. This tied in nicely with the theme of Michael's 'Lollapalooza' article.

The one and only gig review, of Fugazi's second Hobart concert in the abandoned Hoyts cinema where his mother had once fallen asleep during *The Sailor Who Fell From Grace With the Sea*, was ditched because the gig was boring compared to the first, and because Michael now associated them with too much PC crap, and anyway, you can't step in the same river twice.

As for the interviews, responses had been disappointing - they sent off nearly a dozen, but only one was answered, by Hannibal Flea of the Canadian band FASCES IMPERIUM. He answered promptly, but the guy was everywhere, giving interviews to a lot of underground zines. Shiv's questions, seemingly naive, cut to the meat.

So with a name like FASCES IMPERIUM, are you

hoping to create an empire? If so, what kind of empire? Will you be emperor yourself, or will someone else be? If the latter, then what role would you prefer to play: vizier or court musician?

Flea responded: 'The Reich we refer to is nothing so plebeian as a real empire, with its attendant soulless pomp…it is an empire of the Spirit, and exists wherever Great Men and True Spiritual Warriors unleash their power on the inferior, soulless hordes of undermen. You must read the complete works of Julius Evola in order to understand the true nature of such a spiritual vision. It is not for the worthless men of today.'

Shiv, disappointed with this patronising reply, had been hoping for something more.

'This bloke's more *your* cup of tea, Michael, but at least you know what kind of empire you want to create. Spaceships and all that. Me, I'm just a humble anarchist, and Flea probably regards me as lumpenprole cannon fodder or something. He's pushing Mithraism, but if Mithraism had won then he'd be pushing Christianity. No values,' sniffed Shiv.

'Humble? Come on Shiv, we need to be hungry for victory.'

'Humble *and* hungry then.'

They decided to run the interview in any case, imposed across the collage of butchered dreadlocked trendies which now formed a grotesque visual backdrop for the imperious words of Flea.

At one point they had considered using butchered Scottish junkies as a backdrop, for there were now hordes of middle class kids quoting lines from the movie *Trainspotting* in exaggerated Scottish accents, some even becoming junkies to emulate it, although heroin was almost impossible to get in Hobart at that time, morphine being the best available substitute. They considered writing an article about that as well, but ruled it out as too boring.

Shiv penned a piece on the Demidenko affair, however, giving a new take on the issue. Paul Radley (winner of the same award Darville had won) had confessed he hadn't written a word of his own prize-winning novel.

'So where was the Radley Controversy,' Michael had wondered aloud, not having read either book. *Zionists*, hinted Shiv darkly, and Michael remembered Uncle Reg saying something to the same effect. But both Michael and Shiv were puzzled as to how 'awards' of any kind could be conferred on art, as if it were a running race or chess match, with clear winners and losers. They penned a satirical piece to that effect, depicting establishment professors measuring peoples dreams and visions with a yardstick. Demidenko was lost in the mist somewhere, brushing her hair and doing a Ukrainian peasant folk dance.

*   *   *

A few days later, the front page of the paper carried a screaming banner headline about the Order of the Holy Knights of Sion and the New Temple.

A disgraced disciple had formed a breakaway group, then killed the sect's founder, hacking him up and feeding him into a sausage machine. A new breakaway faction had announced another offshoot, which also wanted to take over Tasmania, before deciding on Invercargill, NZ, as the best place to avoid the forthcoming apocalypse.

They decided against writing about what they had witnessed in the zine, for fear it would come to the attention of the police. Michael was paranoid Hendriksen would tell the cops he had been near a murder scene. What the fuck was Hendriksen even *doing* there?

All was insignificant, however, compared to Anika. He *really* wanted her to notice him, his fame the ultimate revenge. The zine would be ready in a few weeks, just in time for his twentieth birthday. No longer a prodigy, he nevertheless thought it an auspicious age to be famous.

15

STIRRINGS

'So, I went to the impound yard to get the Thresher back...Mark II, I mean...and the fucking thing'd disappeared!'

'What?!'

'Seriously...the duty cop said they'd look into it, like file a report or something. He was literally yawning.'

'No shit.'

'I reckon they chopped it up for firewood, or laughs.'

'Someone has it in for you.'

'So, The Thresher Mark III is all we have now...until Mark IV arrives.'

'Mark IV?'

'The band.'

'You still up for it?'

'Shit yeah...just a matter of time.'

They had called a meeting to discuss the impact and lessons from issue one of the zine.

It had not caused nearly as much of a stir as they were hoping. Despite being distributed widely in Melbourne by a distro who plastered their day-glo sticker on each cover, and despite Shiv and Michael putting copies in every shop in Hobart that would agree to take it, they received less than a dozen letters in response. Some were confused over the fact that it was called The Thresher Mark III, and wanted to know whether the first two issues were still available.

A letter from an angry goth girl took them to task for mocking Cradle of Filth, and another asked where they got their 'crazy music', and if they could tape-trade a copy of Above the Ruins. But there was no sign of a cultural uprising brewing, and they vowed to make the second issue far better, in style and content, so that it could no longer be ignored. The butchered trendies collage had not shocked anyone, and they were now faintly embarrassed by it.

They had also soured on Hannibal Flea, after Michael had discovered he was close friends with a musician who wrote songs extolling the virtues of 'torturing little children and crushing their skulls'. Shiv was going to break into the university chemistry department and send Flea some anthrax in the mail to punish him for keeping such company, but Michael talked him out of it.

'I have big plans for The Thresher, where will they be if you go to prison?'

'How would they know who sent it?'

'They'd see the Aussie post mark, and put two and two together.'

Though Michael couldn't admit it to Shiv without losing honour, in his heart he already felt disillusioned by the project. A list of article ideas he had penned had already ended up in the bin. They were clichéd and ungenuine, typical obsessions of '90s counter culture – Yukio Mishima, Friedrich Nietzsche, *The Wicker Man*, crop circles, Charles Manson, Black Metal, *The Silmarillion*, the Kali Yuga. Others round the world were writing about the exact same things, and Michael wanted to distinguish himself from them. But how? How could he light the taper that would ignite his inner flame? He already felt dampening.

Music was the way – playing it, not writing about it. Other bands were increasingly disillusioning him. The one band who had responded to an interview for the second issue were arrogant, like Flea without the intellectual pretensions, writing several times asking when 'their' interview would be out, an interview so lame and boring that Shiv had considered changing their answers to a piss-take. More enemies, was that the way to kindle inner fire?

Shiv's problems were different – he was puzzled by the way in which all the bands, from metal to 'intellectual' power electronics to mainstream ones like Tool, seemed to have a hostility to Christianity, though for varied reasons - could it be a thinly disguised hostility to 'normalcy'? In case of Norway, the state church's egalitarianism had led to a levelling, dumbing down, tall poppy syndrome (Scandinavians called it the Law of Jante). Same in Australia, though not linked to religion. There, perhaps, the landscape did it.

Michael explained patiently, feeling the retardedness of his own cliches, that Christianity was a 'slave religion' foisted on Europe by Jews to extinguish the native European religions, but Shiv wasn't buying it.

'Christianity isn't Jewish,' he would say, 'because Christ kicked those bastards out of their own temple. And it isn't a slave religion – look at the crusaders.'

'By then it already had vast amounts of paganism mixed with it. Catholicism especially still does.'

'Hmmmm. Maybe.'

One thing they both shared was a contempt for those power electronics bands, mainly British and American, who glorified serial killers, talked about their 'interest' in sexual violence – but who went out of their way to distance themselves from Hitler, who was too crude, too proletarian for their delicate sensibilities. Authors of Might is Right manifestoes, hailing self-will as father of all…twenty years later where would they be? Michael doubted if they would ever create anything worthy of the gods. But that led him back to his own problem.

'What about an article on goth chicks?' he said suddenly. 'Delicious to look at, disappointing in reality. They're ultra-normal conformists, so much I actually feel sorry for the dumb bitches, though not too much.'

'Smacks of bitterness, mate. No, what about an article on the Commie Jew, Albert Langer? Sure, he's a Maoist scumbag, but he's performed a valuable service of late.'

'How so?'

'He's been imprisoned for contempt of court for telling people they don't have to allocate voting preferences. They can write a '1' next to their favourite, then put all the others as '2', equal last in other words.'

'Isn't voting that way illegal?'

'No! The vote will count. It's just illegal to *tell* people about it. But why should we be forced to give preferences to candidates we reject, anyway?'

'Weird...maybe we can do a short piece on it. Voting is for sheep, anyway.'

'I only vote because I don't want to pay the fine,' admitted Shiv. 'Though I'll probably be voting for the red-head bitch.'

'I'll be putting in a blank ballot. But what about music reviews? Music Man's grant ran out and I can't afford many discs these days. I wanted to write about John Lydon's solo album *Psycho's Path.* Or is that more your line?'

'Too weird for me, didn't like it much. I was gonna do one of Horde.'

'The 'Christian Black Metal' band? Ha ha.'

'I've got mixed feelings about it. I respect the guy's balls, but it's a bit contrived.'

'They're going against the grain at least. What's the actual music like?'

'Not too bad, actually. Reminds a bit of Veles. Any other reviews? I don't think music reviews should be the focus of the zine.'

'*Dots and Loops* by Stereolab. It's fucking fantastic. Also the new Graveland, *Following the Voice of Blood.* It had this kind of surf guitar that reminds me of stuff my old music teacher was into. A bold move! It's kind of like the Dead Kennedys without the annoying vocals.'

'I can't stand the DKs,' snorted Shiv, who hated American punk. Michael wondered briefly what his erstwhile hero Jello was up to...had a feeling that he probably hadn't evolved much.

'Did you get those politicians' responses? I suppose not or you would have told me.'

'Prime Minister's office sent back a form letter. The Malaysian PM hasn't responded at all.' Michael had interviewed John Howard on why he had backflipped on immigration since the 80s, and Mahathir of Malaysia on his recent debate with Singapore's Lee Kuan Yu on multiculturalism and assimilation.

'If communities and neighbourhoods governed themselves,' opined Shiv, 'there wouldn't be any immigration problems in the first place. That's anarchy…a patchwork of autonomous communities.'

'Sounds boring,' said Michael. 'You need an emperor, a high king.'

'You, I suppose.'

'Who else? Surely not your beloved redhead.'

'Her, an empress?'

'You trust her?'

'Course not, she started in the Libs. She's establishment to the core. But I wouldn't mind fucking her.'

'You sick bastard.'

'Didn't say I'd do it, mate. I'm chaste, celibate.'

'We'll see how long that lasts. Your thoughts are already turning to disturbing fantasies.'

'She's not *that* bad.'

'Her eyes are too far apart.'

'She's *cute.*'

*   *   *

Despite Shiv's dismissal, there was something sufficiently anti-establishment about the redhead to have unhinged many, and a poll gave Tasmania as her second-biggest base of support.

Shiv and Michael decided to go to the big protest at Parliament Lawns, having missed the redhead's own appearance at Hobart's City Hall a few weeks earlier, where the hall had been invaded by protestors who had managed to drown her message. The police had apparently allowed the protestors in, with the obvious intention of bringing the meeting to an end, and with it a situation they didn't want to waste the time and resources dealing with. They learnt from this at Ulverstone a few days later, charging a door fee and making the meeting private, thus affording it better police protection, along with the fact that northern Tasmanian cops were generally less corrupt than Hobart ones. Two journalists had apparently been heard planning to start a fight to rile the protestors up. Aboriginal elder Albert Deverell had presented the redhead with a bunch of flowers, again in complete contrast to the Hobart mob of ATSIC-funded lowlifers.

But today no redhead-supporters, only protestors, and on reaching Parliament Lawns a sea of signs and banners but no violence. The main organisers, Youth Revolt, were having their day in the sun at last. Many schools had been given the day off on condition they wore plain clothes, and the girl speaking now on Parliament Steps, a smug attendee of the Quaker-run Friends School, was chirping something that sounded like 'racism bad…racism bad', though most of her fellows seemed there merely as a pretext for skipping class.

Michael estimated the crowd was sixty per cent students, but on the Steps flanking the speaker were the soldiers of Youth Revolt, no longer quite so ebullient, as if success had taken something from them. Silverlashes looked positively haggard, had lost her potency, potential…had become fixed, though not in a decent way. Daniel was absent; had he succumbed to her lures and done away with himself? Dorry Wendle was there, however, right up the front, trying to look important. Michael glared at him with festering hatred, and no further guilt for his fallen state. Dorry had spread it around town that Anika had moved to Sydney and had been posing for a pornographic 'girl-next-door' mag, every part of her visible to those paying the prodigious sum of seven dollars and ninety five cents. The malicious gossip was made worse by the fact that it happened to be true. To his eternal shame Michael had bought a copy and jacked off over it, before throwing it away in disgust.

No doubt she thought of it as performance art. He wanted to kill her for being so shallow…had actually *planned* to kill her for hurting his honour, and in front of 'Dog' Wendle of all people, the very exemplar of slave morality. One day, these people would fear him.

Dorry and Silverlashes weren't the only faces he recognised. There was the weaselly, swaggering 'Aborigine', crutches gone, who had hobbled after Reg. And in the more staid and respectable 'older people' section at one side of the protest, he was shocked to see…his mother! She spotted him also, giving a kind of benign grimace. He threaded his way over.

'Did you get the card I sent for your fiftieth?' Was she really half a century old? It was scary.

'Yes, thank you.'

'What are you doing at a protest? I didn't think you went in for that sort of thing.'

'Someone has to show that horrible woman her views aren't welcome here. Who's your tall friend?'

'This is Shiv, from Burnie. My mother.'

'Good to meet ya, Mrs. Glendower.' She smiled, nervous with a touch of frost, and Michael knew immediately that she disliked him. But who cared?

'What are you carrying a tape recorder for, Shiv?'

'Good, isn't it? I found it at the South Hobart tip shop, it's voice activated and all. I brought it to interview some people, to find out why they hate the redhead so much.' A goat-faced chap of around sixty turned around.

'I'll tell you why I hate her. She talks about 'one nation', which sounds like 'One Reich' to me…but what she really wants is to divide people.'

'Paul Keating put out a statement called One Nation.'

'That's right,' said Michael. 'And Howard had a One Australia policy in the 80s, which makes him a hypocrite for disendorsing her.'

'Anyway, isn't it good that people have divisions?' continued Shiv. 'Something I actually disagree with her on is that everyone should be treated the same.' Michael noticed him slide the recorder switch to 'voice-activated' mode, and wondered if they would be able to use any of it for samples in their future band, or if the carnival sounds of the background noise would make it unintelligible.

'She *doesn't* want everyone treated the same,' said the man petulantly. 'She wants to discriminate against Aborigines and Asians.' Shiv disagreed, and began detailing her actual policies.

'Return of funding direct to Abos on a needs basis only, accountability of those handling it, zero net immigration until unemployment down, moratorium on foreign investment, no overseas aid til our own probs sorted. All common sense stuff. It's autarchy, but on too big a scale. And that's where I disagree with her. I'm an anarchist, mate, and I think communities should govern themselves.'

The man looked at Shiv like he was crazy, no longer prepared to take him seriously on anything. Michael's mother had turned away, embarrassed. She turned back briefly, giving a 'what's happened to my little boy' look, actual tears at the corner of her eyes.

'He was bottle fed, that's what's happened to him,' Michael wanted to retort, but held his tongue.

A big, loutish-looking fellow who might be called chubby if not for a permanent-seeming sneer on his face, had overheard Shiv's last remark and turned to face him. Almost as tall as Shiv, with broader shoulders.

'You call yourself anarchist? And you think communities should adopt the views of that dumb fish and chips bitch?' he sneered. 'You're a fascist, dipshit, not an anarchist.'

'I beg yours?' growled Shiv, hackles up. If there was one thing he hated it was any insinuation his anarchism was insincere. But the thuggish mutt repeated his last sentence, with added words to the effect that he would beat up fascists 'wherever he found them.'

'Belligerent, aren't you.'

'Defending myself against racist scum.'

'Attacking.'

'Defending myself against racist scum...*racist scum*.' A

mantra, it seemed to increase his power levels. He put his hand on Shiv's shoulder.

'Scum, am I? Been called that all my life. Don't need it from you, faggot.' Shiv stepped back just a tad, and punched him in the solar plexus. The windbag deflated at last, crumpled and coughing, but the cops had seen it.

'He assaulted me,' Shiv yelled, putting his hands up as if to air them clean.

'That's right, I'm a witness,' said Michael importantly. An old one behind was yammering. 'I saw it, officer. They were *both* to blame.'

'Well, well, it's the one with the skateboard thing. Whatever happened to it?'

'Disappeared from the impound yard. Would you happen to know anything about that?'

'I dunno, mate. You'd have to ask whoever's in charge of the yard. Now then…you'd better leave this area, the pair of you. We don't want any trouble here today. I appreciate that you want your democratic say…'

'We're not here to pro…' began Michael, and Shiv nudged him, already knowing the Hobart cops better than Michael himself did. The cop glanced disdainfully at the thuggish-looking character now rising painfully to his feet.

'Get out of here, we'll say no more about it.' They left.

'He punched me,' they could hear him saying, sounding deeply shocked, as the cops moved him towards the periphery of the protest.

'Never let on you're an independent thinker,' hissed Shiv. 'They don't like it in Hobart…they want you fitted in a slot.' The comment fitted in its own slot, and did rather well there.

'Thought Christians believed in turning the other cheek.'

Shiv glared at him. 'None of us is perfect.'

*   *   *

Listening to the violent sounds from the tape recorder.

Michael enunciated his earlier thought. 'We should use this as a sample, build a song around it. Like Ministry's 'N.W.O.' or something.'

'Too weird.'

'It's a bit ambiguous maybe, but...'

'You're right we need to start doing music, though. Preaching from the stage will give us greater reach than a zine. Street theatre. Look at all the people at the protest today. All that energy! If we get reds like that cunt attacking us, all the better. Bring it on.'

'It's what I've said all along. With a band we can impose our vision on the world, even if our vision isn't exactly the same.'

'We can tap into the energy the redhead has tapped into.'

Political upheaval had been in the air ever since John Howard's over-the-top anti-firearm laws a year ago. Graeme Campbell had formed a party called Australia First, which triggered some weird half-memory in Michael, of what he didn't know. All he felt was a deep relief that they didn't have to do the zine anymore. To be a rock star was what he really craved, had sought in his secretmost dreams, ever since the '80s.

16

BY ANY MEANS NECESSARY

'This is sin in your religion,' whispered Michael.

The Thresher Mark IV – the band – had been activated, and they were burglarising the music department of Hobart College. Their needs were simple – an electric guitar and amplifier for Shiv, and a keyboard for Michael, in light of the smattering of piano lessons he had had as a kid. He realised there was no way he could compete with Shiv as a guitarist and frontman, and was determined to be the architect of the band, as keyboardist and chief songwriter.

'No, it isn't,' whispered back Shiv. 'It's like when I stole the truck. It's God's will. God willed The Thresher Mark II, and Mark III. Now God wills The Thresher Mark IV. Who am I to question His command? If our will is weak, worse wills wax stronger.'

'What d'you mean?'

'I mean, if *we* don't step forward to blow the other bands out of the water, the masses will continue to listen to the bands of lesser, more irreligious men.'

For Shiv, the band was a vehicle to fight the New World Order.

Michael, on the other, wants to *create* a new world order. Creation and destruction – yet they were on the same side, for now. Ships passing in the night.

The zine – Mark III – had been abandoned. It wasn't reaching enough people, or causing enough controversy, though one of Dorry Wendle's friends had apparently been making outraged enquiries about them, wanting to know where they lived. Other than that, the response to issue two had been virtually nil.

People complained it was all over the place...Michael despised them for not seeing the hidden thread linking everything together. He was also heartily sick of bands not responding to interviews. Then, their Melbourne distro had dropped them because of Shiv's review of Horde. Shiv had written them a letter with menacing undertones informing them they were conformist wankers.

'With a band, we don't necessarily need to worry about distros,' he told Michael. 'Even if we can't get a record out, we can just blow the masses away with live concerts. Although it'd be good if we could have a record too, of course.'

But that might never happen now that Michael was a criminal, paranoid at every noise. A security firm did the rounds each night. Real danger of jail if caught, first offence regardless, suffering for Art. Would prison food malnourish him? The chance to ask cheese grater man, Bryant, if he did it. Shit, when would this purgatory be over, out of the darkling woods?

*   *   *

Sitting relaxed, snug on old hessian draped on milk crate, writing songs on a fine Roland keyboard, black paint disguised. Red Jackson guitar, also black, Marshall amp serial number filed off, 'property of Hobart college' liquid paper patiently scraped away. School insured, no doubt, would pay only modest premium.

He could remember only a little piano theory but his fingers found the scales. A smattering of theory would be his engine, infinite imagination his fuel.

In some ways he was happy to be playing keyboard, and

any residual jealousy he kept to a dull frown. He knew a good thing when he was onto it. He was the engine all right, rigid and aloof, while Shiv was the chassis, mudguard, hotted up exhaust pipe and mag wheels.

They had agreed to write separately, their main initial influence being *Songs of the Wolf* by Above the Ruins (in Sol Invictus, Michael had finally introduced Music Man to a band he had never heard of – 'it's dreary stuff,' MM had said approvingly). But his chord progressions sounded unique, at least to his ears. Then Shiv would improvise over the compositions, and he over Shiv's. Their first official rehearsal was in a week.

The Thresher name had been good so far...their music, too, would 'thresh the wheat out from the chaff', per David Tibet, an artist they both (more or less) admired. Shiv was expanding his knowledge of the guitar, had borrowed a tablature book of obscure chords from the library, which he was plucking as well as strumming, generating power from the contrast.

He had consciously modelled his style on John McGeoch, who had played on several albums by Siouxsie and the Banshees, but Michael thought privately that it sounded quite different to McGeoch, more abrasive and sinister. With the amp, and three scruffy pedals found at the tip shop, Shiv had created a guitar sound cold, beautiful, and menacing as a winter morning on the final day of the world.

They argued over minimalism, and a three chord limit...Shiv had at first claimed it would make them more disciplined and intense, but after borrowing the chord book he came round to Michael's view that the chords should form a forest, a mysterious soundscape for the listener to hike through. Shiv's view had been tinged by his discovery that changing from minor chords to major actually sounded sadder than the reverse.

Michael had also brought Shiv around on the 'anti-rock star' thing that both PiL and Death in June had failed at. Shiv believed punk had failed in its rebellion because the musicians were on a raised stage...he wanted to play behind a curtain, or with each musician wearing an potato sack and interspersed with the crowd, but Michael convinced him that his weird charisma should be utilised, as it would get their message across more powerfully (*what* message, he thought privately…am I just a fame whore desperado?).

'What if people confuse our personalities with the message?'

'Don't worry…*I'll* be the anti-rockstar. I'll stand behind the keyboard like a member of Kraftwerk, giving off disciplined German vibes, while you impress the ladies with your proletarian grandeur.'

'Eh? Oh well, if we impress the chicks, then they'll convince their boyfriends and so on. Whatever it takes to get the message out.'

'Yes, but what message?'

Shiv looked at him like he was obtuse. 'Overthrowing the New World Order, of course. Haven't you been listening to a word I've been saying?'

*   *   *

Rehearsals and songwriting were going well, now they must try with a drummer. Shiv's flat was above an electrical repair shop whose owner had no objections to musical noise, and there were no other residential flats within half a block.

Michael had managed to enlist Tom Hammond, a friend of Leighton's, whose main influences were Primus and Tool. Tom attended Hobart College, and Michael hoped desperately he wouldn't recognise their stolen equipment. His father dropped him off, having brought his drum kit in the van. He was looking forward to 'jamming', he said, as he was 'between bands' at the moment.

Shiv frowned.

'We need you fully on board,' he said. 'It's alright if you play in other bands on the side, but The Thresher must take precedence.'

'Wow, you guys are really serious, committed. Good! All right, let's jam, then.' He rubbed his hands together and rolled up the long sleeves of his pristine Soundgarden t-shirt. Shiv nodded.

They launched into their newest song, mainly Shiv-penned, called 'Crisis'. Shiv's jarring, crunching riff conjured up a *Clockwork Orange* atmosphere of violence before Michael's haunting keyboard line merged with it to create a black nocturnal rainbow of ominous harmony.

They were just entering what they called 'the zone', an area of white heat where the instruments began playing themselves, when Tom stopped them by waving his arms about.

'I think a 9/8 metre would be better for this part.'

'What?' growled Shiv.

'If you change the riff a bit, make it groove more. And you really need a pumping bassist.'

'You got me out of the zone to tell me *that?*'

'No, I mean, I think you guys have some potential. I'll do a 9/8 beat, and you can change the riff to fit it.' He started playing a beat whose energy was so unlike the riff that the room seemed suddenly drained of meaning,

'Ringo takes over the Beatles.,' whispered Shiv. Michael sniggered.

'You'll have to get out of here, mate,' Shiv yelled over the percussive calculations.

'Pardon?' Tom stopped.

'Just get the fuck out, mate. You're not right for the band. Though your drum kit is nice.'

'Are you serious?'

'Yeah. Just get out. Now, please. You're cramping our vibe.'

The drummer's face turned cold.

'Fine. I'll send someone to pick up my kit.' Michael felt bad for him, not recognising vision unless presented by a label, but there you go. At least now they had a drum kit.

*   *   *

They moved the kit to the obscure bedsit Michael had just moved into, so Tom couldn't get it back. Shiv wouldn't answer the door to him, and would go out the back way if necessary. The cretin didn't deserve such a lovely kit, but fate had placed it in his hands so he could donate it to the higher cause that was The Thresher.

Now they were rehearsing with Fiona Appleyard, Hobart's only female drummer (at least, the only one who could play in time). She wasn't outstanding, but they needed only functional drumming in any case. As for a bassist, one would turn up eventually…the important thing was getting a set ready for performance.

Fiona had the odd, slightly endearing habit of tracing the beat in the air before each piece, then carefully, so as not to upset it, transferring this 'air beat' to the kit itself. She wasn't political, either, which was good. The energy generated by the tension between Shiv's anarchism and Michael's cosmic 'space fascism' felt unique, and both felt instinctively that any third vision would deplete it.

They spent a week really getting down 'Crisis', til they could play it blind and deaf. The haunting, skeletal riff, mushrooming over the course of the song, would hold the audience spellbound, they believed. Fiona honestly liked it, too, was excited about it in fact, and it was good to have a third, objective opinion convincing them that they were creative geniuses. Their star was finally on the rise!

*   *   *

Key rattling in door. *What the fuck?* Landlord letting in two bailiffs. Big men, very big.

'We're here to get the drum kit. Our client won't go to the

cops if you hand it over now. So, where is it, you little shit?'
The other had already pushed past into the bedroom.

'Here it is!' They began to carry it out, snare by cymbal,
as Michael fumed. There was nothing he could do…if only
he had a gun. *He would join a gym, work out, turn his body into a
weapon.* How dare they take the kit providence had
bequeathed to The Thresher! Blasphemous fools. Who had
told them his address…Leighton?

'I'm giving you two weeks notice,' the landlord said
somewhat pompously. 'The one carrying the kick drum is my
brother-in-law, and if you're not out in a fortnight, they'll be
back.'

*   *   *

Homeless again. He had to move to the lounge room floor
of Shiv's immaculate flat, for now at least. Shiv didn't mind
the company, but complained Michael had destroyed his
cultivated minimalism with the mess of clutter that now filled
two thirds of the room.

The remaining third was all that was left for band
rehearsal. Fiona had brought her own drum kit along, not
nearly as good as the one the bailiffs had stolen, but
functional. It had a snare, crash, hi-hat, a single kick drum,
and one very dull sounding tom. Shiv approved of the
minimalism, which reminded him of how his flat had been
before Michael's chaotic entry.

'If you can't play what we need with that stuff, you'll
never manage with more.'

'How's   the gig-hunting going?' enquired Fiona.

'I've been knocked back everywhere so far. We need to
record a demo to play them, then they'll see how good we
are.'

'Did you try the Empire?'

'Never heard of it.'

'It's changed its name to the Republic Bar,' explained

Michael.

'Oh, that snooty place. Bunch of commies, I wouldn't even bother.'

It was true that the former Empire Hotel, haunt of prostitutes and drug dealers, had now begun attracting a more noxious clientele.

'We'll just have to get a demo together, then.'

'I've got a theme for it…the Chemical Wedding.'

Shiv had been reading about Rosicrucians. As the Isis Mysteries were intended to prepare for the Piscean Age, when fire descended and water rose, so the Rosicrucian were to prepare for the coming Aquarian Age, or so Shiv held.

'So Christianity is going to be superseded?' asked Michael with interest.

Shiv looked ever-so-slightly offended. 'I never said that,' he said calmly. 'No doubt it will be *renewed*.'

'But with something added.'

'I dunno. Anyway, let's jam.' Shiv seemed unusually anxious to change the subject.

They ripped into the new song, 'Surgical Mirror', a savage ode to inner city Hobart and its denizens. Despite its three minute brevity, they were exhausted by the finish.

'That verse riff reminds me a teensy bit of a song by Joy Division,' panted Fiona, already drenched in sweat.

'What?!?'

Neither Shiv nor Michael had heard a single note of Joy Division, but both were so alarmed at the possibility of plagiarism accusations that they threw the song out then and there, despite it being one of their best tunes.

Damn it. Even bands they had never heard were turning against them.

'Only when we have the entire establishment against us, only then will we succeed,' muttered Shiv, before launching into the next song, 'Warpath', more determined than ever.

'We must be ready to die for our beliefs!' he screamed, and Michael was frightened by the way he found himself pounding the keys in response. He had told Leighton and others ad nauseam that this was not a band but a weapon, and to sceptical smirks…but now it hit home for the first time that perhaps he really *would* have to die for the band. He hoped at least to make a good looking corpse.

17

'HOBART IS DEAD'

Fiona had borrowed a four-track from an ex-boyfriend, and they were recording their first demo. She winked as she led in the song. Michael kept rigid warrior posture, didn't wink back. Shiv had been annoyed when he found out they were sleeping together, but was determined not to let it interfere in the dynamics of the band.

'As long as she doesn't start interfering in the songwriting,' he muttered. 'She's not a warrior, we just need her to keep time.' But Fiona wasn't creative, she just wanted to be part of something. In older times it would have been a crochet circle. She 'didn't really want' a 'formal relationship' in any case…but that didn't appease Shiv, who thought they should all be celibate during recording., Sex without fertility possibility (she was on the pill) seemed a travesty of nature – but so did celibacy. Michael tried not to think too much about it.

How he had changed! A year ago he would have been bragging to someone like Leighton how he was 'banging' a 'cute chick'. But The Thresher had morphed him immeasurably. Anyhow, Leighton was barely on speaking terms with him since he'd learned of the theft of Tom's drum kit. Michael suspected the real reason was that he hadn't been asked to join The Thresher. But Leighton couldn't understand, *would* never understand. He hadn't the flame. A drummer without the flame was one thing, but a guitarist…

The other recent event in his life, his discovery of Joy Division and early New Order, was equally ambiguous. After Fiona's comment he had to hear them, and was filled with admiration and envy. In many ways it was the sound he wanted, only The Thresher should be more aggressive. If only they could sound half as good...but he was determined neither to ape their style (impossible without a bassist anyway) nor consciously avoid it...just let things develop organically, then their star would shine.

Shiv, on the other hand, had been listening to Masonna's *Spectrum Ripper*, which Fiona was horrified by. Shiv spun her a bullshit story about how the artist got Buddhist monks to tear his organs out and stomp repeatedly on the nerve fibres joining them to his still-conscious brain - the greatest level of pain possible - leading to a transcendent state called 'Diamond Thunder Consciousness' - the ultimate bliss. She looked like she was having second thoughts about being a part of The Thresher.

She didn't actually *complain*, though, and that was good. This was not a feminine group, unless one considered the lush reverb of their guitar sound as feminine. Shiv looked like he was going into battle, not singing. The vitriolic strain he gave off, coupled with the cold autistic demeanour cultivated by Michael made it hard for her to concentrate on generating basic beats, but she tried, alas, she tried. Their all-out harsh abrasive sound and no bass made it sinister somehow.

'The music will still bewitch people through the harshness,' Shiv maintained. They used the delay pedal to get a slapback effect, as in early '60s music like Roy Orbison...or like The Church, one of Michael's favourite bands. Shiv was now using hypnotic arpeggios rather than punk power chords, and it improved his sound immeasurably.

The first two tracks had Michael-penned lyrics, though the music was collaborative. The first, 'Caves, Hills and Shadows', anticipated the adventures awaiting him as a committed musician:

When wolves descend from the stars
And land on all fours in the cold southern sea
And pick up their ancient guitars,
Watching the world as it falls on its knees.

A winding path leads to the stars
From the crooked streets of my hometown.
Beneath the grasses and up above the arches
The stormwinds whip and drag me down,

While up above the mountain sighs
And throws its tears upon my face;
I leave my fears up the altar of the hillside
And tear away to face my fate.

The second, 'My Little Sociopath', secretly about his Rhodesian ex (gods, how he despised her...would that she would disappear forever), magnanimously writing of wanting to rescue her:

My little sociopath, you're a living cenotaph
You gather flowers for your own black heart and soul
You live on entropy, and its secret energy
You draw the curtain on all friends and on all foes
You've got no one to hate, just the fear of being great
And sometimes your own blankness scares you.

Come and tell me where your heart is
Come and show me where it used to be

My little sociopath, yeah, you pretend to laugh
And turn your minutes into lasting tyrannies
You're never gonna live, you're fucking negative
I see your weakness for the curse it is
I've got no time to lose, can't vanquish what I choose
But I never wanted you to fade into the dark.

Shiv felt weird singing that one, until Michael convinced him it was abstract and could apply to any number of fallen people.

Shiv's non-Rosicrucian-themed songs were anti-Howard, anti-Clinton, and very much opposed to the new British PM Tony Blair, a creepy and sinister-looking man who had done a Bob Hawke on Britain's Labour Party, modernising it at the expense of its soul. Shiv's lyrics concerned Blair's hidden backers...like Hawke, he was an ardent Zionist, something Shiv hated, and Michael wished he could understand the obsession some had with that tiny country he had once had trouble locating in his Junior Encyclopedia.

Shiv's lyrical flair was no match for Michael's but his grim but angular words fit the music well enough, making it if anything more sinister, more '90s. The music was what would hook people in, not the lyrics, which hardly anyone paid attention to anyway. And the music was *good*.

'It's going to crush everything,' they agreed.

They had placed ads for a bassist, but were undecided on whether they would answer responses.

*   *   *

'When the disciple is ready the master appears.'

Yet the disciples were for once in a way drunk, and *they* were really the masters, yet the wise one was experienced. He had played in England, in a band that had recorded an *actual album*...and he *was* English, which alone made him ancient and real. A full decade older than them, he would be the anchor, the ointment, the 'still point of their turning world'. The circuit was complete. Only the drummer was expendable; they kept *her* round because they liked her, and because there was no one better.

They met him, of all places, at an '80s theme night they had crashed without an invite.

Michael had admitted to being inspired in his keyboard

composition by '80s pop, and both he and Shiv sheepishly admitted to having a crush on the Kylie of 'I Should Be So Lucky'. The party was billed as a big drunken retro night, as the host's expensive German sound system cranked 'Time After Time', 'She Sells Sanctuary', 'Down Under', 'Our House', 'Fade to Grey', 'Vienna', 'Sweet Child O' Mine', 'Never Tear Us Apart', 'The Final Countdown', and 'Livin' On a Prayer'.

Given it was only a decade ago, weren't they jumping the gun, thought Michael. But this stuff seemed organic and real compared to the new pop he was hearing in buses and supermarkets. With the Spice Girls, a new note of falseness had crept into top 40 pop, which mades him feel old at 21. Compare to Kylie or Cyndi Lauper it sounded awful. Would the '80s be seen as a golden age some day? He laughed at the idea, it wasn't that great, ABBA were better anyway, and they were '70s. The '90s had more promise, he thought, had the first true esoteric underground, from it the seeds of a mighty empire would grow. Oh yes, people would long remember the '90s...wouldn't they? The '80s stuff had a wise innocence like an earnest child; but the '90s would be the decade of THE THRESHER.

Fiona was making eyes at the English bassist, but Michael didn't care, he felt nothing for her, nothing at all save a patronising affection. She was a cat, untrustworthy like all women. Even if Anika herself walked in the door, he wouldn't care, wouldn't...*no*, don't go there.

Colin, the bassist, was politely ignoring her anyway, face craggy and weatherbeaten, he was alert and open-minded as Shiv played him their demo on a walkman in the garden, impressed enough to request a jam, would stay in Hobart instead of returning to Sydney then London if he was right for them...*he longed to be in a band again.* He played them a tape of his main inflence, Neu!, and now they could see where Stereolab got it from. 'It's all coming together!' cackled Shiv gleefully. Michael nodded in drunken agreement. The circle was complete.

* * *

He joined. He had no choice, the music entrapped him in its enthusiasm, Shiv's persona entrapped him in its belligerence, and Fiona entrapped him between her legs. *She'll have to go at some point*, thought Michael coolly. *She could damage the integrity of the group. We'll just wait til a suitable replacement comes along.* He had come around to Shiv's position.

In the meantime, he concentrated on improving his keyboard technique, like a painter of old experimenting with light and shadow, ecstasy and foreboding, seeking the musical equivalent of the golden ratio.

As for his lyrics, while Shiv greatly admired his ability, he was against his more personal approach, tolerating it 'if it's the only way you can write.' Shiv felt awkward singing 'Everywhere and Nowhere', seeing it as more proof of Michael's megalomania, but it fit the music so well he agreed to keep it:

Loss is when you see it as if branches off,
The path you know you won't be ever taking.
If everything existed there'd be no creative power
In the cosmos: what's done is done forever.

Don't believe those theories that there's endless parallels,
Universes splitting every instant.
It's rubbish. The ticking hands of Time would lose their power,
And we'd have no worthy foe to strive against.

Remember, then, the first time that you met her?
You knew it even then, the hint of future hopes and fears;
And you too shy to speak, stupid puppet in a trance.
It was like that all throughout those early years.

Purple flower draped in softest black, intangible;
The eyes downturned and gentle smile pervasive.

Power and surrender in the strangest glance;
The smile will never die, was indefinable.

And now it's back there just the same, unreachable.
The always-barrier holds you fast, your limbs outstretched
For brutal rapist Time to have his way with.
'Never' is a word too cold and black to comprehend.

But *if* you could have grabbed her at that instant,
Most beautiful and warm and dark and fierce and shy;
And *if* you'd given *all* for her to be, to grow;
Who'd say she'd not just wither anyway?

And now you'll have her always there in memory,
The 'her' who'll never be again in flesh.
Too much has happened since, too little innocence.
What never was ends up more real than all its real effects.

But that's no consolation, waking terrified at night
And sliding into nothing, into Time's black maw,
And crying out to hold her but she's never there.
Only one way left then: *be a warrior.*

That laughter flickers coldly from the past,
Glittered-white like orphaned sunlight in antarctic air;
It sinks and fades and falls before it freezes.
But her smile is always everywhere.
      And nowhere…

Shiv liked the lyrics to 'Hobart is Dead' a lot better.

Hobart's dead around me where it falls;
Nothing but the smell of empty flesh.
All ruins, and the light blanched out of everything.

None has any reason still to be,
And those that did are faded into signs,
Invisible to prisoners of the 'binary-men'.

Nothing but the stench of money, purpose gone.
Kindness gone and love a faithless word.
Joy and terror gone and nothing left but lack of pain,
Making money for the flickers-screens to feed on.
There's nothing, just museums and an empty glare
And cars that hurtle endlessly to nowhere.
No mystery where the blind ones stop and feed:
For Hobart choked too long on its own greed.
It let its shadow blur its own uniqueness
And lost the balance delicately held;
It vomited its sickness to the four winds
And forged the chains that suffocate the world.
Creation may have crested here at one point,
And woke the gods themselves from darkest dreaming,
But now the wave has broken and the binary-men have come
Dismantling all, hardwiring people's inner freedom;
Luring them to sleepwalk in the crowded empty street;
The consciousness that crested sinks away again.

But can the wave resurface?
If it will, then not in Hobart.

Hobart has to die to live again…

'Cool…but who are the binary-men?'
'They're like robots, they don't have inner music. They don't see that *life itself* is music, or something very like music. They're caught in their little ideologies, subcultures and fashion trends, and can't see the bigger picture.'
'There's no hope for Hobart?'
'I thought there was. I thought it was the city destined to change the world, a new Athens. But seems I was mistaken,' said Michael somewhat pompously.
'How will it 'live again', then?'
'In my heart, my songwriting. I'm the fruit of the tree.'
'We're on the same wavelength, then.'

'I've got a new song about that. Just the words, I haven't been able to come up with any music...perhaps we could work on that when the demo is finished.'

'Can I see the lyrics?' asked Shiv eagerly.

Rise again from winter's shaded embers little bird
And let us deck ourselves for fight, so may it be the last.
We dance on Hobart's grave.

Our tree rose out from frozen soil and concrete throwing seeds
And flowers to the wind, to disperse where no one guesses.
We die (stirb und werde) die to live.

In the far arc of the future different music may take form,
Growing out beyond the elder staves from which it softly sprang,
Far song and battle cry.

We'll shelter something through the night, through war's black storm;
Who knows where it will nest and spread its feathers next.
'Ours' but to never know.

Through time deprived of meaning it will guide and bring us forth,
Through suffering its light will only harden.
Then: clearer than the sky.

Transfixed will stand one day a growing child on ancient walls
Keeping lookout for his people; to the past as well.
He stands upon the spiral's dancing crest.

A new twist of the cycle: let each round surpass the last;
Let the arc's exacting swing be never wasted,
Or the fall will murder all.

Our spiral leads where star-geese shiver, over Time's grey
halls,
    Wheeling straight in arrows through the sunwheel.
    They cry and circle home.

Impatient for the years when other souls will join the
surge,
    Overflying darkened rivers for the greenest land.
    It shimmers in the dawn.

Then haunting springs of echoed pain will crystallise again
And Time will come full circle, possibilities intact.
    All suffering made joy.

When wasted land and cancer-shadowed cities never heal,
Still the ever-ruined soil may yet bleed forth a secret stair.
    For we die (stirb und werde) die to live.

Shiv liked the part about suffering. He thought it would
bring them redemption, whatever that meant.

'We *will* suffer for this band, Michael,' he prophesied. 'But
it will bring great things.' Michael shuddered. He hadn't
known *what* he had meant when he wrote that line. Was it
really prophetic? Was he *ready* to suffer greatly? But one day it
would turn to joy…

'I've also got a ballad planned about my late uncle and
aunt.'

'Just put as much work in on the music as you have on the
lyrics,' said Shiv, 'and our next demo really will crush
everything.'

18

THE ZONE

The Watchorn Arms, spacious pub where they were supporting Rob Weed's cover band, was alive with punters that night, but not Weed's kind of audience. Many in gothic attire, even a couple of Darkthrone t-shirts. The photocopied flyers had paid off.

They had literally bribed Weed's band to open for them, paying a slab of beer for the privilege – and Weed was posh now, he didn't drink Cascade Bitter but some pricey European brand. Nevertheless, the crowd, which Michael estimated nearly a hundred, was mainly here for them. All was proceeding according to plan.

Weed in his arrogance thought they were his, however. He thought the vague sense of tension and excitement was due to his cover band, which ruled the roost of the Hobart pub circuit, not the unknown weirdo outfit called The Thresher (the good reviews for whose latest had only appeared in obscure overseas zines). The stack of demos left in local shops sold out, but who had bought them? Perhaps those here tonight, or perhaps they had been lured in by the flyers. For they had adopted Vlad Tepes as their mascot using his image on their flyers, imposed over the silhouettes of a forest of impaled Turks.

Weed was apparently fuming that they had given themselves first billing, with his own (headlining) band in tiny letters – the opposite of his own flyers, more professional but fewer in number, for Shiv and Michael had been busy, plastering every power pole from Sandy Bay to Glenorchy with the Impaler's image. The 'Dracula' connection would hopefully pull in the goth chicks – and had, by the looks of it, but Weed thought they were here to hear his Living End covers. Weed, like Spinal Tap, would jump on any trend going to get his end wet with the groupies as he put it. Yeah, there were cover band groupies, but that was Hobart. Michael looked at Weed and his men warming up, and thought 'what a bunch of fuckheads'.

Hayden Burn, passing him, said something withering, along the lines of 'who would have thought little Michael would have his own band.' He bit it down, focusing on blowing them away. Rob Weed's girlfriend had literally laughed at Shiv's 'mullet', as she called it – but Weed used to have one in high school.

A quick soundcheck. The mixer up back, pub's own hired man, signalling okay. Michael felt butterflies, unexpected. People *looking* at him. Shiv grim, determined. Michael swallowed calm. Must be Übermensch, blow crowd away. *They* were the event, not Weed, arrogant non-entity to be blocked, cast out from future empire, fake art – punished with exile!

The mixer put on the tape of their opening music as they climbed onstage. Originally this was to have been Wagner's 'Entrance of the Gods Into Valhalla', and Michael had envisioned them striding onstage like gods...but the stage was raised and they had to scramble up so perhaps it was a good thing they had changed it to an excerpt from Janáček's Glagolitic Mass, which united pagan and Christian atmospheres, anarchic and imperialist moods (pan-Slavic as a substitute for pan-European), the creative impetus of the band in miniature.

Then someone yelled, 'Nice mullet!', killing the atmosphere they had sought to create, and the crowd began to laugh.

Michael clenched his teeth. He would teach these shallow fools not to follow fashion...all fans of The Thresher would be indoctrinated in anti-trend ideologies…but that would be a trend itself. He was disgusted that he himself couldn't help feeling a faint aversion to Shiv's working class hairdo. But Shiv was Shiv, oblivious to fashion, and a true punk. A soldier for his beliefs and an inspiration for Michael to be likewise. He pumped himself up. Even with their merely competent female drummer they must utterly blow off stage the arrogant cover band they had *paid* to let support them. Shiv's intensity and Michael's haunting keyboards would do it, but the two had to harmonise, lock step covalently and enter the Zone, the floating region, and rain fire on the audience.

And now it was really happening. Fiona clicked her sticks together four times, and they launched into their brutally heavy opening song, subtly titled 'Fuck the New World Order - Smash It and Destroy It!'

All Michael had to do for this one was hold down menacing chords to underpin the two scourging guitar riffs, verse and chorus (Shiv having jettisoned the bridge section as 'too bourgeois'), and he tried to look like a solider or a member of Kraftwerk, a frozen menace. *The lights were too bright*, he thought irritably, we should be shrouded in a greater layer of mystery…is the keyboard high enough in the mix, is it *too* high, is the sound engineer doing his job right, is that nice goth girl staring as me, can't look must be Soldat, fight for the future empire, fatherland, chicks don't understand, wonder what shape her breasts are, all the cigarette smoke is making me cough, place stinks like beer, drink of the masses, Nietzsche said never trust anyone who drinks beer, Nietzsche was a pussy, insane with jealousy of the superior genius Wagner, is this song too minimalist, would the audience prefer more complexity, fuck the audience, who cares what those trendy sheep think, do they even think anything, perhaps I *am* the only mind, solipsism, don't go there, remember schizophrenia runs in your family, remember Sylvie, no really, Ved Buens Ende are a good band, so are Beyond Dawn, would like to hear more by them, The Third and the Mortal would have been better if Kari stayed, dumb bitch left Storm because they were non-PC, maybe if we're big enough she'll beg to join our band, we'll tour Norway, play in Tromsø, Fenriz wants to make it capital, I wonder if it's as grim as they make out, what about the gulf stream, what about…

Somehow, it was over. The final chord came crashing down. The crowd were completely silent. Michael's heart sank down to his surplus GPs. Had time slowed? Was he doomed to failure in everything he did?

Then, amazingly, the crowd *roared*. No other word could describe it. The silence had actually been astonishment. They weren't expecting such intensity from a local band. From *any* band. Now they shouted and screamed and whistled in approval. Michael and Shiv looked at each other briefly. *It was happening.*

'This one's called 'Hobart is Dead',' growled Shiv, as they launched into what they already regarded as one of their finest tracks, destined to be a classic. The crowd honked and cackled loudly as Fiona counted in. Fascinating, thought Michael, cheering their own demise. He could see eyes looking at him through the smoke-haze. Since he'd stopped smoking, considering it a sub-habit for Untermenschen, he had become sensitive to the smell of tobacco smoke, and now it was coming at him in gusts. He was coughing as Shiv crooned, then, bellowed the final words:

The consciousness that crested sinks away again.

But can the wave resurface?
If it will, then *not in Hobart*.

Hobart has to die to live again…

The crowd seemed to take in the last line – or did they? – because they cheered even louder than before.

And now they launched into 'Everywhere and Nowhere', in feel and meaning vastly different, not abstract, but personal.

That laughter flickers coldly from the past,
Glittered-white like orphaned sunlight in antarctic air;
It sinks and fades and falls before it freezes.
But her smile is always everywhere.
     And nowhere…

The cheers more restrained and respectful this time. No one was laughing at Shiv's haircut now. Fiona was sweating like a pig, and Colin looked like an ancient crow, wise and grim, his bass sewing the wound of the music roughly shut. Song after song they played, until the world was all aswirl, energy peaked, and they went into *The Zone*. And now they felt the presence of the gods, of God on earth. Michael was no longer himself, but the universe was playing through him. They all felt it except Fiona, who just kept plodding along. Could a drummer enter The Zone, Michael wondered later, or did the earthbound nature of percussive activity prevent them? Or was it because she was a girl? Women could achieve mystical ecstasy, like Hildegard von Bingen, but the Zone was beyond ecstasy, was beyond beyond. He hoped Fiona could one day enter, but now he knew her tenure couldn't last. Perhaps they should just replace their drummer every six months, like servicing a car. She was their timing belt, outside the engine…

He remembered little about the last few songs, but when he came to and noticed Rob Weed staring at them with a mixture of wonder and discomfort, he no longer cared. He no longer wanted to blow the arrogant cover boys off stage because they no longer mattered. And when they set up and launched into their opening cover of The Offspring's 'Pretty Fly (For a White Guy)', a pisstake song about a white kid trying to act black to be cool, just like their cover band tried to act 'grunge' and now 'punk' to be cool, the irony passed over him, because it too no longer mattered. His only thought was to get Shiv out of there before he became violent…Shiv *really* hated Triple J 'punk' like The Offspring.

But Shiv was in an expansive mood, generously inviting the audience back to the flat for a post-gig meet-and-greet.

'Mine would be better, more room,' suggested Colin, and dozens straggled back to his shared Victorian era rental house, shabby but spacious. Michael was glad, as he wanted the chance to take another look through Colin's esoteric library, stored in a room with big rusty meathooks hanging from the ceiling, no doubt a meat larder in earlier times. More than half the audience followed, and Michael almost felt sorry for the members of Sure Thing, that accursed cover band of halfwits.

He saw to his surprise that Music Man was there, talking to Colin, who was talking about synchronicity, and the schizophrenic cat paintings of Louis Wain. The flat was littered with issues of *New Dawn* and *Fortean Times*. Music Man was listening politely, perhaps sceptically, eating a paddle pop, explaining that he wanted to win something on the match-the-sticks competition…Michael had no idea they still had those, an '80s thing. And then he saw, good grief, Silverlashes of all people, looking lost and washed up. She was talking to Shiv. Had she been at the gig? She must have been! What would someone like her make of it all? Or was she bored with democratic socialism? Shiv was telling her about the illegal gig he planned to do at Tunnel Hill, an abandoned railway tunnel on the eastern shore that had once been used by the university's physics department to 'harness cosmic rays' as Shiv put it, though Michael thought it was only used to detect them.

Michael moved over, slowly, bit by bit, to get close to Silverlashes. He wanted to see how the last few years had ravaged her face.

He could hear Shiv saying: 'Esoteric Christian belief is the same thing as Nietzsche's philosophy, just using different terminology…that is if you ignore the materialist stuff in Nietzsche. But he probably just put those in to deter the unready.' Michael, having become a convinced Wagnerian, now affected to despise Nietzsche, the chronic masturbator who had betrayed the greatest artist that ever lived. He was going to butt in rudely and tell her so, when someone clutched at his arm.

It was Fiona. Now she was finished with Colin, sexually, she was being friendly to Michael again, telling him how she'd been listening to Ulver's William Blake album he had taped her while painting the caravan she rented in someone's backyard. Michael was a bit cold, but congratulated her on her performance – do you think you'll stick the distance with us? Oh yes, definitely.

He scanned the room for a potential girlfriend who would help him realise his artistic visions, but none of the numerous females present seem to fit. He could hear Colin telling Music Man: 'We have an email address now, with some website called 'Hotmail', we're getting professional. We're getting a Geocities website, too, in the Nashville district…we're a country band at heart…Shiv's from some small town up north, actually.'

Then Fiona said: 'Actually, no, I'm probably moving to Melbourne. I want to learn to design websites. That's where the future is, not music. I thought I should let you know now so you can find another drummer.' He knew it, knew she wouldn't stick the distance.

'Okay,' he said politely. 'It won't derail us.'

'Good.' But she looked a bit disappointed. 'I haven't told Shiv yet…bit scared to.'

'I'll tell him…but what about the Tunnel Hill gig?'

'Depends how soon. I'm going in a few weeks.' Some notice. But she *couldn't* derail them, nothing could. Soon there would be a knocking on the door, something grand and gripping would happen. He was cold, changeling cold.

19

UNDER THE HILL

All of them were secretly relieved Fiona was gone – her looseness had sapped them in indefinable ways. But Hayden Burn from Sure Thing was not who Michael had envisioned as a replacement.

He was initially outraged, remembering how Hayden had drummed him out of assembly when he had been expelled.

'But there's literally no one else,' said Shiv. 'And he's enthusiastic about it, he says he'll try and fit in.'

'Hayden's an absolute fuckwit. He was ribbing me before the gig, like 'Little Michael's got a band, awwww,' or something. He might be a good drummer, but he's everything we stand opposed to. I went to high school with the guy, trust me.'

'Keep your enemy close, then you know what he's doing.'

'Not *that* close.'

'We can put him through a harsh trial, to make sure he's committed. He doesn't know how desperate we are for a drummer, so he'll probably agree to it.'

Michael was reluctantly persuaded.

'Alright, but he's got to be subordinate. There's no way he has any creative input.'

Shiv agreed. 'Drummers are earthbound, a necessary evil, but they have to know their place.'

They confronted Hayden that afternoon.

'Me and Michael have both stolen for the band, risking

prison. Colin has given up his ties to Merrie England's green and pleasant land and doomed himself to stay here in the land of convict bastards. So what are *you* going to give up for The Thresher, little drummer boy?'

'Hayden just wants the groupies, he isn't serious,' sneered Michael. Hayden looked daggers at him.

'I *am* serious. I like youse guys' style, that's all. And Sure Thing isn't going anywhere, especially after you blew them off stage last week.'

'Them? So you're already betraying your comrades. How can we be sure you won't betray *us?*'

Hayden looked confused by all this talk of 'betrayal'. It was just a band, wasn't it? Albeit one that might, just might, be headed for success. And now Shiv and that insufferable little prick Michael were talking about some medieval trial by ordeal, boiling water or something, what the fuck?

'I have a better idea,' said Michael suddenly. 'Break into Rob Weed's flat while he's sleeping and restring his guitar with the strings in reverse order.'

'What?'

'Then reverse his autistically-arranged alphabetical CD collection. Yeah, I've heard about it. Take a photo then get out.'

And in the end, Hayden actually went through with it.

Michael was surprised. Maybe he *was* the right drummer for them. Maybe the edge of having someone in the band he felt uncomfortable with, even (he scarcely dared admit to himself) *intimidated* by, would be a creative stimulus.

He and Shiv stood on the street outside Weed's flat while Hayden did the deed, arguing for the umpteenth time about *The Wicker Man*. Once again their positions had reversed, and they were channelling poles. Colin, meanwhile, was the calm one, the magnetic bar connecting the poles and giving them form (Hayden was just a pile of iron filings).

'Howie was looking for a missing child, so his actions were justified,' said Michael, pleased at how his mind had been expanding of late.'

'Ask your friend Hannibal Flea about that,' retorted Shiv.

'Flea's no friend of mine. His music is totally derivative, anyway. But I don't buy your view that Howie should have *known* the islanders were bluffing with the girl. He's a cop, not an historian, so how would he be expected to know that the stuff about Celts burning people alive was all made up by Julius Caesar?'

'He *should* have read up on it. It's more about the islanders' way of life, and them just wanting to be left alone.' So Shiv the Christian was defending the pagan islanders, and Michael the pagan was defending the 'Christian copper.' He had a flashback to childhood, Reg divesting Sylvie of membership in his Order. *If outside interference is brooked, where will it end? Will Papua New Guinea insist via the UN that cannibalism be tolerated in Australia?* There must be laws, empire. But again he felt his uncle's enormous shadow and wondered if he had even broken free of it.

'Anyway,' said Shiv, 'You're fine with the Moors Murderer references in Death in June's 'Runes and Men'.'

'I don't even know what that means.'

'Incidentally, I went to see 'Night and Fog' at the Bavarian Tavern with a bunch of art fags, because you said there was a DIJ album named after it. I was appalled when I saw it. It was just some shitty Zionist propaganda film.' Shiv had been listening increasingly to Muslimgauze, and had been corresponding with the musician behind it, Bryn Jones. He had also been reading anti-Zionist books by Israel Shahak, along with Gaddafi's 'Green Book', and Michael sincerely hoped he wasn't going to do a Cat Stevens.

One result of his new reading was that he wanted to drop the Vlad Tepes logo, and they argued over this. Michael wanted to drop it too, but for different reasons. It had become a cliché in the black metal underground, and now a bunch of crappy 'intellectual' power electronics bands were using the famous visage due its alleged sadism, not because Vlad was a European loyalist who knew how to deal with Turks.

Michael despised industrial music in general, except for some of the Swedish stuff. He had recently heard the 'mighty' Throbbing Gristle and was stunned by how flaccid they were, how much their reputation rested on media midgets regurgitating their name rather than artistic depth. He had been amused to read of the 'anti-bourgeois' Genesis P-Orridge's million dollar lawsuit against some Hollywood producer.

'Look,' said Shiv suddenly, pointing at a face peering out from the front window.

It was Rob Weed, looking spooked.

They smiled and waved, and he disappeared. A light came on. Now sounds of shouting and violence ensued, and a few minutes later Hayden Burn emerged with a black eye. Perhaps he wasn't as tough as Michael thought – it gave him hope he would be able to bash Burn himself if he got out of line. Michael had been working out at the PCYC gym, and felt more confident in general, even against Shiv.

'I only took the strings *off*, ' Hayden was blathering. 'I didn't have time to restring them before he caught me.'

'It's alright, you pass. You took a blow for the band.'

'Rob thinks I've gone insane.'

'You've just joined The Thresher. You *have* gone insane.'

*   *   *

Dorry Wendle was drunk and in attendance. Why had he paid $3 for a ticket if he just wanted to abuse them?

'Fuck homophobia!' he was screaming incongruously. It was weird, because The Thresher had never said a word about homosexuals. It was probably the 'Not Sorry' flyers that had attracted him here. Between songs all they could hear was Dorry's raucous screeching. Most of the punters seemed amused, though a few clearly sided with him.

Hayden walked out from behind the kit and looked at Shiv, like a dog begging for a treat. Shiv ignored him, which he took as permission to grab the mic and start insulting Dorry, resulting in hilarity from the crowd, as one dog baited another.

'You were always a wanker in high school, 'Dog'…even Michael beat you up, remember? Fucking gannet…' Michael felt a renewed twinge of guilt, so much so that he ignored the insult when he should have pushed Hayden into the crowd and taken over the drumming himself. He could do a straight eight, at least. But keys were indispensable for their current atmosphere. It was the combination of their melancholy and Shiv's aggressive guitar that made the thing work so well.

Shiv gently but firmly took the mic from Hayden.

'First, matey,' he said to Dorry, 'if you come here wearing that kind of crap,' he nodded at Dorry's 'Man is the Bastard' t-shirt, 'you're asking to be ridiculed.' Shiv hated American punk. 'You're not a victim, cobber, you just think you are. My father pulled a gun on me when I was five years old. He kicked the crap out of me, and after he left my junky bitch mother kicked the crap out of me too. Do you hear *me* whinging about it? People like you make victims out of the Abos, so you sound off about what a great white knight you are, protecting them, and what happens? They *turn* into victims. You don't give a fuck about the Abos.'

But Dorry wasn't listening. He was repeating his 'fuck racism, fuck homophobia' mantra tirelessly, so that Michael standing behind his keyboard trying to look aloof and mysterious wondered how his throat could endure it…surely Dorry's vocal cords must be pissing blood by now?

'And what happened to the Tasmanian Indigenous Council?' thundered Shiv above Dorry's hysterics. 'I asked them here to debate with me, or to make an official treaty, between the Thresher tribe and theirs, and they laughed in my face.' From Shiv's description of the official in question, Michael knew it had been the ferret-faced one who had chased his uncle long ago. It was pure coincidence that this gig had fallen on the first ever National Sorry Day, but Shiv was capitalising on it to good effect, with the flyers (many of which had been ripped down by persons unknown – Dorry? – but the crowd was a decent size anyway) and now on stage.

'Let me tell youse why we're NOT SORRY. Because we don't want to be part of the New World Order's plan to breed snivelling half-men. That's how they do it, divide and conquer. Turning Euro against Abo, woman against man. Corporate wankers in their high towers. Anyway, this one's for the megafauna.'

Shiv was being naughty, but no one seemed to understand the reference anyway, as they launched into 'Hobart is Dead'. There were rapturous cheers on completion of the song, and Dorry was nowhere to be seen.

*   *   *

After the set they were approached by a little blob-shaped man who was a correspondent for a Melbourne music paper, down for a week on assignment to write up the 'thriving Hobart scene'. Michael let Shiv handle the interview because he was busy chatting to the two plain-but-cute goth chicks, Erica and Pamela, who claimed they were The Thresher's groupies. Michael was ashamed that he had a boner while trying to give them a 'moral talk'.

'We're not interested in sex with groupies,' he said, gritting his teeth and forcing the words out. 'We're interested in educating people, and attaining the heights of fame so we can reach more people. We want to pave the way, culturally, for the demise of the current system and the start of something much better – a galactic empire.'

'And, uh, does Shiv feel the same way?'

Yes, they were more interested in Shiv…surprise, the singer always got the girls. He swallowed the bitterness, surprisingly easy. Hey, maybe he *was* getting better at suppressing his ego. Still, he was attracted to them. He would really get a kick out of their loyalty, if it was genuine. Were females capable of loyalty, though? Even Sylvie hadn't stayed true to the TUL, albeit she had to Reg personally.

Sandra Good and Lynette 'Squeaky' Fromme were still loyal to Charles Manson after three decades. But Michael had little interest in the deep ecology of Manson's ATWA cult. If you wanted to preserve the environment you needed an emperor to back it up, and Manson, while maybe a talented songwriter, was certainly no emperor. Emperors don't write songs about eating out of garbage dumps.

Michael liked the quieter one, Pamela; she wasn't what you would call 'pretty', but was feminine and therefore attractive. Still, he must remain celibate until he knew more about her. A future emperor must never spill his seed in an inferior vessel, as the future crown prince would have half her DNA.

He asked if she would like a drink, she smiled shyly and said yes. At the bar Shiv was talking to the blob, loudly over the house music, and the blob was saying in a somewhat patronising voice that he would get them a good write up in 'Circle of Fifths', a free weekly music magazine that relied heavily on advertising. Shiv went on a rant about how shit those kinds of magazines were, and the journo pretended to sympathise, getting political information out of Shiv without his realising it. Michael wanted to interject, remembering how his uncle had been treated, but couldn't be bothered…and Pamela was waiting for her drink.

*   *   *

'Hobart Band Spews Hatred Against Indigenous Australians From Onstage,' Blob Man's article read. It barely mentioned their music, briefly describing it as 'competent' with 'weird melodies' before delving obsessively into Shiv's 'confused' and 'facile' views.

'While Hobart's indie scene is indeed thriving, the presence and popularity of The Thresher casts a serious question mark over its fundamental soundness.' All the Hobart indie bands making cassettes in their lounge rooms must be pissed that an article about them had turned into a hate rant against The Thresher. Still, any publicity was good in a sense, and as they were supposed to be playing in

Melbourne soon, and hopefully the controversy would translate to a hyped audience.

The downside was that they had been unofficially banned from every pub in Hobart that accepted indie gigs. Hayden was angry, and wanted to beat up the journalist. Shiv told him not to worry, they were going to conquer the mainland.

'I wish you wouldn't get mixed up in politics,' muttered Hayden.

'Remember, you're a hired hand, you don't understand the band like Michael and I.' Michael felt a glow of pride as he said this. He had thought that Shiv had been closer to Colin lately, but now it was clear the old creative partnership was the core of the band again. Pagan and Christian, imperialist and anarchist – the opposites created the energy….Heraclitean.

And now they were playing the only gig open to them in Hobart – Tunnel Hill. They had prised open the rusty gate to play an illegal gig with about a dozen audience members, including the loyal Pamela and Erica. No PA system, And Michael and Colin had to share the bass amp, but even the muffled, muddy sound couldn't dampen their spirit.

'Christ *is* the only force stronger than Time and Gravity,' growled Shiv, as they launched into a new song called 'String Theory'. Would they be zapped by 'cosmic rays'? A rumour had circulated that something supernatural would happen. There were further sinister rumours about Shiv; he was bringing criminals there to shoot the audience; no, someone was going to shoot *him*. Michael was annoyed there were no rumours about himself, then annoyed at being annoyed. Again, he felt a sliver of self-doubt – were they trying to be rock stars when they should be teachers, or what should they be? He tried to suppress his ego.

It didn't matter, because halfway through the cops arrived and shut the gig down.

'Not you again!' one of them grinned catching sight of Shiv.

Ten minutes to get out or charges would be pressed.

They grudgingly complied, not wanting instruments

confiscated. Quite a way from the nearest house, so who complained? Were the cops now keeping tabs on their activities?

The old tunnel yawned, sealing tight its memories of cosmic rays.

Interview with The Thresher in 'Cursed Winter' zine (Szczecin, Poland), January 1999.

Answered by Shiv (vox, guitar) and Michael (keyboards).

About your band I have known from English 'Metal Hammer', which was a demo of the month! I have also read that there is a black metal available for 5US$D.

Shiv: If you mean our second demo, it's available from the same address, but it isn't black metal. Just the guitar sound might remind some people of that, but it's a richer more esoteric sound than any BM bands.

Your vocals they are very unique. Do you use two singers or one?

Shiv: It's all me. I'm not very versatile, I basically have two styles: the harsh, abrasive one, and the melodic one.

Did you know any Polish bands? And which of the bands you have heard? What do you think about them? In my region Pomorze Zachodnie (West Pomerania) there is not much also.

Michael: I like Graveland, Veles, Infernum.

Shiv: Michael played me some of those, they're atmospheric enough.

Tasmania is very eerie, far away, not known for me. What can you tell of it? The landscape there does haunt you?

Michael: Yes, absolutely…from the skeletal dead eucalypts of the midlands to the dense, forbidding rainforests of the south-west, Tassie's landscapes are imprinted on my soul. And beyond them, you can feel the presence of the Antarctic. *Tekeli-li.*

Shiv: Convict ruins haunt me the most. My ancestors were dragged there by the British government for poaching to feed their starving families, but they triumphed in the end didn't they, because their descendent is in the soon-to-be biggest band in the world!

You sing of Man's lost heritage?

Michael: I'm interested in European history, and educate myself for two hours a day at the state reference library.

Shiv: Atlantis, Lemuria, Mu. That is man's lost heritage. Before the Flood. Only God can give it back.

You play keyboards. But it still sounds good!

Michael: Yeah, keyboards suck I know. But in a shop today I saw a computer that looked like a day-glo plastic bubble. Is this heap of shit the future that started in the basement of my parent's…debased, dead plastic aesthetic?

Shiv: Keyboards enable a melancholic sound that gives depth to the anger of our songs, depth that's lacking in most punk bands, or metal bands for that matter.

What do you think of 'Satanism' in the scene?

Michael: Satanism is a semitic ideology from the deserts of the Middle East, and thus of no interest to me. I'm of European descent and prefer forests and mountains. The Order of Nine Angles had some okay vigilante ideas but I lost interest after Myatt converted to Islam, the most boring religion in the world (though Shiv probably disagrees).

Shiv: Bands mainly sing about Satan to be rebellious. I wish they would wise up and channel their rebellion against the real enemy: the New World Order and multinational corporations.

One of your songs is about Andreas Epp. Are you interested in the UFOs? Do you think they are Nazi Technology stolen after the war?

Shiv: All I know is that I saw eight red orbs above the South Burnie hilltop making erratic movements, like the dance of a collective intelligence. No manmade vehicles could move that way. The red visitors rose and went through the clouds. They may be watching us, the tall ones…but someone is watching them.

Do you want to be kult band, or big band?

Shiv: We want to incite the masses to rebel against their puppet masters, so as big as possible.

Any trouble with authorities?

Michael: This is where I'm supposed to brag about how one of our gigs was shut down by the police. Actually, it was quite a sordid affair, and we weren't dragged away in chains or anything.

Shiv: More to come, no doubt. More lies from the media, too.

Views on the democracy. Are you right-wing?

Michael: For the record, I'm not a fan of One Nation. A One Nation spokesman lambasted the memory of my uncle, Reginald Murchison, whom he described as a crank, and (disgustingly) a 'traitor'. Whatever one thinks of Reg's views, he fought for his country during World War Two, and was a committed patriot. Not to mention David Ettridge's recent stupid statement about 'printing more money' to boost the economy.

Shiv: I'm not 'right-wing'. So-called 'conservatives' seem to be all about getting rid of national institutions, like our prime minister selling off Telstra. In what way is that conservative? I think decision-making should devolve as much as possible to the level of the community, then the corruption and evil that now hides in plain sight can be dealt with more easily. That makes me anarchist.

So-called democracy is a bunch of shit. At the last Aussie election One Nation were doing well, but were kept from getting seats by our preferential voting system. You had Jewish groups lobbying the big parties to put them last on their 'how-to-vote' cards. There was a way to defeat this, called the 'Langer Method' after the commie Jew who was imprisoned on a contempt of court charge after he'd been forbidden by a court from communicating it to the electorate. But they recently changed the electoral act to make it fully preferential, so votes made using the Langer Method won't be counted.

Pollies break most of their promises, anyway, they do what they want when in office. In America you have Clinton ordering airstrikes on Iraq to distract attention from his sex scandals. Any healthy human being should be outraged by this. I have developed quite an affection for Hamas (which isn't exclusively Muslim, by the way, and has spoken in defence of the Palestinian Christians). Also, Muammer al Qathafi's *Green Book* is good. He talks about replacing so-called 'representative democracy' with popular congresses, that choose the administrators so a fixed bureaucracy doesn't develop, kind of like the old Anglo-Saxon 'folk moots' Michael was telling me about recently. When people have a say in their own destiny, they are no longer alienated.

Influences growing up?

Michael: Funny you ask that, because I was going through all my old stuff recently at my mother's house, after someone I knew in high school committed suicide. I blame myself for the suicide…but at least blaming myself means I have a soul, unlike my mother and her dipshit second husband.

Anyway, I found my dad's old computer from the late '70s covered in a thick layer of dust. It seemed to speak of what will happen to those who go with the flow, and who don't, you know, carpe diem. They are lost, wandering in a Niflheim of their own making.

I also found my Junior Encyclopedia - a big influence because it opened a world of learning and knowledge. And the *Australian Women's Weekly Children's Birthday Cake Book* certainly influenced me, because the constant disappointment at not having the various cakes made taught me that food isn't important beyond basic sustenance (unlike my mother and Clive, who are developing an unhealthy obsession with restaurants and wine).

But most pertinent of all I found my old drawings of space battles between Saturn and Earth. Fighting Saturn to me means overcoming fear, fighting unjust tyranny. Which is appropriate, because right after looking at them I punched that pompous twit Clive in the face. He had threatened to 'give me a good hiding', but in the end it was he who was beaten, ha ha. Going to the gym has certainly paid off.

Shiv: I'd rather not talk about my early years. The

Thresher is where it's at.

What are future plans for The Thresher?

Shiv: We're doing a tour of the Australian mainland later this year. We'll be living out of a small panel van our current drummer Hayden Burn owns (if Hayden lasts the distance, that is).

Now is your turn to ask <u>me</u> question I think!

Michael: Why do Polish women have such pale creamy skin and raven hair?

Cursed Winter: I don't know, perhaps it is the motherland's beauty? No, seriously, I think that not all of them do!

Shiv: What are your thoughts on Kosovo?

Cursed Winter: I am Slav, and I am by the Slav's side (Serbians). In my opinion, they have a rightness. But the most of Polish people are other opinions! Yes, there are organised a gathering of clothes, food and medicines for the people from Albania. The Polish government admitted an outsiders from there now, they are in a located asylum. The monthly payment is about 400$. Scandal!!! The middle payment for a job in Poland is about 200$ but it sometimes below! A good job is only for friends of a company! Now I am without work and I am still looking for a good job. I have not a grand!

Thanks for the interview!

Michael: Thank you.

Shiv: Thanks! Fight the culture war, my friend.

PART THREE

THE CRUCIBLE

20

MELBOURNE

They drove off the boat in bright late winter dawn. Michael had never left Tasmania before, and it hit home as he craned his neck to look at the dizzyingly tall buildings of Melbourne's central business district. The Kennett government were in the process of stripping Victoria of its public assets. Water, railways, the lot, all flogged off to multinationals, reinforcing Michael's anti-democratic inclinations, for by voting to be robbed the majority had demonstrated they didn't deserve a say, he thought. Still, it was unreal to be here...you never knew what you might find in a city this size.

Shiv's plan to stay with an old acquaintance had fallen through, and they had flipped to see who stayed in the van (which could sleep two fully laden) and who in the dorm bunks of the Central City Backpacker's. Shiv and Colin had drawn the hostel, and while they were checking in, Michael wandered down to the Theosophical bookshop he had spotted on the way.

Hayden followed, dogging Michael with irritating questions like a child. He looked uncomfortable in the unfamiliar surroundings of a bookshop. Michael glanced at him contemptuously, ossified brat of the televisual age. He himself had been obsessing on whether the fan who had agreed to run the band's Geocities page had updated it with news of the Melbourne show, but here, lost in a labyrinth of books, such vulgar thoughts crumbled like a sun-struck vampire…and Hayden had the nerve to look sullen and bored.

He found an interesting-looking treatise called *Hamlet's Mill* in the second-hand section. He bought a copy of Patrick White's *Voss* because they would soon be crossing the outback, and on a whim got *Five Shakespearean Tragedies* for Shiv, thinking perhaps that *Antony and Cleopatra* would convince him of the inevitability of Imperium. Shiv had been moody of late, dwelling on the death of his penpal Bryn Jones, supposedly of a rare blood infection, which Shiv regarded as highly suspicious.

Heading for the checkout, a voice in the next aisle caused Michael to pause and listen.

'Yeah, Jarl Grimslade's going to try and kill this Tassie band called The Thresher…'

'He tries to kill a different band every year,' yawned a second voice. 'It's getting a bit old now.'

'But this is different. He's made a solemn vow to kill someone before the year 2000, to usher in 'a new millennium of hate and fear'. This'll probably be his last chance to do it before Y2K kicks in.'

'Can't he just kill a homeless beggar or something?'

'No, it has to be a band…no one would care if a beggar was killed. Besides, The Thresher singer's rumoured to be a Christian. Plus they're Tasmanian, so probably a bit slow, ha ha.'

'He wants to be the Grishnackh of Melbourne, so let him.'

Michael smirked at the name 'Grimslade', taken from one of the *Fighting Fantasy* gamebooks he had enjoyed in primary school. Well, they were The Thresher, and some skinny Black Metal kid shouldn't be a problem.

*   *   *

The crowd continued streaming in.

Michael observed them, different cliques. The Thresher had generated a small amount of hype. Or was the crowd merely here to see Jarl Grimslade butcher them live on stage? He had told the others…Shiv and Colin hadn't taken it seriously, but Hayden had, and was now scanning the crowd with a look of pure paranoia on his thuggish face. Michael hoped it wouldn't detract from his timekeeping duties, for as drummer, the little rat virtually held the band together.

Holst, the manager of the club, who claimed to be an old-school goth but looked like a clean-cut businessman, was saying something to him. He strained to hear above the thumping bass notes of Sisters of Mercy's *Floodland* booming from house speakers.

'You've drawn a lot of people here tonight who would normally hate each other. Different subcultures.'

'Good, I like that. Shiv'll be overjoyed, too. I don't approve of subcultures. Everyone needs to come together into one big empire, ruled by me. In Tassie, we listen to nearly anything, or did at some point. There aren't clearly defined cults like here in Melbourne.'

'Yeah? Well in bigger cities like London it's even more extreme. There are Death in June fans who hate Current 93 fans and vice versa.' Michael was astonished by this, for he had thought of those bands as Siamese twins.

'I see Black Metal is still a thing here.'

'Yeah…it's not like *Dogs in Space* anymore.' Holst sighed, remembering lost days. 'Black Metal's the biggest thing going right now.'

Black Metal was utterly dead to Michael, however. The last albums of big bands were a parody of their former selves…*Ravishing Grimness*, *IX Equilibrium*, *At the Heart of Winter*, just going through the motions. Decent riffs, but feeling gone. Corporate sharks signing the dumber bands like Dimmu Borgir, giving them a makeover, sanitising them for fans of *Buffy the Vampire Slayer*, emphasising cheesy Satanic elements and suppressing nationalist themes. Corporatisation of Black Metal for greenbacks. Surprising it was possible, but one should never underestimate the vampire crowd. Weird he'd lived to see it, though. He felt so old. He'd be 23 soon, and Black Metal had died, The Thresher was the only show in town. All else was white noise, dead static, whereas The Thresher was light and life.

Michael would fill the local youth with galactic ideals, help them move (partly) out of the shadow of their parents, realise if they were to be cogs, then they could be cogs in something much greater. Shiv probably wanted to preach to them about the evils of earthly empire or something. But that was compatible with Michael's vision, because the degenerate rulers of the present must be swept away before the Star Conquerors took stage. Shiv's vision was negative only if taken alone. Anarchism and local community could never fill the gap in the human soul from the 'death of God', yet for those who couldn't or wouldn't believe in the gods of Asgard as Michael did, help was at hand…for a new god was coming, or a new Face of God. *Something* was coming, he felt it in his bones.

This interregnum wouldn't last forever.

Somewhere in the thick Tasmanian rainforest was a hint of what lay ahead, the forest where he had once seen the Nothing.

Nothing was now pregnant with Something.

*　　*　　*

They played 'Hobart is Dead', Shiv changing the lyrics to 'Melbourne is Dead', and the crowd went wild. A cheap gimmick, thought Michael, irritatedly…they should never stoop to such. The song was written about Hobart and only fit that city. Shiv, from Burnie, couldn't understand. Michael hated people tampering with his lyrics. It wasn't worth starting an argument over, but if it happened again in Adelaide he would have words on it, he decided.

On the other hand, Shiv's haircut wasn't seen as a problem here, as there was a big '80s-metal retro mood in

Melbourne at the moment. He caught glimpses of an attractive goth girl in a velvet dress swaying cobra-like to the music as she stared approvingly at Shiv's hair. He decided he would seek her out after the show. The celibacy thing was a joke, and he knew for a fact Shiv had banged both Erica and Pamela on the boat on the way over. How could he concentrate on his musicianship if he was thinking about sex half the time? Appropriate thoughts, as they launched into their new song, 'The Metaphysics of Sex', about the Platonic forms of female and male, and what they actually meant, cosmically speaking. Michael had penned it after skimming Julius Evola's book of the same name, which had found in a Sufi bookshop Shiv had taken him to, tucked obscurely away in Hobart's Liverpool Street. Michael had no idea it existed, and was miffed that an out-of-towner had discovered something about Hobart he didn't know himself. This, apparently, was where Shiv had been getting his supply of anti-Zionist books. Michael had little interest in the Middle East, and said loudly, in misanthropic Black Metal tones, that choosing between Islam and Israel was like choosing between two piles of shit.

'Maybe,' said Shiv politely, 'but one pile smells worse.' Michael, wishing to avoid arguments with Shiv at all costs, let it drop, but was pleased to find a book by Evola, whom Hannibal Flea kept namedropping. The book itself was difficult to read, so he had been forced to use his own ideas of the metaphysics of sex for the song lyrics, hoping they made sense and wouldn't be ridiculed by erudite philosophers at some later date when he was galactic emperor.

Halfway through the song, something went wrong with the sound. Guitar was down, keyboard way up, bass booming and distorted. Shiv apologised to the crowd as they stopped playing, but no one could hear him as the mic had also been turned down. They made their way over to the mixing desk to find out what the hell was going on. The manager was there, talking to someone. Apparently, a skinny Black Metaller had been seen lurking near the unmanned desk, bullet belt glinting.

'Why was it unmanned?' demanded Hayden.

'I don't know,' said Holst. 'I can't see Bill anywhere.' Bill was the house mixer. Colin had a go at adjusting it as the rest of them soundchecked, but couldn't seem to get it right. Where *was* the house mixer? The impetus had been lost, the crowd bored and restless. Shiv uncharacteristically got annoyed at them. A scuffle broke out in the crowd. Shiv went to try his own hand at mixing, while Colin tested his bass.

Then someone cut the house lights.

Light from the door only, where bored punters were leaving.

A sour, rasping voice from behind Michael's left ear screamed: 'You will *die*, virgins!' Michael spun, but no one was there. There were thumping sounds from elsewhere on stage, and a loud yell of pain, Colin's voice. Wood thwacking on flesh and another ghastly shout. Michael moved forward wondering what to do, hoping he wouldn't fall off stage. Then the house lights came on and he blinked. Colin was holding his leg, which was bleeding broadly. Hayden clutched a broken drumstick.

Their assailant was nowhere to be seen.

*   *   *

They waited at the Royal Melbourne Hospital for Colin's thigh to be seen to. The casualty ward was packed, overdosed junkies and fight victims galore...the triage nurse who examined Colin merely told him to 'hold the wound shut with your hands til a doctor can clean it out. And sit over *there*,' she pointed to a dark corner, 'so you don't bleed all over the floor. We just cleaned it. Put *this* down.' She threw him a towel. A cleaner with a full body protective suit like a Chernobyl worker's hurried out to mop up the trail of blood behind him. Presumably it led back to the nightclub, fortunately only two blocks from the hospital. Shiv darkly muttered something about 'capitalist medicine', but Holst, who had insisted on coming with them, was extremely apologetic.

'Jarl's annual attempt at assassinating a band...he failed again. I'm just sorry it had to be you.'

'Maybe Thrall would be a better name for him,' muttered Michael. 'Anyway, he can't stop us, no one can. Colin's tough, he'll be better soon.'

'Right as rain,' rasped Colin through gritted teeth.

Hayden bragged about how he had 'stopped the nutter' singlehandedly by conking him with his drumstick, which may or may not have been the reason Grimslade had fled. Shiv said he would pray for his enemy, but vowed to beat the shit out of him regardless when they came through Melbourne again after the tour.

'I think we'll get a song out of this, though,' said Colin. "To Turn the Bitter Knife', or something like that.'

'Not a bad title,' Michael admitted.

'The lyrics would be about how no adversity can hold us back, or something along those lines.'

'A melody just came to me,' said Shiv. 'Listen: va-va-VOOM, va-voomty-voom, va-va-voom, va-voom-va-voom-va-VOOM. Epic grandeur...proud melancholy.' He hummed the riff repeatedly and Hayden tapped out a rhythm on the plastic hospital chair with his hands. Now lyrics floated into Michael's head and he began to chant them aloud.

To turn the hand that bites
In a sick world of fear...

'*Excuse* me.' A sour nurse tapped his shoulder.

Half-dead junkies, larrikins and their pugnacious girlfriends were staring at them in amazed contempt, but also a sort of nervous wonderment. 'If you want to make that kind of racket you can do it elsewhere, there are *sick* people in here.' M looked around him at the low-life, many of them scarcely in pain.

'So, the comfort of Untermenschen comes before the needs of Art?' he growled. 'I think *not*.'

'It's alright, Michael,' said Colin. 'We'll finish the song at the hostel. If we can just stop at a late-night chemist on the way for some peroxide and a bandage, I'll treat the wound myself. We could be waiting hours here.'

'Yes, I think you should do that,' said the nurse. 'Or I'll have to call security.'

'Call them then,' sneered Michael, 'you philistine hag.' Her eyes widened and she stumped off. Was he overreacting, would the others think him pretentious? But thankfully they were grinning, including Erica and Pamela.

'Don't come between Michael and his art,' bellowed Shiv.

Sikh security guards manhandled them out the door, singing and in high spirits. Despite the curtailed gig, even Hayden seemed cheerful. The 'Jarl' had failed to stop them, and now nothing could...

21

THE CAMERA

'We sanctify the energies of this place, making them fuels for the Logos.'

They were in Engelbrecht Cave, a sinkhole beneath the town of Mount Gambier where blue-greenish waters welled from the depths. The ritual was intended to harness earth energy and put it in the service of something higher, transcendental, rarifying the earth and spiritualising it. *It is the white man's dance.* Dance of Kennewick Man.

What would Sylvie think, he wondered? For her, the earth was sacred in its own right, but for Michael as for Shiv, its mysteries must be interpreted...consciousness gave meaning to cosmos, not the other way around. Sylvie was part of the earth herself now, yet Michael continued to perceive her soul, to give it life, all the more as he felt he knew better than her. Hers was a female soul, and his was...what? A man's? He didn't feel like a man, which was a problem. Initiation rites of old done away with, young 'men' trapped in eternal boyhood, young women in turn shallow. A scary feeling - that he knew better than the older generation, poised to overtake them, yet didn't even feel a proper man. This tour would *make* a man of him, it *must* make a man of him. Something would happen, he willed it to happen. He willed earth energy of the grotto to give him wings, give him balls, give the sceptre needed to rule over it, the earth.

But before the grotto could answer, Hayden said loudly: 'I

need to take a piss.'

'Why has this vulgar halfwit been allowed a presence here when he isn't even part of the inner core of the band?' blurted Michael. For a second he thought Hayden was going to swing at him, and tensed himself ready to hit back, but the others backed him up.

'He's right,' said Shiv. 'You should show some respect for what we're doing, even if you're a benighted atheist.'

'I'm not an atheist,' stammered Hayden. 'I dunno what I believe. Anyway, didn't know I wasn't supposed to talk. I'll fucking well go, then.' He stalked out of the cave, no doubt seething deep down that 'little Michael' from high school outranked him in the band. But Michael was not so little anymore. Indeed he felt very calm.

'It's alright,' said Pamela, touching his hand and smiling sweetly. 'He was the one in the wrong. And you were right to come here, too. It's beautiful.' She was referring to an earlier argument between Michael and Hayden; Hayden had wanted to drive the Bordertown way because it was quicker, but Michael had put his foot down as he wanted to see his grandmother in Mount Gambier. Finding the sinkhole and creating an impromptu and heartfelt ritual proved it was the right decision, but shallow, bored and sulky Hayden shouldn't have been there.

'Do we even need a drummer?' he wondered aloud.

'I'm not sure he isn't cursing the tour in some way,' muttered Shiv, unexpectedly. 'What d'you think, Colin?'

'Ah, I don't know. She'll be right, as you Aussies say, I suppose.' Colin was in some ways a giant shrug, and Michael wondered if he had the requisite energy to see things through. Unlike Hayden, however, he had made important contributions to the songwriting, and Michael had trouble imagining their sound now without his booming, headchopping bass waves. But when it came to rituals, Colin, despite his esoteric proclivities, was low of energy, and Michael worried this would hamper them for the big one - the 9/9/99 ritual to be performed outside (or near as possible to) the American military base at Pine Gap, in order to spiritually bind the forces of NWO so a *new* new world order could be born. Shiv had no vision for its replacement other than a world of self-governing communities, but Michael saw the ritual as a cornerstone for the creation of an aristocratic, Hyperborean empire. Anyone hampering it must be cast aside...musicians, groupies, all insignificant next to his grand imperial vision, a vision steadily replacing Odin and Thor in his conception of the divine. Or rather, reinforcing them, a new conception of Asgard, post-Ragnarokian...for religion that ceased to be renewed became mere dogma, sinking into the void of Ginnungagap.

*   *   *

He had never met his grandmother til now. His parents had often talked about coming here for a holiday yet somehow had never gotten round to it, or it had turned into an argument. His father attended the funeral when old Grandfather Glendower died in '89, but Michael and his mother had stayed home. Now his widow got a shock when her grandson showed up on the doorstep.

'Well! So you're Michael! I still have all the Christmas cards you sent me.'

'Eh?'

'Yes, look...' She pulled down a biscuit tin. The handwriting was his mother's, in Michael's name. He wondered if she realised this and was testing his reaction, but decided to say nothing. As they finished their Earl Grey tea and the conversation petered out, he fidgeted for a bit before gathering the courage to ask for his father's new address. Her look changed from one of blankness to disapproval.

'You don't know where he's living, then?'

'I figured he didn't want us - my mother and me - knowing where he is. But I'd like to see him once before the turn of the millennium. I don't know if this Y2K stuff is true, but if it is, then...we could be in for a Mad Max type scenario. The temporary end of civilisation. I might never see him again. Anyway, surely he's had time to sort out his…issues…by now. It's been a few years, after all.'

'The place he's living is what they call a…commune.'

'Yeah? Is he still with what's-her-name?'

'If you mean that floozy Conny, I'm afraid so. I never cared for your mother much…no offence, Michael…but compared to Conny she was like a Rolls-Royce Silver Shadow.' Michael had noticed pictures of luxury vehicles on the walls, although the car in her drive was a small Honda hatchback. Still, he decided he liked the old chook. She was forthright, more so than his parents. Maybe he had inherited his cockiness from her.

She wrote something on a sheet of notepaper and handed it to him. 'That's the address…it's near Port Pirie. Virtually on the edge of the desert. I wonder if you could tell him what a disappointment he is to me. Though I think he already knows.' Prim and grim now, the nice old lady who'd poured the tea gone. But when Michael asked what his father had been like as a boy her face softened.

'I remember he always wanted a computer,' she murmured. 'That was in the late '50s, when they were as big as a house. When you were a baby he finally got one, and he wrote to me telling me how awful it was. That's Paul all over. Wanting things and being disappointed when he gets them.'

'But isn't the chase what matters? Then we move on to something else.'

'I see you're a bit of a philosopher, Michael. Perhaps you can help me with the cryptic crossword?'

'I can't stay long. The others are waiting in the car outside. My band, you know. We're doing a show in Adelaide tomorrow night.'

'Oh? You don't look like a musician! You don't have long hair.'

'Did my father have long hair, in the '60s? Did he go through a hippy phase?'

'Oh no…he was 'square' as they call it in appearance. I always thought he'd end up working with computers, but now here he is, living on a commune, and it's nearly the year 2000.'

'And his computer is gathering dust in the basement.'

'Yes. Isn't it funny how things turn out?'

*   *   *

Listening to Arckanum's *Kostogher* as the miles went by, Michael felt an abiding loyalty to the good old-fashioned cassette walkman. Hayden's discman skipped every time they went over a bump, making it impossible to listen to on a trip like this. Sometimes old technology was better, he thought, staring out the window at the windswept, shrub-speckled waterway. This was the haunting landscape of the Coorong, where the Murray's mouth lay hid in a wide spread of mazy, swamplike channels. In a few hours they would be in Adelaide, a city he knew little of, other than that many of its original settlers had been German.

He glanced at Shiv, but couldn't fathom what was stirring inside the other's hairy head. Was he praying, meditating, mentally fasting? How long would this band last, and how long could Michael use it as a vehicle before it came crashing down? Surely their impending fame was too good to be true. And what would Erica and Pamela do when a thousand other groupies were clamouring to replace them? Michael's heart went out to them, actual tears forming behind his eyes which he quickly blinked away. He hoped he wasn't falling in love with Pamela…it could hamper his plans.

*   *   *

The gig was a pub in the CBD, audience less than a quarter that of Melbourne…still, it was a smaller place. The wide belts of parkland between city and suburbs felt artificial

251

to Michael, who disliked the idea of a planned metropolis. But how would his imperial capital be built, and which planet would it even be on? Earth was too far gone; ask Sylvie, he thought, plugging keyboard into amp.

The crowd were dull here, drunken ockers in the most generically Australian of cities, Adelaide, also the City of Churches. Shiv should feel at home here…but no, he remembered, Shiv hated the church, regarding it as Antichrist. Well, they would have to play intensely enough to wake the locals from their consumer slumbers, he thought, trying a few test chords.

'Keys too high in the mix,' he heard Hayden whinging passive-aggressively, but no one paid heed. Ah Hayden, still pretending you're anything other than a hired hand. The tension between them had been strong since Mount Gambier, but Michael had done his best to ignore it, concentrating assiduously on his push-ups in case it came to a physical fight. He felt sure Hayden was still stronger than him…but for how much longer?

Hayden would be out of the band after this tour, anyway, he thought, relieved. Michael looked forward to telling him the news himself, and maybe punching him in the solar plexus for good measure. He noticed Pamela in the audience, sweet and sad, the innocent slut…what a contrast to baleful Hayden. He tried to shake both of them from his mind…he must concentrate. They were opening with a new song tonight, a catchy, punchy Shiv-penned one, a protest against the NATO bombing of Serbia, called 'Field of Blackbirds'.

Shiv began introducing it now to the audience.

'Wesley Clark has been saying, and I quote, "There is no place in modern Europe for ethnically pure states. That's a 19th century idea, and we are trying to transition into the 21st century, and we are going to do it with multiethnic states." So by that logic, he's gotta open Israel's borders next, right, eh? Why stop at Europe?'

'Just play some fucken songs,' yelled someone. Ironic whoops, drunken roars. Shiv shrugged. 'Tough crowd,' he muttered, 'but we're tougher.' They launched into the new song.

At the end the crowd cheered, but undoubtedly at the punchiness of the main riff rather than the words. Did anyone even pay attention to lyrics? It was *atmosphere*, atmosphere they must put across, Michael realised more than ever. They must *soak* their ideas into people's subsciousnesses. The direct approach was wrong. He would discuss this more with Shiv when the tour ended; it wouldn't do to be arguing now, at a time when they must be unified.

*　　*　　*

Zonk was the name of the guy hired to make a clip for them. He charged a thousand bucks, which came out of the tour money. He didn't have an office, he said, he would meet them in Port Adelaide where he wanted to film the clip. After Shiv played him part of their demo down the phone, he claimed to have developed a 'feel' for their music, and knew the perfect location to shoot it. It turned out to an abandoned industrial area which reminded them a bit of Burnie.

Not a bad backdrop, but the producer-director was another thing entirely. A friend of a friend of someone in the Cosmic Psychos, who had once roadied for INXS at a gig in Wollongong or something, his beer gut and straggly beard seemed out of line with their vision.

He claimed to have done a couple of clips that had been played on *Rage*, but Michael remembered *Rage* were obliged to play *any* clip by an Aussie band. Still, he got the feeling they would refuse The Thresher, especially when the song in question was called 'Zionist Pest State'. He shook his head at Shiv's bluntness. He wanted to do 'Hobart is Dead', though it would be weird shooting it in Adelaide, but 'Zionist Pest State' was too punky, not mysterious enough. Perhaps it suited their current surroundings, a bank of decaying warehouses. But if they were going to do a Shiv-song, the crushing 'Fuck the New World Order - Smash It and Destroy

It!' have been better, or the killer riffage of 'Field of Blackbirds'. Shiv had insisted on 'Zionist Pest State', though, 'so our beliefs are on our sleeve, where they should be…no pussyfooting around these issues.' Michael yawned, having little interest in the Israel-Palestine conflict. The Jews could keep their pissy little country for all he cared, as long as they ceased meddling in the affairs of Australia and other nations. He wondered idly what he would do with the Jews when his own empire got going…Saturn would be a good place for them, perhaps; or one of its moons, rather. Titan supposedly had methane oceans, and even a bit of an atmosphere. Possibly they'd be at home there. Methane would be cleaner than the Dead Sea, in any case, which he had heard was full of germs from people spitting in it.

In any case, Zonk (or Shonk as Michael privately thought he should have been called) turned out so inept the rushes he showed them looked more like something from *Australia's Funniest Home Video Show* than a serious film clip.

Michael ended up taking over the camera, even though he wanted to be in it himself.

'As long as I get a production credit at the end of the clip, I guess I don't mind,' he said. Michael realised with immediate and awestruck simplicity how much he loved using a camera. It was an old Russian camera, a Krasnogorsk, from the Soviet-era. Spring wound rather than electric. A 100' roll of film lasted around three minutes, then it had to be changed, and the camera made such a noise that even if they'd wanted to record live sound they couldn't, so mimed their instruments to be combined with the demo track in the studio Zonk had apparently booked for them. Pamela pretended to play keyboard in Michael's place.

The weird camera felt made for his hand, and eye. Yes…his right eye. Reading *Voss*, he had been struck by a character saying the land (Australia) was his *by right of vision*. Was Michael's inner vision stronger than that of the Abos? If so how could he prove it? Surely his clip would be better than *The Phantom Menace*, at least, which he had seen with Pamela at an Adelaide cinema yesterday evening. The CGI had struck a distinctly false note. Was that the future of movies? He hoped not.

At one point he went into a kind of trance and 'floated' the camera, panning it across the band. It would look amazing in the rushes...but unfortunately Colin injured himself again, falling off the concrete stump where he was pretending to play bass and twisting his ankle.

'Stabbed in Melbourne, now this,' said Erica, tending to him.

'He's not having a very good time of it, is he?' said Zonk nervously.

'Leave it in the clip anyway,' said Shiv. 'It shows we've got fortitude.'

'You'll have to have fortitude,' said Zonk. 'You've only got an hour to edit it, that's all I could get us at the studio. Hey, you don't want to buy the camera, do you?' he asked Michael. 'I was gonna sell it anyway, and you're pretty good with it.'

'How much?'

'A grand.'

'I dunno...'

It looked good. It smelt good. He ran his hand along it.

'It's a 16mm, not some crappy Super 8. I'll chuck in a dozen film rolls, too. A grand's a bargain!'

Shiv agreed to deduct $900 from the tour money to pay for it, to Hayden's protests. Shiv demanded the $100 discount because Zonk hadn't directed their clip.

'Fair enough...'

Shiv thought they could use it to make other films clips, and also a kind of tour diary, which could be amusing. It could be the start of something big, Michael thought, already feeling proprietary towards his noisy new machine.

22

PORT PIRIE

They stopped near the river docks to vomit.

The docks were a short stroll from the greasy, run-down takeaway shop where it appeared they had contracted a kind of food poisoning from their chicken burgers. How was the place still in business? Maybe the locals were impervious to it, and the germs would only take effect on out-of-towners. They clutched their stomachs and groaned. Only Shiv seemed happy, and after vomiting appeared to get it out of his system. He was used to it, he said - there was a takeaway in Burnie that was worse. He was more concerned about the mechanic where they had left the van, which had started overheating as they entered town. After carrying all the musical equipment the kilometre or so to the pub where the gig was, they had staggered back in the heat to be told by an arrogant troglodyte the van probably couldn't be salvaged.

'It's only a bit of overheating, but no coolant leaking. Probably something wrong with the thermostat.'

'*We'll* be the judge of that. Anyway, don't get your hopes up. There's a scrapyard round the corner, ha ha ha.'

'Probably owned by his mates,' muttered Shiv as they left. They had no choice, though. They couldn't go into the desert all the way to Alice Springs and beyond with a faulty vehicle. Even on the main highway there was often little traffic in those regions, or so they'd heard, and payphones for a breakdown truck were hundreds of kilometres apart.

Meanwhile Hayden, in addition to suffering the ravages of food poisoning, was in a black mood because he had phoned his girlfriend back in Hobart and learnt that she had left him…for Rob Weed.

'Fucker must have seduced her deliberately, for payback,' he growled. 'It's just the kind of thing he'd do.'

'Oh well, there's other fish in the sea,' said Michael, trying to be reconciliatory. 'Try and find one more loyal.' Hayden took this the wrong way, however, and flew off the handle.

'Fuck you, Glendower,' he snarled. 'What the fuck would you know? You've only had one girlfriend and she turned out to be a literal whore.'

'Actually I'm with Pamela,' he said, a little too smugly.

'That's two whores, then.'

Pamela shrieked in protest, and Michael despite his wish to put an end to intra-band conflict, had little choice but to punch Hayden in the snout. He expected to be punched back and tensed himself to block it, but was unprepared to be grappled to the ground, which was what Hayden did - and he was every bit as strong as Michael had feared. Thousands of push-ups hadn't prepared him to throw off the weight of their fit drummer. It might have ended badly if Shiv and Colin hadn't been there to pull them apart.

'Truce, truce,' Shiv bellowed, asserting authority. 'We already have the government and corporations against us, without worrying about you two scragging as well. Now get the fuck over it.'

'Focus your energies on the gig,' admonished Colin. 'It's in less than two hours, in case you've forgotten.'

Hayden muttered something and Michael panted, staring at him resentfully and silently vowing to do twice as many push-ups.

'And there's more to worry about than the gig,' frowned Shiv. 'If they can't fix the van in three days at the latest, we're gonna have to steal another vehicle, or we won't get to Pine Gap in time. It's either that or hitchhike, which is hard with all our gear.'

'Come on Shiv,' said Hayden. 'You don't want to go to

prison. The band wouldn't exist without you, you're the natural leader.' Michael sneered inwardly at such shameless suckholing.

Shiv said if caught he would ignore the summons and skip interstate.

'Relax, I'll never go to prison. There's a freedom charm in my birth sign.'

'How d'you know?' demanded Hayden.

'I just *feel* it.'

*　　*　　*

The audience that night was a small crowd of working class males of late middle age, somewhat intoxicated, yelling for Rolling Stones covers. Soundchecking, they realised the PA system was terrible and something was also wrong with their foldback. A frantic discussion took place as to whether they should even go ahead with the gig.

'It's gonna sound real bad.'

'Doesn't matter, the crowd will hate us anyway. Hey, we could cover 'Wild Horses'.'

'Fuck off with that shit,' growled Shiv, who hated stadium rock with a passion.

At that point a couple of teenagers dressed in black sidled in, hunching surreptitiously in a corner as if afraid of being noticed by their beery elders.

'We'll do it for *them*,' said Shiv. 'It sucks growing up in a town full of Rolling Stones fans. I should know, 'cause Burnie's like that, too.'

They proceeded to play, but due to the lack of foldback could only guess what they sounded like. After the first song there was polite applause from the youngsters, but the old coots were covering their ears. Two or three left, to 'get some quiet,' as one of them put it.

During the next song, Hayden stopped playing halfway through and doubled over to vomit on stage. There was uproarious laughter from the workers, and even the teens were chortling. Michael was mortified, but Shiv tried to make light of it. 'Don't worry, he does that, don't you, Burnsy? Although, d'you think you could try and get to a toilet next time?' He threw a beer mat at Hayden, telling him to clean up the mess. 'Drummers,' he said, rolling his eyes, getting another laugh from the crowd.

They managed two more songs before the PA gave out. They shrugged and began packing up to ironic applause from the 'crowd'. One of the teens began looking at the anti-NWO brochures Shiv had placed on a table near the door, and between trips to the toilet with vomiting and diarrhoea, Michael could see Shiv talking to them, or ranting rather, about black helicopters, crop circles and sundry other topics. Far from a warrior, Michael felt weak and shaky, in no mood to confront his father tomorrow, with whom he wished to have the upper hand. At least they had gained a couple of converts, he thought, seeing the teens listening respectfully to Shiv. Or would they forget about it next day and resume their parochial ways? No, seeds of thought *may* have been planted. One had to hope. Gig by gig they could reach all the youth of Australia, and then the world. He must get some galactic imperialist brochures printed he thought, before spewing again.

*   *   *

In the morning, against all hope, they found the van was fixed.

'Water pump was rusted and stiff,' said the mechanic, unexpectedly friendly. 'Put a new one in, she'll last a bit now.' He then looked pointedly at the Tasmanian number plate. 'I won't make any scar jokes, but you'd better settle with cash if you're from out of town.'

It turned out to be $320, mainly labour costs, and their tour fund was starting to look decidedly empty.

'We should try and get Sydney and Brisbane shows after Pine Gap, just so we've got enough to get the boat back to Tassie,' said Shiv.

*   *   *

Hayden grumbled at the prospect of yet another Glendower family reunion.

It wasn't actually the edge of the desert, but it was dry, scrubby country. It looked as if the earth has been wrung out by thirsty giants, then pan-baked.

The commune itself was surrounded by high fencing with razor wire at the top, and to their surprise there was a guard at the gate, reading a magazine in a small, air-conditioned shed.

'You need a permit to visit…you have to arrange it by phone with the Prophetess.'

'I see…and have you got her number?'

'No.'

'C'mon, let's go,' said Hayden. 'We're wasting time…what *is* this fucked up place, anyway?'

But Shiv had wire cutters in his pack.

'Never know when they'll come in useful.' One of everything, that was Shiv. Why not one pair of wire cutters? They stalked round the perimeter and found a deserted spot to cut a gaping hole in the fence. They walked towards the dongas which radiated out from a cluster of wooden huts in the middle. A cold brass bell sounded, summoning the inhabitants to different tasks.

One woman was threshing wheat by hand…a different kind of Thresher. In the next shed, others were grinding the grain in large hoppers to make flour. It looked like hard work, but they seemed content. Everything seemed to revolve around bread, and the loaf symbol was everywhere…a mural of the loaves and fishes miracle on the side of a donga, but no other obvious religious symbolism.

'Are you newcomers?' smiled a lady with long auburn

hair.

'Uh, yeah.'

'Has the prophetess given you the Speech of Welcome yet?'

'Not yet, no.'

'Ah. Not to worry, I'm sure she'll be with you shortly.'

'Do you know where Paul Glendower lives?'

She frowned and pointed. 'I believe he's in that donga over there, the one that's slightly askew.' She dropped her voice to a whisper. 'But I think he's out of favour with the Prophetess.'

'Oh…that's no good.'

'No, it's no good at *all.*' She walked off with a wave and a less friendly nod.

'Man, this place is creeping me out,' said Hayden.

'There's a sickly vibe all right,' conceded Shiv. 'We should play a gig here, advance the Kristos energy against it.' Michael agreed heartily, but called it Odin energy. A moment of pure brotherhood.

Conny in the distance, Michael noted, walking shoulder to shoulder with a man, who didn't appear to be his father.

The reached the skew-wiff donga, and knocked at the door. His limp, deflated dad, Paul Glendower, got a shock. As did his son at the sight of the straggly-bearded anorexic figure. Did the carbohydrate-intensive diet disagree with him?

'You remember Hayden, dad?' A squint indicated that he may have seen him, centuries ago. 'And this is Shiv and Colin. My bandmates. We're on an Australian tour.' Michael could finally talk to him as an 'equal', but couldn't still his nerves entirely.

Long silence. 'So what are you doing *here?* And how did you get in?'

'We cut the fence,' Shiv beamed.

Glendower frowned. 'You shouldn't have done that. It will lead to more trouble with the Prophetess. Trouble for *me.*'

'How's Conny?'

'Conny's happy here…and so am I.'

'I just saw her with someone else.'

His socially conservative father suddenly became defensive about 'free love'.

'So *you've* got another woman?' He muttered something, embarrassed.

How had Paul Glendower's life come to this nadir, wondered Michael. Embarrassing, yes, but instructive. How not to live.

Shiv asked if the communards were allowed to leave.

'Of course we are. But depending on the circumstances we might not be allowed back. *I'm* thinking of leaving,' he muttered, exhausted, soul spent. Michael doubted he would. Where would he go? Too hard to begun afresh with null energy. He felt a sudden painful pang of pity for him, and with great difficulty stifled it. A woman did this to my father...he vowed never to care for a woman so much he would follow her anywhere. But part of him knew Paul Glendower had done this to himself.

He told his dad about the band, their lyrics, dreams and ambitions...his dad showed no sign of interest...another bitter defeat. No Reg, no dad. His elders would never recognise his gifts. He felt on the edge of a void, emptiness lapping the back of his skull.

Colin lit a cigar.

'No smoking in the commune,' said Glendower tiredly.

They left.

The others seem to feel sympathy for Michael, even Hayden.

Once out through the hole in the fence, they went to fetch their instruments.

*   *   *

No electricity in the commune - the handground grain should have tipped them off. Only the security guard's hut had air-conditioning. What would it be like in summer, in a metal donga? It already felt overheated in August.

They brought two acoustics (Colin had a battered one that would serve him as a bass), kick drum, hi-hat and snare. The Thresher, unplugged. Michael's instrument would be the film camera.

They started with 'Silent Weapons for Quiet Wars'. Halfway through the song people began streaming in. Michael turned the camera on the crowd. They were a strange bunch, mostly female, faces lost and inward-looking, confused, having seemingly found no answers there. Michael felt a bit sorry for them, and hoped the music would give them some spiritual uplift. Then a woman who could only have been the Prophetess appeared, looking a bit like an angry witch, barking orders at the security guard in an American accent...he thought it sounded like a New York one.

He got it all on camera, the guard's comical attempts to snatch the guitars away from Shiv and Colin, who played on stoically, even as the guard drew them in a long dancing tussle. He then turned to the kit, but backed off when Hayden drew his stick back menacingly.

The Prophetess herself marched up and began shrieking at them, spitting venom.

Shiv and Colin were too strong, spiritually...the other denizens seemed spellbound...Michael worried that Hayden would be helpless before her witchery, but was pleased to see him ignore her, concentrating on his rhythms with a grim half-smile.

Paul Glendower put his head in the door. He looked puzzled, as if trying to remember something from a long time ago.

'Why aren't you playing an instrument?' he said in Michael's ear.

'Normally I play keyboard. Today I'm filming, that's all. Can't plug the synth in here, can I?'

His father looked sceptical, and Michael felt a sudden wave of hatred towards him. The Prophetess stormed out, spitting on the camera lens in passing. Michael wiped it on a tablecloth and turned it off, as the reel had ended anyway.

The band continued, playing three more songs, clearly enjoying themselves. He felt outside it. His father had gone. Perhaps The Thresher was not his destiny? Uneasy chill as he thought it.

Eventually two cops arrived and ordered them to leave. They clearly knew the place, and disliked it. Being called here to shut down an acoustic concert made it weirder than ever.

They didn't accede to the Prophetess' demands the band members be arrested. The senior cop said they would be issued with a trespass notice (Shiv gave a fake address in Port Adelaide), and warned them not to come back, that was all. No summons would be served on them.

On the way out they passed Paul Glendower again. Despite his newfound anti-Nietzscheanism, Michael couldn't help saying to him:

'The desert encroaches. Woe to him who has a desert within…'

All cocky and full of malice as he said it, the last words he ever spoke to his father.

But whom did they apply to?

Glendower, in any case, didn't react. He gave a limp wave and shuffled back to his donga.

23

GUBBA GUBBA

They stayed the night at hostel in Port Augusta that smelled of sandalwood, leaving early next morning for the drive through the desert.

The land became arid very quickly, and soon they were in a savage country like a drunk dreaming fitfully, half-conscious of the hangover that would make his day a misery beyond words.

The sun hit them with full force. And they drove through the same scene for hours, and Michael couldn't see the slightest difference in anything. I mustn't be looking hard enough, he thought. That's wrong, for a film director. And he strained his eyes until they hurt, trying to pick out tiny differences in the landscape.

*   *   *

When the sun was at its height, the van started making funny clicking sounds. They pulled over, only to find a hissing puddle of water beneath the engine. Shiv, after examining it, declared that a radiator hose had burst.

'Can you fix it?'

'Mending the hose won't do any good…the engine'll be cooked.'

'Why weren't you watching the heat gauge?'

'The heat gauge doesn't work.'

'Oh, great.' Hayden melodramatically pacing up and down slapping his forehead.

'Calm down. We can sell the van for scrap, and…'

'You mean it's fucked completely?'

'It'll need a new engine block. What with the cost of transporting one out here to woop woop, it'd be just as cheap to buy a new van. I'm guessing we'll have to finish the tour by hitchhiking. No matter, I thought it'd probably come to that, anyway.'

There was much grumbling from Hayden and Erica, but it took only ten minutes before a small truck approached them, and stopped. It was dual cab, and it looked like they could all get in at a pinch.

'Where youse going?'

'Alice Springs.'

'I'm only going as far as Gubba Gubba. You won't get further tonight, anyway, not unless you get a long distance truckie.'

'Is there accomodation in Gubba Gubba?'

'Yeah…leastways, there's the pub.'

'Awesome. Can we fit our gear in the back?'

'Yeah. That's where you'll be riding anyway…the cab's full of stuff.'

They loaded their gear in, finding it was a butcher's truck, the back full of hanging meat.

'You're musos? No shit. Woah, is that a video camera?'

'It's a film camera'

'Can you take some footage of me?' He held a couple of cold chickens to his chest. 'Channelling my inner female.' Michael felt a burst of unease.

'I haven't got much film left.'

'Never mind, then. Now, have we all got proper footwear?' He inspected their feet. 'Alright, get in.' He shut the door on them, like the door of a tomb. At least it was cool.

'I don't like this,' said Erica, agitatedly. 'He seems weird, what if he's a psycho?'

'What if he padlocks the doors shut?' said Pamela.

'Well, there's a gun here,' said Shiv, picking up a rifle, 'so we can always blow the lock out.'

'Is it loaded?'

Shiv inspected it. 'No,' he said disappointedly.

'Why would he have a gun in here? Isn't it supposed to be in a safe or something?'

'For killing the animals, of course. He's probably a mobile butcher. Now relax. Nothing can go wrong on this tour. It's our destiny.'

Time had little meaning in the enclosed world of the meat van, but after what may have been an hour, during which little was said, they slowed, turned a corner and stopped.

The butcher let them out with a chuckle and a grin. They thanked him and unloaded their gear onto the footpath outside the town's largest building, a brutalist edifice once an odeum and cinema, had fallen into decay, if brutalist buildings *could* decay. From such a centre the rot had spread through town in wide strips of uncare, threading the shiny bits. Dust reached its fingers to the centre, relaxed in the knowledge it would take all back. *The desert encroaches.* Next door was an old block of council flats with a jagged stair at side, and a large fire danger warning, probably permanently on high, though what would burn with no trees Michael couldn't guess. Across the road was an IGA, with a pub next to it.

'Welcome to Gubba, boys and girls. Your luxury hotel's right there.'

Shiv said he would go to the garage tomorrow to see if he could arrange a tow truck to go out and take the van for scrap.

The Hotel Invincible, the town's only pub, had two bars and a few upstairs rooms. The landlord seemed friendly, and booked them in for the night, but warned them under no circumstances to set foot in the 'coon bar'.

'White bar's down the end of the hall,' he said matter-of-factly. Hayden looked taken aback, but Colin seemed amused. A radio somewhere was playing the Red Hot Chili

Peppers' 'Californication', and the lyrical reference to Bowie's *Station to Station* made Michael think of Anika. In what glossy Hel was she now, as Michael ascended to a dark Valhalla? Perhaps he could redeem her, make a virtuous woman of her? Not a wife, not after the entire world had seen her naked body, but she would be his personal servant, and pour water on his feet.

Water in the hot, hot desert.

* * *

As soon as the landlord was out of sight, Shiv announced he was going into the coon bar.

Hayden, who was still unsure whether Shiv was racist or anti-racist, begged him not to go into the coon bar.

'But I was born and raised in a coon bar,' whispered Shiv, and only Michael got the joke, having read Enid Blyton's retelling of the Uncle Remus stories as a child. Shiv disappeared, leaving the others to lug all the gear upstairs.

To their surprise it was a dorm room, with eight bunks, and no other guests save the cockroaches, of which there were hundreds. As soon as they turned the light on the walls turned from black to a dirty off-white as the roaches scurried into cracks and behind cupboards. Pamela was shocked, and demanded to share Michael's narrow bunk, which he acquiesced to whiteknightedly wondering how on earth he was going to breathe. And roaches, crawling into his mouth in the night…he shuddered, resolving not to sleep.

Downstairs again they hear Shiv roaring Gabriele D'Annunzio's war cry: 'Eja Eja Alalà'…which Michael taught him from a Laibach album. It seemed he was teaching it in turn to the Aborigines, for there was a mass of drunken bawling. Michael and the others didn't dare go in, and headed for the white bar instead. The girls stayed in the room, not wanting to go to an outback bar, saying they would guard the clothing and gear against roaches.

The bar certainly was an outback one, trying for a cultivated eccentricity in the hope of luring tourists. In this case it was a large collection of gumboots, nailed to one of the walls.

A shelf behind the bar was filled with ships in bottles (which demonstrated a more genuine humour than the boots), and a barometer on the wall was shaped like the obligatory naked woman. Michael noted its reading and thought it must be broken, as it seemed to indicate rain. There hadn't been a cloud in the sky all day.

Locals at tables, and one at the bar. Only the latter gave the traditional stare one receives entering a rural pub, a little man and thin, not at all intimidating. Hayden muscled up to him, and made some patronising remark about 'what've you got to do to get a beer around here?' and the man told him to 'shut the fuck up, you misbegotten poofter.'

Hayden bristled, but a much bigger man came in, reeking of sweat, and sat next to him at the bar, affable but powerful, curly-haired with a sense of potential menace.

'G'day, Chris,' said the little one. 'Looks like we got some city fellers here tonight.'

'Where youse from?' said the curly one, turning to them.

'Tas,' said Michael.

'That tiny little island, covered in snow?'

'Where's your other heads?' smirked the little one, scanning Colin's shoulder for scars as he searched the dim recesses of his mind for any other Tasmanian jokes he might have heard.

'*I'm* actually English.'

'Pommy, eh? Touring the provinces. How the fuck did you end up in Gubba? Not much going on here, mate.' Colin pulled a cigar from his shirt and lit it, cool as a cucumber.

'We stopped on the way to our concert, which is further north.'

'No shit...you're in a band?' exclaimed Chris.

'I thought I saw them carrying some instruments upstairs,' muttered the little one.

'Sing us a song,' said Chris. 'Something we know.'

'We don't do covers, only originals,' said Michael, somewhat pompously.

'You mean you can't play a recognisable tune,' said the little one, scornfully. 'What's the use of being in a fucking band, then?'

'Esoteric reasons,' said Colin.

'Political reasons,' said Michael.

'Money, tits and cunt,' said Hayden.

'Hey, watch your language,' said the little one, then looked shiftily around. 'You get much? Cunt, I mean.'

'Not yet,' growled Hayden.

'Gah, what's the use of it then? Can't play a tune. Can't get any cunt. Eso-politi blah blah. *And* from bloody Tasmania. What the fuck did you want to wash up in Gubba for?'

'To film the locals,' said Michael, cheekily. 'I'll get the camera…I can interview you for our doco.'

'You got a film camera? No shit. Yeah, go get it mate, I'll tell you *all* about my sordid life.' He laughed nastily, amused by the idea.

Michael went upstairs to fetch it, while Hayden and Colin set up a game at the eight ball table. He needed to piss, but the toilet, amazingly, had tiny green frogs hopping around in it, so he pissed out the window instead.

On reaching the room, he found it locked.

'Who is it?'

'Me.'

'Just a minute.' Shifting of furniture. They ushered him in, cupboard and drawers as temporary barriers.

'Someone taped *this* to the door.' It was a note saying: *WATCH IT.*

'*Really* creepy and disturbing.'

'I'll take a look round.'

'No, please stay here.'

'We're scared.'

'It's just a note. Some drunken dingbat.' Nonetheless, he was happy to 'comfort' them, sliding cupboard against door again.

Every man's fantasy, two at once. Not so long ago he would have been ecstatic, gloating, but he had changed…all he could think about banging them was responsibility. What if one became pregnant? Condoms broke. What if he made *both* pregnant? He would marry them both. They would go to one of those camel countries Shiv was so fond of, and he would legally marry them, even if unrecognised in Oz. Could he be a strong enough husband for both? He could, was sure he could. The two could take care of childminding and homemaking duties, while he concentrated on his empire. And he would have a future son to pass it on to…

Lying postcoitally entangled they heard a loud and unexpected noise: sudden torrential rain. The barometer had been right. Come to think of it, the air had felt sticky. And now it had discharged, just as he had…a weird synchronicity. Cold rippled his back.

He dressed and went downstairs, hand in hand with both. In the white bar, everyone was looking out the door at the pelting rain. The flies had gone, and to his surprise, Colin and Hayden were being hailed as 'rain gods'. 'Bloody Tasmanians, you brought the weather with you. Good on youse!'

The desert people were ecstatic about the rain, and barely noticed Erica and Pamela as a result. Colin and Hayden had finished their game, and all returned to their room. A new message had been taped to the door: this one mentioned sacrificing the 'rain king', and ended with a fake quote:

Confucius say: he who piss out window should expect trouble.

Michael admitted to the mentioned act, and Hayden became incensed.

'Why're you causing trouble with the locals?'

But the girls explained about the first note.

'It seems we have a stalker,' said Colin thoughtfully. They searched the entire top floor, but found no one. All the other rooms appeared unoccupied. They went back to their roach-infested lair and rebarricaded the door. Hayden complained the room smelt like 'cheap sex', and an argument with

Michael ensued. When it finally settled down they took turns watching.

In the deep hours of the night, listening for scuffles outside, Michael wondered the same thing they were all wondering.

Where was Shiv?

24

AT THE CLINIC

There were wildflowers everywhere after the rain, including the Sturt's Desert Pea, which he recognised from his Junior Encyclopedia all those years ago. The place looked subtly different, a tender yet tough fecundity replacing the bone dry broodiness of yesterday. A small lake had formed in the wasteland at the end of the block which before the rain had been a salt flat. Michael wondered how far they were from Lake Eyre, which was technically Australia's largest lake but only filled briefly once a decade or so. He wished he had brought a map.

Shiv was still AWOL, but they soon found the mechanic's (attached to the petrol station) and paid a visit. It was already scorching hot at 9 a.m. As predicted, the van was undrivable. Not only the engine, but the brake discs were worn completely down and the rotors were scored - hundreds of dollars to replace out here. The engine itself, assuming they could find a compatible one, would be at least a grand, probably considerably more.

'Not worth it,' the mechanic said dismissively.

Hayden demanded to see the rotors, a pompous and useless act which only confirmed the mechanic was telling the truth.

'I don't make up lies, mate.'

'But how're we gonna hitchhike with all our gear?'

'There's a bus once a week. It left yesterday.'

'Do you know anyone who can give us a lift to Pine Gap, with a bunch of instruments and stuff?'

'Pine Gap? What you want to go there for? That's a Yank base. Aussies aren't allowed to set foot there, not even the prime minister.'

'We're doing a gig outside it,' explained Michael, 'and it has to be on the 9/9/99 because of the Ragnarokian symbolism of the number nine.' Hayden looked embarrassed.

'If you say so,' said the mechanic. 'But you're gonna get arrested playing there. They say there's an underground city there, built by the CIA in case of doomsday. Huge trucks go in and never come out again.'

'Yes, but how can *we* get there?'

'You'll have to hitch. Here's the cash for your wreck. Take it or leave it.' They accepted a hundred dollars and a receipt, having little choice. They turned to go, disappointed, but as they were walking away, he called to Michael.

'You the one who pissed out the window?'

Good grief…it seemed his casual act was known around the town.

'They say it brought the rain, but I think it's bloody disgusting. This is a decent place for the most part, so it's best you push off to Pine Gap or wherever you're going.'

'There's just a narrow lane outside, no one could possibly have seen me.'

'You were *seen*.' He said no more, retreating inside his workshop.

They turned to leave again, but a dog ran out of the workshop and began growling faintly. They ignored it, but it followed and tried to herd them. It looked part collie.

'Shoo off,' said Hayden, waving it away. Interpreting this as aggression the dog snapped at his hand.

'Ow, fuck it,' he yelled. 'You stupid mutt!' The mechanic emerged, whistled it indoors.

'Did he get you?'

'I'm bleeding.'

'Yeah, sorry mate…but you shouldn't of waved your hand in his face. I saw you out the window,' he added, as if expecting Hayden to deny it. 'You want to go to the Health Clinic for a tetanus jab, you do. It's down that way.'

They followed his pointing finger several blocks.

'Did he set the dog on us deliberately?'

'Was *he* the one who put the notes on the door?'

'Check the writing on the docket.'

'Looks different, but the note was in capitals.'

'I wouldn't put it past you to have written it yourself, Glendower, so you could get a sympathy shag from the spooky goth twins.'

'They're not twins, and don't talk about our only groupies like that. Have some respect.' The girls had stayed at the hotel, barricading the door again.

'We'd better go and see if they're all right,' said Colin.

'The clinic's just here,' said Hayden. 'Let me get my fucking finger bandaged first.' The modern-looking building housed the town's veterinary surgery as well, which shared a waiting room with the human clinic.

They sat down. There were several Aborigines in the waiting room. One, in an Essendon Bombers t-shirt, was talking about his various diseases, while a gin had what looked like herpes sores around her mouth. Across from her, an old white woman with a mangy dog sat glaring at them, and the dog began growling at Hayden.

'Dogs don't seem to like you,' said Colin, amused.

'I've got it on a *leash*,' rasped the woman, as if accused otherwise. '*And* you're dripping blood on the floor.' A well-forged axe of a nurse passed through and Hayden got her attention.

'Excuse me, I'm bleeding from a dog bite and I might need a tetanus shot.'

'Just wait a minute. Ross Olsen has flown in from Oodnadatta.'

An emergency patient, they assumed. But no, Ross Olsen turned out to be the local Member of Parliament who had turned up to tour the clinic. He hurried through, shaking the hands of the staff, but when it came to the patients he forebore, perhaps not wanting to come in contact with blood and herpes.

'The Liberal Party have as an utmost priority the creation of new opportunities for rural youth,' said the block-like visage, making a grand jabbing gesture at Michael. 'We're in the process of creating more jobs in this district, so these kind of, er…'

Michael was sure he was going to say 'layabouts' or 'scroungers', but he was through the soundproof door now, so it was anyone's guess.

A sudden bloodcurdling howl made everyone jump, even the placid Aborigines, who had been ignored completely by the MP.

'I've been bitten by a bloody *redback*,' screamed Hayden. 'Look!' He pointed a shaking finger at an untidy web in the crack between wall and the back of his fold-down seat. A black spider with a streak of red was disappearing from view.

The axe-nurse was back. She was displeased, and told him to wait.

'But it's a fucking *redback.*'

'Don't swear at me. No one's died from a redback bite in decades.'

'Yeah, because they got prompt medical treatment!'

'Just hold your horses, young man. Now what did you want to go and put your hand on a redback for?'

'I wasn't expecting it to be there, was I? This is supposed to be a clinic, why isn't it fumigated or something?' She chuckled sourly, as if having heard it all now, and left the room.

'It's all right, mate,' said the blackfeller with the transmissible illness. 'I been bit by one of those. Nasty little cunts. Just tip some grog on the bite…'

'Everything's going black,' whined Hayden, sounding genuinely frightened. Colin looked concerned, Michael pretended to look concerned…but the nurse reemerged with a packet of over-the-counter pain-relief tablets.

'He's jumping the queue,' complained the herpes female.

'Never mind, Kylie,' said the axe-nurse. 'You're in here so much, surely the rain god can go first for a change.'

Did the whole town know of their alleged rainmaking powers?

'Here's some codeine. We're not going to waste good antivenom unless you show symptoms of anaphylaxis. It's expensive. Now, we'll put you in the quiet room for observation while we get your tetanus jab ready. Did you know that your ears are full of wax? Disgusting! I'm surprised you can even hear anything. We'll have to syringe your ears out, too.'

'What?'

'Oh yes, I *love* syringing ears out. They call me Twisted Sister, you know.' She looked straight at Michael, and winked as she said it.

He felt a chill.

The school nurse at D'Entrecasteaux had said exactly the same thing.

Was it a standard joke for nurses, or *could it be the same nurse?*

She looked different, but memory can play tricks. Or had time gone backwards? He had noticed an ad on the wall for an 'indigenous film competition' in Melbourne. He double checked the date. 2000, described as 'next year'. He sighed with relief. For a minute he thought he was in some horrible time loop, like the Ladies of Versailles.

Perhaps he could enter the film competition himself, with the tour documentary? He would put some footage of the Gubba Gubba blacks in it, that would make it 'indigenous'. Hold on, he was born in Australia, and as Reg had never succeeded in making Tasmania an independent nation, then that made *him* indigenous. Just as indigenous as the black youth who now walked in the door, wearing a Cannibal Corpse t-shirt.

The youth sat next to him. To take his mind off Twisted Sister II, Michael made conversation based on the shirt even he disliked Cannibal Corpse.

'What's your favourite song, then, 'Hammer Smashed Face'?'

Everyone knew that one, thanks to Ace Ventura.

'Nah, that shit. 'Fucked With a Knife'…way better.'

All right. Silence.

'I'm an Odinist,' said Michael after a bit. 'That's the indigenous belief of *my* people, northern Europeans.' The youth glared at him.

'Nah,' he said, shaking his head vigorously. 'Bullshit.' A nurse called and he left the room, leaving the gin sweating and shaking her fist that again someone had been summoned before her.

Why had the youth been so hostile? Had his head been filled with shit by white leftists? Mistook Michael for a dreadlocked trendy claiming to be in touch with 'indigenous spirituality?' And yet *he* was using white culture like Cannibal Corpse to express his own brand of tribalism. The thought rankled Michael, indeed the black's dumb belligerence in the face of his confiding in him his innermost beliefs filled him with anger.

Another door opened, and an older, neatly-dressed Aborigine entered.

'G'day Kylie,' he said. 'Ready for the dance-off next week?' She muttered something. 'Hullo,' he said, taking a seat beside Michael. 'There's a big dance-off next week between our boys, the Morbid Angel Mob, and these Cannibal Corpse bastards. Even whites can watch it if they want.' Florida Death Metal, the shittiest music around, and these people had based a whole neo-tribalism around it! But the new arrival was better spoken and seemed more intelligent than the other blacks there, so Michael retreated from his anger and made conversation. It turned out the man, who called himself Mr. Magoo, and who was there getting his eyes checked, was an elder of the Morbid Angel Mob, based in a township some fifty kilometres away with a strict alcohol ban. The ban meant the blacks there were more orderly and prosperous than the Gubba ones, and Michael decided he would take the side of the Morbid Angel Mob for this reason, and also because they were a better band, even if they did promote Lovecraftian chaos demons. And wasn't David Vincent regarded as a suspect 'fascist' by the left? Okay, he would take *their* side.

After all, Londoners had the Death In June Mob and the Current 93 Boys, he snickered. Even whites were tribal...but Michael would lift them out of that, while retaining their positive differences...just as Abos might find 'unity within diversity' once the Cannibal Corpse boys laid off the drink.

Then a dream came back to him, received last night in the fitful sleep between watches. In it, scientists had received a broadcast from outer space, saying 'help me.' Michael, who did not worship science, spoke to them haughtily. Scientists, especially today, were technocrats, nothing more. Their arrogance would be curbed once he took power, he told them. They were slaves, already slaves...but under him would be made to realise and acknowledge it. Their function was to provide the (inferior) physical backdrop for the cosmic drama of the higher spiritual men, the men of the gods.

But they ignored his insults, and kept telling him excitedly about the alien contact. Computer analysis showed it was in Mudcambrian, the most ancient known language of mankind, hitherto conjectural only, like proto-Indo-European but far more ancient. The language was so guttural it sounded a lot like the vocals of Cannibal Corpse. What did this signify? Some ancient astronaut theory of the kind Anika had subscribed to, a race with interstellar tech who lost it in the Flood...or something more profound...the white man's burden? Couldn't he be rid of the Mudcambrians and flee into the shimmering rainbow vacuum of space? Or did he have to sort their problems out first? Weird he had had the dream before even learning of the Cannibal Corpse Boys' existence.

'You're the rain makers, aren't you?' said Mr. Magoo. 'Noah's Ark landed here once, you know. This used to be the seaside. They've found fossils of sharks near here. You heard of Atlantis? It was an island that sank, but Gubba Gubba's the opposite...it's the bottom of the sea that rose up.'

'Could it be a remnant of Mu?' said Colin.

'Say what?'

'Mu, the lost continent of the Pacific.'

Kylie, the herpes gin, thought this was hilarious, as it sounded like a cow. 'Mu, Mu…MUUUU!' she bellowed, screaming with laughter. Mr. Magoo said something in her own language and she simmered down with a snort.

'You don't speak our language too good Mr. Magoo,' she said in English. 'You too flash for us, with your studio and car.' She gave him the finger.

'It's true I've got a dot-painting studio,' he turned to Michael. 'It's a money making scam. Rich whites can't get enough of it. They use it to show off their status. Weird, huh?'

'I thought the dots had some spiritual significance, or showed hunting grounds and water holes and whatnot.'

'Maybe once. Now it's just a bunch of dots. We churn them out, make plenty of money. Oh yes, Morbid Angel Mob is *much* better dressed than Cannibal Corpse Boys. But rich whites wouldn't come out here and see real Aborigines.'

'I like Albert Namatjira,' said Michael, truthfully.

'Who?'

Just then the door to the clinic swung open, and they could hear Prince's '1999' on the radio. Michael realised with a sudden chill that it *was* 1999, they had a gig they were meant to get to, and the world might end.

He could hear Hayden arguing loudly with Twisted Sister II. Apparently he doesn't want to be injected in the arse.

'I wonder where Shiv is?' he said out loud.

'He's in there,' said Mr. Magoo, pointing to another door. There sure were a lot of doors coming off the waiting room.

'Eh? You mean he's *here?*' said Colin.

'Yeah…I thought you were here to see him. He had a bit too much to drink with the Cannibal Corpse boys last night, ha ha.'

Just then a nurse walk in with a man in a shirt and tie, and they entered the door where Shiv was said to be.

'The coroner's here,' she called to someone inside. Michael and Colin rose, alarmed, and raced in.

'Don't worry, he's here for Jimmy from the CC Boys,' said Mr. Magoo, but they didn't heed him. They looked in the rooms coming off the corridor until they found Shiv, lying on a white bed with a drip in his arm. He looked at them weakly.

'Metho poisoning,' he said faintly. 'Someone spiked my fucking drink.'

'Will you recover?' asked Michael. 'We've got a gig to play.'

'They put me on some machine that cleaned my blood and put it back in me, or something. Now I've got to stay here for a bit with this thing in my arm til the blurred vision and stomach pain stops. It's lucky they had the machine here. The Cannibal Corpse Boys need it from time to time.'

'You know the CC Boys, then.'

'They're mates, or they were til one of them spiked me drink. I suppose they thought I'd like it. Watch out for the Morbid Angel Mob though, they're a real bad lot apparently. Uncle Toms or something.'

Here Michael felt superior. 'No, they're actually the better of the two mobs. Their township is dry, so they can string a sentence together.'

'Yeah?' Shiv was too weak to argue.

'Hayden's been through the wars. A dog bit him, then a poisonous spider.'

'No shit. God's sign he doesn't belong in the band.'

'But he's suffered for us. Isn't that a sign that he *does* belong?'

Shiv was about to answer when the local Liberal member flounced in, bustling with import. Desiccated, dephlogisticated, he reminded Michael strongly of Clive.

'Ah, the musicians from out of town,' he said. 'I've just been hearing about your shenanigans. I doubt the people of Gubba Gubba welcome it very much.'

Shiv laughed, and began to sing softly 'Kill the *Parties* like it's 1999', then changed 'parties' to 'pollies'.

'So…terrorists,' sneered the MP.

'I'm a Christian Anarchist, Michael's a Pagan Imperialist or something, and Colin's an esoteric pommy cunt. So fuck off, you old fart.'

Olsen barged out with a patronising laugh.

'Why do you hate him?' said one of the nurses. 'He's not a

bad old stick, really.' Shiv began to lecture her about globalism, how it disrupted and distorted the various God-given energy currents in the world.

Then Twisted Sister II came in, looking sombre for a change.

Hayden was pissing blood, and the Royal Flying Doctors were airlifting him promptly to Adelaide.

Shiv dragged himself out of bed, and soon they stood on the baked fly-blasted airstrip watching Hayden being bundled into the plane. Their drummer gone, they would be a three-piece for the 9/9/99. Although it seemed to fit numerically, without the percussion to give them the link they needed to the earth one of the four classical elements would be missing.

'Bye,' said Michael, raising his hand.

'Don't pretend you *like* me, Glendower.' Hayden was wild-eyed and angry.

'You were our drummer. At least for a while. So I honour you for that.' He felt he'd grown enough to say that, at least.

And Pamela and Erika were going, too.

Pamela already seemed distant to him. They had done their duty as groupies to a failed band, and little more could be expected of them. Loyalty beyond that was not for earthly women, only supernatural ones like Sylvie. And even then...

He could hear Shiv talking to one of the Flying Doctors, asking if another plane could be wrangled to lift them to Pine Gap with their equipment, describing it as a 'spiritual emergency,' and rebuffed with amused certitude. But what would happen to Hayden's drum kit? It was dead weight now.

The plane door was shut, and Michael banged on the hatch, but an airport employee shook his head and herded them towards the tin hut that passed for a terminal.

The plane began to taxi.

In the terminal the clinic nurse who had escorted Hayden stood smoking thoughtfully.

'Are you Michael?'

'Yeah.'

'The head nurse told me to tell you she thinks you have Asperger syndrome. She thinks you should get checked out by a psychiatrist next time you're in a city.' Twisted Sister II...still causing trouble, even when she wasn't around. He almost suspected she had *made* Hayden piss blood somehow, part of a plan to take the band out one by one, Gubba's revenge for having peed out their precious window. What the hell was Asperger syndrome, anyway?

His thoughts returned to the themed album he was planning based on *Hamlet's Mill*, which he had only glanced through (reading time on this tour being far less than he had hoped), but which perhaps revealed the secret meaning of The Thresher. The Thresher was the cycle of the Great Year, the Precession of the Equinoxes, of which classical paganism (Aries) and Christianity (Pisces) formed only parts, as did the looming Aquarian era. This was the secret meaning of his and Shiv's differing religious views, both of which would be subsumed and transcended in the coming age by a new current, perhaps represented by Colin. Was Colin a bearer of water? *Or did this refer to the Grail?*

Shiv was sceptical about all this. For him The Thresher was about separating the wheat from the chaff, that was its mission, not an endless cosmic cycle (though he didn't disbelieve in astrology, he wasn't terribly interested in it). He also hated the idea of a concept album, which reminded him of '70s prog rock bands he hated (or was officially supposed to hate as a punk, Michael thought cynically). But Michael remembered King Diamond's *Abigail*, *Them* and *Conspiracy*, which he liked despite their cheesiness. They were heartfelt...as would be The Thresher's debut album, *Hamlet's Mill*, which would crush everything preceding it.

*   *   *

Shiv had received interesting information from one of the Flying Doctors, viz that there was an immigration detention centre a kilometre out of town. They walked there in heat and flies of late afternoon with camera, guitars and floor tom from Hayden's kit. They would play outside the camp as provocation, to curse NWO multicult *and* war, and to give reffos the gift of music.

And in exchange for hearing the mighty Thresher, they would agree to go back when the wars in their countries (if wars there were) were finished. Sans keyboard power, Michael filmed again.

They weren't the only ones filming, either. A busload of Japanese tourists, who seemed to have taken a wrong turn, were busy taking footage of what they thought was a standard Australian prison. A refugee stared sullenly out at them from the razor wire-topped exercise yard.

One of the Japanese handed Michael a disposable camera, asking if he could take his photo with the refugee in the background. He introduced himself as Hikaru Shibuya, intelligent and contented. He liked Western literature he told Michael proudly…Dostoevsky and Tolstoy.

'Yukio Mishima?'

'Ah, no. I don't like Mishima Yukio,' he muttered, a frown of distaste momentarily indenting his contented brow.

'C'mon, where's your samurai spirit?' said Michael cheekily. Namatjira, Mishima, Hamas…what the hell was wrong with these non-whites, he wondered. The white boys of The Thresher mob appreciated their own culture-heroes better than they did.

'What if the millennium bug causes a collapse?' said Michael. 'Then you have to go back to samurai lifestyle, warring clans, right?'

'There won't be any collapse,' said Hikaru, very sure of himself. 'Hydrogen fuel-cell technology…probably already developed…use hydrogen from natural gas to make electricity and water vapour.'

'Water vapour means more clouds. Could lead to a new Ice Age.'

Shiv walked over to them. 'Can you do taiko drumming?' he asked Hikaru.

'Ah.' He shook his head.

'Just a simple 4/4 rhythm then.'

'Sorry?'

Shiv imitated the beat.

'I try,' he smiled obligingly. Shiv handed him the floor tom.

Just then a somewhat battered Holden Commodore pulled in. It was Mr. Magoo and another Aboriginal who went by the nickname Tuxedo, although he was wearing a t-shirt and shorts. He seemed more aggressive than Mr. Magoo, but in a laid-back kind of way. They were on the way back to the township, having finished their business in Gubba.

'What are youse doing here?' said Tuxedo. 'This is the bloody reffo camp. Full of no-hopers. Go back where you came from,' he yelled to the man of Middle Eastern appearance, who was still glaring at them.

'C'mon now,' said Shiv.

'Hey, you like that redhead sheila?' said Tuxedo. 'I like *her*, she wants to get rid of them Asians.' He made a slanty-eyed gesture, which Michael found embarrassing. But if their new drummer Hikaru understood what was meant by the gesture (Michael had heard Asians didn't think of themselves as having slant eyes, and Hikaru's weren't particularly scanty in any case), he didn't show it. But this was 1999, not 1997, and One Nation were in the process of tearing themselves apart, to the delight of their many enemies.

Tuxedo wasn't their only Aboriginal supporter, of course. A blackfeller called Ron Holten was standing as One Nation candidate for Wyong, in New South Wales. He had been quoted in the rural press (the *only* free press) as saying: 'We Aborigines have developed a terrible name for hypocrisy by claiming land which we say is holy and essential to our spiritual well-being and then flogging it off to developers like second hand car dealers as soon as we get it.

'Not one of the people on the Darkinjung Land Council is a genuine tribal member of this area. They are all outsiders and they have the audacity to turn me out, the only genuine

285

tribal member of the area amongst them, simply because I believe in fairness being the only road to true unification of all Australian people.' Michael appreciated his honesty, but thought Tuxedo impolite.

'Hey,' yelled Shiv suddenly to the refugee over the fence. 'Where you from?'

'Ramallah...in Palestine.'

'What the fuck are you doing here? Shouldn't you be fighting for Hamas? Kick the Zionists out of your homeland, you useless cunt.' The Palestinian's eyes widened in surprised outrage. He had never been spoken to so rudely, not even by a Jew.

'No, I stay here...drive taxi in Sydney,' he sneered. He was cold, fast-talking, a stare that took many things in. But while Shiv was trying to hie him on to fight for his motherland, another car pulled up. This time it was a carload of protestors with Victorian plates, including a fair-skinned 'Aboriginal' woman with blonde dreadlocks. There were two other whites, a chubby male and a hard-faced female. The local cop pulled in right behind them, presumably monitoring the protest. Quiet, inscrutable, but looked like he meant business.

'It's the rainmakers,' he muttered. 'What are you lot doing here?'

'Hey you...you can film *us*,' the blonde with the black power t-shirt said to Michael.

'All right,' he snickered, sticking the camera in the face of her chubby compatriot.

'So, what are you doing here in the desert?'

'Protesting the Howard government's heartless and barbaric immigration policies,' the hatchet-faced female answered for him.

'But this is economic migration. He wants to be a taxi driver in Sydney,' Michael said, gesturing at the Arab, who continued to glare at them. The chubby one smirked into the camera, an all-knowing smirk that Michael got the impression he practiced a lot, while hatchet-face merely rolled her eyes, muttering, 'Oh God, it's the local rednecks come to gawk at refugees. They're even filming them. Hey, boy,' she said to Michael in a loud, slow voice as if he were thick. 'They have a right to live wherever they want, yeah? Borders are for *fascists*.' Now it was Michael's turn to smirk. But she had turned away, was inspecting the fence and ignoring the glaring Arab, while chubby continued to smirk.

The Japanese tourists were very interested in all this. They seemed to think it some kind of open air kabuki theatre. But Hikaru wasn't so sure.

'*You*, a blackfeller?' Mr. Magoo said sceptically to the blonde one. 'Don't look like one!'

Tuxedo laughed. She gave an angry speech at them, which sounded well rehearsed.

'I couldn't go to school for years because they teased me for being a 'dirty boonger'. I've identified as indigenous since my early teens. *No one* can take my identity away.'

'People, people,' said Shiv calmly. 'All your problems are due to the enforced multiculturalism of the corporate New World Order. Please allow The Thresher to offer a riposte to its assaults on our God-given right to live as free peoples in communities of our choosing.'

He and Colin launched into an acoustic version of 'Fuck the New World Order - Smash It and Destroy It!'

The blacks listened in respectful silence, while Michael heard the 'white Abo' from Melbourne saying to her friends 'Unbelievable...as if a crappy punk song is going to do anything to solve the refugee crisis.' The chubby one's smirk raised up a notch.

On finishing, Tuxedo and Magoo clapped politely, as did all the Japanese tourists, and even the silent cop. The Melbournites, however, had stalked off in a huff to explore around the perimeter of the camp.

'That's quite a good music you got there,' said Mr. Magoo. 'Tell you what, we'll initiate you into the Morbid Angel Mob. Hey, maybe we change our name to The Thresher Boys!'

He initiated Colin and Shiv by hugging them and patting them on the back. Michael was disappointed and a little bit hurt that they didn't consider him part of the band. A faint bitterness welled up in him, partly at Shiv's hypocrisy, for hadn't he told Michael that Abos weren't really capable of following Christ, they just paid him lip service for the imagined reward of heaven? Michael had replied that most white Christians were like that, too. Shiv said the Abos were pagan like Michael, earthbound, trapped in the earth energy not transcending it; Michael had patiently (for him) explained that Odin was transcendent, not earthbound. Would Sylvie have liked the Abos because they were earthbound? But they had made the megafauna extinct, and their forest-burning hunting practices turned once lush Gondwanan Australia into the arid land it was.

'You boys wanna come and play some tunes at Utnapishtim?'

Utnapishtim, named for the Sumerian prototype of Noah, had once been a Lutheran mission station called Wilhelmina. It was an hour and a half up a dirt road, past an abandoned uranium mine.

'Can you fit our cameraman and drummer in the car?' *Cameraman.* Michael ignored the insult. The drummer, it seemed, was Hikaru, who hadn't touched the drum at all during the recent song.

'Yeah, no worries.'

Hikaru seemed resigned to being part of the band, and put up no protest, but giving a polite farewell to the other tourists, saying he would meet them at Alice Springs, and make his own way there.

The Abos seemed a bit nonplussed to have an Asian in the car, but made room for him.

Michael was pleased to see there was a spare can of petrol in the back.

'I s'pose you think we're gonna sniff it?' said Tuxedo mock-fiercely, and they all laughed at the joke.

'Some white do-gooder from Canberra's been snooping around lately, trying to get the alcohol ban lifted. He waltz in with a band new ute, number plate says 'BUGGER' like the ad. Fucking idiot. Then we end up like the Cannibal Corpse Boys. Bunch of fools.'

Michael noticed a tape of Morbid Angel's *Covenant* on the floor, which must have come from Adelaide. But instead of metal, Mr. Magoo put on a tape of Kevin 'Bloody' Wilson's 'Living Next Door to Alan', which took him back to his scoutmaster's Troopy. Ah, the '80s. So innocent compared to today. But dark, too…there was the Nothing creature. Could that even exist today? Certainly not here in the desert, in bright Nineties now-time. He thought that even the sun seemed a different colour to how he remembered it from childhood.

It was setting now, however, a desert sunset which seemed to suck the breath out of his body. Like the sky was a giant, dirty eyelid, and the specks behind it a flock of black cockatoos in the merciless distance.

'You wouldn't be able take us as far as Pine Gap, after the gig, with our equipment and all?' asked Shiv. 'We can give you petrol money.'

'Pine Gap…that's up near Alice Springs…no way this car'll make it that far. Too shaky.'

They passed a new-looking sign saying 'Total alcohol ban, $100,000 fine for supplying,' or something to that effect. Kevin 'Bloody' Wilson finished his piece, and just as the sun went down for good June Christy began singing 'Midnight Sun'. It made the hairs on the back of Michael's neck stand up.

And then…they saw them.

Pale lights on the horizon, like pallid discs.

They wove in and out separately, but with unified form, like a swarm of insects. They came closer, and seemed to hover, as if watching their progress. Michael's stomach somersaulted.

'Are those like the ones you saw in Burnie?'

'No…they were big, and in the sky. These are small and stick near the ground. And they're not vehicles.'

'Min Min lights…'

'Are they…?'

'Could be CIA activity…experimental weapons…'

'No, it's the spirits of the dead,' said Mr. Magoo. 'Don't bloody go near them.'

*　　*　　*

The lights followed them for a bit, then disappeared. A few minutes later, the car broke down. Michael could almost have predicted it. The Thresher Mark II was having its revenge for having failed to salvage it, for vehicles and this band didn't mix.

'I know where we are,' said Mr. Magoo. 'Right near the old uranium mine. About halfway between Gubba and Utnapishtim.'

'How far to either town?'

About 60 kilometres, as it turned out.

'Long bloody walk.'

25

THE DESERT ENCROACHES

'Don't fall into the mine pit,' they warned before leaving.

The Thresher had decided to return to Gubba Gubba, while the blacks, who knew their way blindly in the dark, headed for Utnapishtim. It looked like the gig wasn't to be. 'You better off walking in the night. From Tassie, can't take the heat.'

Shiv nodded, and they divided the water up, one two litre bottle for the blacks and one for them. They parted, shaking hands, Abo hands limp, like dead fish.

Before leaving they looked around the ruins of abandoned mine buildings. Much of it had been demolished, the only fully intact building looked like it had been a canteen for the workers. The others were reduced to posts and piles of brick, foundation slabs.

Night fell quickly, moonless and starless, and they could see virtually nothing. Was it going to rain again? The decision was taken, reluctantly, not to walk in case they get lost, as the road was barely distinguishable from the barren country around them. They would walk at very first light, before it got too hot. They were uneasy about spending the night in a possibly radioactive environment, and wished they had asked Mr. Magoo before he left whether it was safe.

'Hiroshima,' said Shiv somewhat patronisingly to Hikaru, who muttered something darkly.

It was cold, though not freezing, and they curled up like

possums in a corner of the old canteen, shivering themselves to sleep. It took Michael ages to nod off, and when finally on the threshold he realised with alarm that someone was walking among the ruined buildings.

'You guys all here?' he whispered. Hikaru said 'Yes,' and Colin muttered 'Go to sleep.' Shiv was snoring loudly.

'Someone's walking around outside.'

'Just an emu, probably. No one'd be hanging out in an old uranium mine. We're the only ones stupid enough...'

But it sounded like human feet. Was it Sylvie? Michael hadn't thought about her for a long time. He remembered the comments in her journal about uranium miners contaminating the blood of the earth. Was mining really contamination? What if it was used for *transcending* the earth? The earth, he thought, was a puzzle game like 'Space Quest' he had played at Adam's house, there being only a finite amount of certain resources, just enough to get *off* the planet and tap the potential of other worlds (limitless...or would there be puzzles there too?). In which case, wasting lanthanides etc. on decadent entertainment needs *was* earth-rape. But using it for space travel was different - like marrying the woman, and sublimating her into something greater, breeding herits. A large moth landed on his face. He kept still, letting it crawl there, and passed shivering into sleep quick as the desert dark.

*   *   *

When they woke it already full light, warm. The flies were active. A panicked feeling. They began to walk immediately.

The clouds of the night had gone, and they looked briefly down into the mine's huge pit. The water at the bottom from the recent rain was bright blue. They didn't dare drink their own water and bottle the blue, for fear it was radioactive.

'Let's go,' growled Shiv. 'We walk *fast*, before the sun gets too fierce.'

They power-walked out of there, past the abandoned car and down the long dusty unsealed road. Hopefully a car would pick them, but they couldn't rely on it.

It was the tail end of the cooler season in this part of the desert, transitioning into the hot (outback Australia has only the two seasons). After an hour's walking whereby they had covered perhaps one tenth the distance, it began to be uncomfortably torrid.

Soon the heat and sweat were become an ocean, glugging him down, arresting every attempt at transcendence. Northern European in his DNA, what was he doing here among flies and oceans of red sweat? What the fuck was winter, just a dream of crystal lattice, faint, deprived of being, imagination couldn't hold it. Suck it, Immortal…Nordic winterstorms would be a pleasant gentle breeze by comparison.

It had rained recently, and wildflowers were blooming, but there was no visible water, and if there was it would probably be salt. Why hadn't they walked at night like the blacks? They could have felt their way along the skirt of the road, perhaps their eyes would have adjusted…

They stopped for a sip of water each, but it wasn't enough. The others were looking as shaky as Michael felt.

Even Hikaru seemed tottery, but he didn't complain, just plodded along saying nothing. All part of the tourist experience.

After a while they noticed a large bird tailing them to the left. They thought it was an emu, but as it came closer they could clearly see it was an ostrich. Michael had heard of feral populations, and this must be one of them. It was huge - emus might be tall, but the ostrich was three metres if it was an inch. It tailed them a while, until they stopped for a short rest in the shelter of some small boulders, then walked right up to them. Somewhat understandably, they backed away. Its body language looked aggressive to them in their weakened state, though perhaps it was just inquisitive.

'You have ostrich in Australia? I didn't know that,' said Hikaru.

'Imported from Africa…must have escaped from an ostrich farm,' said Colin. He was backing away, as the enormous bird appeared to have developed a fascination for him. He was backing away, as the enormous creature appeared to have developed a fascination for him. It beaded around, fixed on him like his head was a lost egg. It began to herd him through the rocks.

'Must think you're a relative of his,' chuckled Shiv, but his laughter was cut short by a bestial roar from Colin. They rushed to see what was wrong. They saw the ostrich disappearing through the crevice between the boulders, and Colin nowhere, a hole between the rocks leading to darkness. Then they heard his voice.

'I think I've broken my leg.'

'Where are you?'

'Down here. It's some kind of abandoned mineshaft. Not uranium, I hope.'

They stared into the dark oubliette but couldn't see him, though could hear him quite clearly.

'Can you climb out?'

'My leg…AHHHHH…no, I can't move it, it hurts too much.'

'You'll have to stay down there while we get help. Someone from Gubba'll drive out. At least you're out of the sun.'

'Yeah. But try and get back before nightfall.'

'Will do…'

'Someone has put a curse on this band,' said Michael to Hikaru. 'Are you sure you want to drum for us?' Hikaru's eyes widened slightly, but he nodded.

'Don't be so negative, Michael,' said Shiv. 'Adversity strengthens. All right, we should get going, we'll see you soon,' he called to Colin.

'Hang in there,' added Michael feebly.

'Okay…good luck then. Cheerio.' Cheerio was the last word they ever heard him speak.

*   *   *

A little down the road they heard a welcome sound - an engine. Sure enough, a white Hilux was coming from the direction of Utnapishtim, slowing in billows of dust, clearly about to stop. Mr. Magoo must have told someone of their plight. As the car slowed to walking speed, they could see clearly the plate saying 'BUGGER'. It must be the do-gooder who was trying to get the alcohol ban lifted. Still, any lift was welcome, even this sallow and humourless looking man.

But to their amazement, when he had had a good gawk at them, he sped up again, headed in a hurry for Gubba. They swore and yelled and shook their fists at him.

'Fucking un-Australian prick!' bellowed Shiv.

Even the stoic Hikaru seemed angry.

*   *   *

Sunburn. Feet blistered, bleeding. Utnapishtim and the plant of immortality…desert becomes the sea floor, mother of mountains. But they were headed wrongly. Shirts round their heads, they had drunk the last drop of water.

'Maybe we should stop.'

Slurred speech.

'Colin. Anyway, can't stop without shelter. Might be more boulders ahead. Something on the horizon there, I think.'

'Boulders back *there*. Wait til night.'

'No point. We're probably over halfway.'

'I don't want to die yet…too much to achieve.'

'You've achieved much already, with The Thresher. Your songs are good. I couldn't have done it without you.' Not long ago Michael would have been honoured by this praise from Shiv, but now his mind was fixed on other plans, plans involving Gesamtkunstwerk.

Please, Wotan, take the ostrich and not me. If freed from

the desert I will prove I don't have a desert within...I will become an artist-tyrant, stamping my will on millennia...

In the harshness of the desert, he even prayed to Anika, then hated himself for it.

Sylvie's face appeared (he hadn't been able to remember what it looked like for ages), and that felt calmer, more wholesome, but she too was aloof to him ultimately...was he shut out of the universe forever? Was he the West in miniature? Ha. Cocky little bastard.

He saw another face too, though...Sally Hemingway. He should have gone with her, but...

Did women even understand what they meant to men? His mother, matter. Anika, energy. Sylvie was spirit. Men could reason, but reason was just a means for the end that emotion wills (yet it took reason to reach that conclusion, he thought wryly). Lower animals were hermaphroditic or female dominant; from the 'viewpoint' of evolution male dominance was a 'recent' thing, so it must be intended by nature and the gods as part of the process of differentiation. Women were like cows or dogs, but men were dead fish and must learn to become Water Bearers...grail bearers. The Grail! It hit him in a flash. The age-old chalice was the key to what was coming. Could the quest for it unite his beliefs with Shiv's?

His head was spinning, throbbing from the heat. Hikaru was singing drunkenly.

'We *will* suffer for this band, Michael,' Shiv had once prophesied. 'But it will bring great things.'

Michael shuddered. He licked the sweat off his arms for hydration, and marched up to Shiv.

'I want to understand your beliefs.'

Shiv glanced at him, aloof as if carrying a great weight. Michael began to reel off a list of internal contradictions in the Bible he had found on a website back in Hobart.

The logic assault failed, it broke upon the rock that was Shiv.

'Maybe we should disband the group if my faith bothers you so much.'

'It doesn't bother me. Like I said, I want to understand it.'

'Stop trying. You can only understand it if you stop trying.'

'Disband the group. Are you crazy? After all this?'

'Everything has to die. Everything shall be born anew.' Was Shiv serious? The Thresher had begun life as a skateboard, morphed into a zine, and would now die here, in the Australian desert. Had it served its purpose? What *was* its purpose? He felt sad.

In the distance, he seemed to see the Nothing creature from scout camp as a child…but it was changed somehow, made smaller. He laughed sadly as it tottered. He grew angry with it, it tottered again. Then, sadness fuelled a deeper anger - and it disappeared. Such a funny creature, he thought blithely, giddy with heat.

'Truth or dare time,' rasped Shiv.

'Truth,' Michael croaked. 'Always truth.'

'What do you really *want* from this band? And do you really want to *be* in this band?'

'What do I want to convey with my art?' The Nothing, beaten by sadness tinged with anger. 'I want a Gesamtkunstwerk, with me in complete control. At least my success or failure will be on a grander scale.'

'So, now it all comes out…'

'You just want to rebel, Shiv. You're a rebel. But where does rebellion end?'

'We *have* to rebel. It's religious duty. The system will turn us into bar-coded slaves. The mark of the beast.'

'Do you really believe that?'

'You *know* it's true.'

Shiv wanted his fans to fight, but Michael wanted to install them with vision of the deep past linked to the far future, a continuum, an everywhen, something like what the blacks called 'dreamtime', but the white man's dreaming - the white man's dance.

When a conflict is repressed, it reappears externally. If they repressed this conflict within the band it would damage the world at large. No, they had no choice but to disband

The Thresher…or Michael, at least, must leave, leaving Shiv with the rights to the songs he had already written.

But a god can seize hold of the ego and compel it to act as the god wills.

The sun is the centre of the wheel, the millstone - it *grinds* the grain that is *threshed*. Is it enough? They would die if not. Hamlet's *mill* wasn't a thresher.

John Barleycorn was crushed to death, John Barleycorn gained life.

Rejuvenation through change, fish into cup.

New, weird lights on the horizon. Like the ones last night, but their colour had changed purple. Was it day or night? Michael couldn't tell.

'Min Mins,' breathed Shiv. So he could see them, too. Ghostly luminance of the Australian outback. Michael wanted to film them, but realised he had left the camera in the car. He cursed silently, then stared in wonder.

The grail was a disc. The discs resolved into one. It wobbled, sliced through the Nothing, and dispersed the Nothing.

Michael slipped into a fertile blackness that was Something.

26

THE WHITE MAN'S DANCE

He woke in agony, having dreamt of someone speaking through a megaphone. To his bewildered consternation there was a drip in his arm. *Where was he?* Some kind of hospital room. Looked familiar. Then it kicked home - it was the room where Shiv had been, in fact the very same bed. The politician would come waffling in at any moment. But why had he and Shiv changed places? The desert, the heat, losing consciousness. What had happened? He had been found, evidently…but his innards had been scoured with sandpaper. And what had happened to Colin?

The megaphone from his dream came back, now seemingly real. To his incredulity it was Shiv's voice, speaking words of anger. Someone had caused two deaths by his actions. Michael hoped it wasn't himself, he would hate Shiv to be angry at *him*…but then he remembered, almost with a sense of relief, the man who had refused them a lift in his Hilux. His own anger rose. Could it be true, what Shiv was bellowing through the megaphone (where had he gotten a megaphone?)…that the mineshaft had fallen in, burying Colin alive? Had Colin been trying to get out? If that bastard had given them a lift…

But whose was the second death? Shiv's ranting gradually revealed that Hikaru would never be returning to his native Japan…had died of dehydration. Michael felt sadness, impersonal as the risen moon. He had barely known their temporary drummer, but his enthusiasm, not phlegmatic by any means, but stemming perhaps from an inner knowledge he was serving a high and worthy cause, had been most admirable. But Colin…how much esoteric knowledge and wisdom had perished from the world with *his* passing?

Colin had been their near-silent mentor, the elder Silenus entrusted with focussing their energies, the glue binding the otherwise divergent poles of the band together. Without him, Michael and Shiv would surely go in separate directions. In this too, a great wave of sadness churned…but suffused with anger, rage that a little man, a *very* little man, a bureaucrat, could have the power to bring the mightiest band that had ever existed to its knees. One man, one solitary man…in an air-conditioned dual-cab Hilux that could seat five or six. Sadness and anger fused, and he entered Thresher Consciousness. Whatever he did now, whatever his artistic endeavours, his ultimate direction would be the erasure of people like that little man from the earth.

Now Shiv was trying to rally the wallabies, like St. Francis. Brother Roo, he asked of them, should this vagabond me fight? It must have answered in the affirmative, for Shiv roared a challenge at the bureaucrat, apparently skulking in the building Shiv stood outside of. Perhaps the townspeople were now asking questions, because Shiv was reiterating his case against the sly-grog lefty. He could hear murmurings that built gradually until they became a fuzzy sea of community spirit, mateship, sincere for at least a minute. In short, the crowd were taking Shiv's side.

Some drunk yelling: 'Where *is* the bastard?'

An Aboriginal voice, presumably one of the Cannibal Corpse boys, members of a drinking tribe at odds with the one into which Shiv had been initiated, saying: 'I'll help you, bro! I'll fight the cunt!'

'This is *my* fight,' said Shiv calmly through the megaphone. 'Nothing less than single combat sufficeth.'

A new voice came to the fore.

'Let go, you have no right. I've phoned the police. They'll be here any minute.' It seemed he was being frogmarched up to Shiv.

'No cops in town,' yelled someone. 'They're investigating two tourist deaths.'

'Which *you* caused,' yelled someone else.

'What are you *talking* about?'

'You didn't give 'em a lift, ya cunt.'

'You saw 'em in the desert miles from nowhere. Why didn't you stop?'

'If you mean those people yesterday, they didn't *ask* for a lift. I figured they had transport of their own.'

'They were waving you down!'

'Form a circle,' instructed Shiv, and the pleasant laughter indicated it was done. Michael wouldn't want to be the social worker or whatever he was for anything. Not even for getting Anika back.

'Fuck that whore,' he growled, knowing in any case that he must help Shiv. He would like to get a punch in, at the very least. He had the right. He might not be a member of The Thresher Boys, a place Shiv was that he couldn't touch, but he was still a member of The Thresher; for a time, at least. And that was better.

He pulled the drip and tape from his arm and rose from the bed, despite the pain in his innards.

'Where on earth do you think *you're* going? It was Twisted Sister II, barring his way, putting meat-slab arms on his shoulders, steering him back to the bed. He wasn't having it, he was going to help his comrade. Next thing he knew she was wrestling him to the ground, riding him like a wild bull as he strained to get up.

'Help,' she called loudly, but he was the injured party. She had put his back out with her immense weight. He tried to throw her off but she was strong. After all the weights and push-ups - to be beaten by a woman. It was too much. He arched with all his might, ignoring the pain in his back, and threw her to the side. She gave a scream as he rose panting to his feet and again headed for the door. But three more nurses entered, including a male one with a face like a fire hydrant, followed by two curious Abos of either sex.

'Give us a hand,' said the male nurse to the male Abo, who nodded. Michael tried to dive to the side of them, but was tackled, more Aussie Rules than rugby, as would have been expected in this neck of the woods. They dragged him, kicking and screaming to the bed, and pinned him to it. He could feel the Abo's alcoholic breath on his face, and wondered why this Cannibal Corpse Boy was against him, when he had heard them helping Shiv.

'Florida Death Metal sucks,' he growled, spitting in the Abo's face.

'Hey, fuck off,' said the Abo and took his hands away to wipe his face. His arm free, he shoved the female nurse on his other arm so she staggered back.

Quick as a flash he tried to wrench his legs loose. But he had reckoned without Twisted Sister II who had been in another room fetching restraints. One of his legs was tied to the bed post, then the two males helped Twisted Sister II grab his right arm and tie it down as well. Then they tied his other arm. After berating him they left the room, but they had made a great big dirty mistake in leaving his other leg loose.

He managed to flip around and heft the entire bed on his back like a hobbling tortoise.

Its light metal clanked against the door as he tried to drag it through sideways, and they came running again.

'This is what these Asperger's cases can be like,' Twisted Sister II lectured them. 'Won't take no for an answer.' They marched the bed with him on it back to its original position. The others held it down, smirking, while she went out for something. A fourth restraint, thought Michael, but no, it was a needle. Shit. He struggled for his life as they injected him with who knew what. After a few minutes he went confused, weak, floppy. His vision became like an old television set, like his parents' old one with its dial for the channels. Static filled the edges, then nothing. The light hurt his eyes. They left him there, presumably to die.

He could hear the man who had refused them a lift pleading with someone, probably an Abo, as there was an 'after all I've done for you' quality to it. Apparently one of them wanted to spear him - but another had come round again, taking his side, trying to placate Shiv. A pair of Cannibal Corpse banderilleros.

It seemed a ring had formed around Shiv and his opponent, and Shiv was waiting for some unknown sign before the fight could begin. Michael had 'Miracle of Love' by the Eurythmics in his head, inexplicably. He thought of Anika again and felt pity. He could feel nothing for the man who had left them stranded, however. It was something in the quality of his voice. Something smug and unctuous about it, even in fear. It reminded him of Clive. He tried to pity his mother, too, but couldn't. He wished he could see out the window, wished he could film the fight. Wished he could film anything. His vision was blurred now, and perfect. His films would not be seen through the harsh light of day ('the desert encroaches') but would start from within, from the fertile flickering womb of the unconscious, and the desert would be *colonised*. The waste would flower again. He would redeem all of them, redeem everything. All with his camera. He just needed to get it. He must bide his time until the next escape attempt. In the meantime, he would plan his epic. A film so profound the world would stand in awe, and people would cry many, many tears.

Things would *change* as a result.

The sterile world of his mother and Clive would be swept away. Cannibal Corpse, those soulless clowns, would be swept away. The world of the baby boomers, seemingly ductile yet brittle underneath, would become a quaking lake, a boiling sea of mud as a new world was born, and that would be the beginning of Imperium. It would all be in his film.

Sounds of pain and terror filtered in from outside through the rough crowd-buzz. Shiv was beating the man, who was trying to escape, Michael guessed, but was it real or hallucinatory? It certainly *seemed* real. Shiv was giving him every chance to beat him in return, was demanding he do so in fact. Shiv was very sporting.

'C'mon, fucker, put up a fight,' he kept bellowing. 'Why

don't you put up a fight?' The crowd roared with laughter. Then there was a brief burst of siren. Twisted Sister II stuck her head in the door.

'The police are back,' she said. 'Any more of your nonsense I'll have you charged with assault, okay? You're lucky to be alive, unlike your friend. You boys are very stupid, going into the desert without water. I'd advise you to go back south as soon as you've recovered. You don't fit in around here, if you know what I mean. It sounds like your friend out there is causing more trouble, too. Well, the police'll deal with *him*.' Michael laughed dryly, but it was true. He could hear the cops addressing Shiv sternly. Shiv was quoting Shakespeare at them, which he had been reading with devouring fascination on the way from Adelaide while Hayden drove the car. And now, knowing he might not have another chance to injure his enemy, Michael heard him roar:

'Out, vile jelly…'

Horror from the crowd. Strained ferocity from the cops. They were dragging Shiv away.

'You'll be charged with causing grievous bodily harm. Should've stayed in Tassie, arsehole.'

The bad man was sobbing and howling in pain, and someone called for the nurses to come out of the clinic.

I am now the last representative of The Thresher, thought Michael, *and I am chained to a bed with my limbs turned to mush.* He tried to feel the heaviness of responsibility but couldn't. Deep down he knew The Thresher had been Shiv's project and Shiv's only. He must create a system or be enslaved by another man's. Michael's time was coming, he was sure. He just had to get loose of these chains, and grasp the cup shining through the mist at him.

It wasn't the blood in the cup that he needed, it was the *chalice*.

The chalice itself…

———

EPILOGUE

'Hey…you'll have to shut up, or the visit's over.'

They had been singing a song, defiantly, but it was finished now.

It was the ninth of September, 1999, and that had been their Pine Gap gig, now relocated here, the visiting room of Port Augusta Prison. Michael feared for the new millennium.

'So, that was our last performance together?'

'How can you keep The Thresher going in here?'

'I'll be out in a few years. You'll still be around, won't you?'

'I'm going to try filmmaking. If it doesn't work out, maybe we can restart the band. Or you can get new members. Did you have to gouge his eyes almost out of their sockets? Whatever happened to turning the other cheek?'

'He deserved it. If thy right eye offends thee. But the heat drove me mad I think. That fucking heat. White men weren't made for that kind of heat.'

'But we conquered it…sort of.'

With water in plastic cups they toasted Colin, and also Hikaru, their one time drummer. Hayden wasn't mentioned.

'So you got our camera back?'

'Yeah. Got a lift out to where we broke down. It was still in the car.'

'It's yours. Keep it. But do something worthwhile with it, eh?'

'I will. I definitely will.'

Michael showed Shiv a clipping from the Adelaide

Advertiser, referring to two tourist deaths, one British and one Japanese, near the outback town of Gubba Gubba. Readers were reminded *never* to go near abandoned mine structures, and never to venture into the outback without an adequate supply of water. It was feared these tragic deaths, combined with a recent spate of violence in Gubba itself (culminating in an interstate visitor being blinded in a brawl), would have an adverse effect on South Australian tourism. A separate editorial urged the government to take action on the issue by means of a new advertising campaign.

To their disgust, there was no mention of The Thresher.

'I'll get that guy who's running our Geocities to post a notice saying the band's on hiatus.'

'Time's up,' the guard told them.

'I'll see you round then, Shiv.'

'All right, Michael. You're destined for great things, no doubt. Catch up for a beer some time.' Shiv looked ever-so-slightly bitter, despite an effort not to show it…but also sad. Michael thought of Solon's words to Croesus. *No man can be happy while alive.*

It would be eight years before they saw each other again.

*   *   *

Camping in the Dandenongs…the vast twinkling plain of Melbourne hidden behind trees was false, held nothing for him. Perhaps Sydney, where he had somehow been before…a garden in the rain.

But no, he must stay here to finish his first film for the competition. With the prize money he could get a proper 35mm camera.

'I will outdo you, Reginald Murchison,' he thought, with a nod at his uncle's ghost. And Shiv…would he outdo Shiv? He didn't like to think.

At midnight, the announcers on his transistor radio pretended to 'crash' with millennium bug, just as he had predicted they would. They soon came back, yelling 'Happy New Year.'

But during that short period of silence, something strange had happened.

The fire, reduced to glowing embers, flared softly up again into a living flame.

It was a secret sign, the millennium was his.

Something *was* at hand.

Sad smell of rain, and the fire flared at midnight!

Michael's adventures (and Shiv's) continue in
Hide the Decline (forthcoming 2021).